MODERN ARCHITECTURE IN AMERICA

❖ ❖ ❖ ❖ ❖ ❖

MODERN ARCHITECTURE IN AMERICA

❖ ❖ ❖ ❖ ❖ ❖

VISIONS AND REVISIONS

Edited by RICHARD GUY WILSON
and SIDNEY K. ROBINSON

Iowa State University Press   Ames

Manufactured in the United States of America

⊗ This book is printed on acid-free paper.

Book design by Joanne E. Kinney

First edition, 1991

Library of Congress Cataloging-in-Publication Data

Modern architecture in America: visions and revisions / edited by Richard
Guy Wilson and Sidney K. Robinson. – 1st ed.
    p.   cm.
    ISBN 0-8138-0381-0 (alk. paper)
    1. Architecture, Modern – 19th century – United States. 2. Architecture,
Modern – 20th century – United States. 3. Architecture – United States.
I. Wilson, Richard Guy. II. Robinson, Sidney K.
NA710.M6 1991
720′.973′09034 – dc20
                                                 90-34402

To LEONARD K. EATON
Architectural Historian
Professor, University of Michigan
A FESTSCHRIFT BY HIS GRATEFUL STUDENTS

CONTENTS

CONTRIBUTORS

ROBERT BENSON teaches history, theory, and criticism and is Director of Graduate Studies in the Department of Architecture at Miami University in Oxford, Ohio. He is a contributing editor of *Inland Architect* and writes frequently in other journals and magazines.

KENNETH A. BREISCH has specialized in American architecture of the nineteenth and twentieth centuries; he currently teaches architectural history at the Southern California Institute of Architecture (SCI-ARC) in Santa Monica, California.

GRANT HILDEBRAND is professor of architecture and art history at the University of Washington; he has written on the work of Albert Kahn and Frank Lloyd Wright.

WALTER C. LEEDY, JR., is on the faculty of Cleveland State University. His book, *Fan Vaulting: A Study in Form, Technology and Meaning,* is the only comprehensive work on that subject. Besides English medieval architecture, his research interests include Polish medieval architecture and the architecture and urban history of Cleveland.

MARK MUMFORD teaches architecture at Iowa State University.

SIDNEY K. ROBINSON teaches architectural history and architectural design in the School of Architecture, University of Illinois at Chicago. In addition to writing on Frank Lloyd Wright, the Prairie School, and the Picturesque, he is a registered architect.

MARY CORBIN SIES is an assistant professor in the Department of American Studies at the University of Maryland. She is finishing a book on the cultural and architectural history of planned, exclusive suburbs in the United States during the pre–World War I era.

THEODORE TURAK teaches art history at the American University in Washington, D.C., and is the author of the book, *William Le Baron Jenney: A Pioneer of Modern Architecture,* as well as several articles on the Chicago school of architecture.

RICHARD GUY WILSON is professor of architectural history at the University of Virginia. His specialty is American and European architecture of the nineteenth and twentieth centuries. He has been the curator of a number of museum exhibitions; the author of books and articles, including *The American Renaissance, 1876-1917; McKim, Mead & White, Architects; The AIA Gold Medal; The Machine Age in America;* and a contributor to *The Art That Is Life: The Arts and Crafts Movement in America.*

INTRODUCTION

In recent years historians of architecture have not only looked at new things, they have also altered their vision of how to "do" architectural history. American architecture is approached with a new seriousness, along with other American subjects. A revision has taken place that includes what is studied and considered important as well as how it is studied. Not only because of the reevaluation of American subjects, but because of changes in architectural history in general, one can say that American architectural history has come of age.

Any active field of scholarly study is connected with its contemporary society and culture; the changes in American architectural history are certainly the result of larger reorientations, some easily understood, others still obscure. The maturing of America in the post–World War II years has shifted the centers of the architectural and art worlds, along with their scholarly study, to the United States. Although many arguments can be made for America's intellectual prowess in the pre–1940 period, the value of American studies, except in a few isolated instances, was downplayed. Since then, the growth of mega-universities, the rise in stature of American scholarship, and the emergence of specialized scholarly groups such as the Society of Architectural Historians founded in 1940 can be seen as ele-

ments in this reorientation. Abroad, as a "Pax Americana" encircled the globe, American architects and scholars followed close behind.

This American hubris has precipitated some striking reorientations in historical perceptions here at home. The American "throw away" culture has not, itself, been discarded; we still destroy far too many historical buildings and replace them with trash. However, the artifacts of America have gained respect beyond patriotic and genealogical ancestor worship by the elite. The historic preservation movement has become a growth industry in the last twenty years as millions of Americans have had their attention directed to the value of older buildings. "Edutainment"–the merging of education and entertainment–as seen in restorations like Colonial Williamsburg, house tours in Frank Lloyd Wright's Oak Park, or the blockbuster, multimedia shows at art museums, is the most striking evidence of the growing awareness and appreciation of American history's panorama. Serious programs on art or American architecture now appear on television. An interest in "roots" sweeps the country: Levittown is being preserved and Reston, a new town of the 1960s, has a historical society.

Architectural history has been intimately involved, as it

should be, with architecture as a profession and a practice. Many of the current interests of architects, from a concern with context to a renewed classicism, have been paralleled by research in architectural history. The ahistoricism and utopianism of the early modern movement has been replaced with an air of retrospection. As the modern movement has matured (or, some would claim, disappeared) in the 1970s and 1980s, the teaching of architectural history to architecture students has advanced beyond providing a layer of culture that peeled away once they entered the studio. Now it is a central feature of their education. Prior to the 1970s most architectural schools either offered architectural history as an adjunct from the art history department or as the personal experiences and preferences of a professional architect with no specialized training in history. Now most schools have professional historians on their faculty.

Concurrently, architectural history has emerged as an autonomous discipline, separate from art history and other historical studies yet retaining ties both of methodology and subject matter to art history and social history. As history has been atomized into economic, social, intellectual, political, and period specialties, architecture has found its own place. Architectural history is a distinct discipline, but it is also part of the larger endeavor of history.

Thirty-five years ago the methods of architectural history largely consisted of collecting photographs and ground plans and then writing from them. Certainly some historians traveled to see the building(s) under consideration; however, the photograph remained the primary document. The historian acted as a connoisseur, assessing the importance and aesthetic value of the specific building. Those buildings meeting a criterion of worth were praised, those falling short were condemned. The building was valued largely in formalistic terms: its mass and volume, space, ornament, and style were the determining elements. A Hegelian spirit of autonomous development imbued most studies; one building led to another in a long chain. A *zeitgeist* directed the historian toward what was important and away from what was dispensable. According to this view many buildings should never have been erected: they were out of step with their times. Forward-looking buildings were approved, while those that were regressive were damned. The air of German scholarship, of Wöefflin and Frankl, hung over much of the architectural history establishment.

This is not meant to imply that all the old methods were wrong and that everything has improved vastly. Aspects of the old methods do survive, and some current architectural history could stand a good dose of formalistic analysis. But the methods of architectural history have irrevocably changed.

Historians now examine firsthand the buildings they write about; increased ease of travel certainly has been a factor, and interest has shifted away from the object in focus at the center of a photograph. Buildings are still praised and condemned, but they are seen not so much as survivors of a relentless selection process exercised along the path of progress but as parts of a more inclusive context of time and place. The most immediate is of course the site: buildings are part of a setting, not just disembodied photographs and schematic floor plans. They have insides with their own particular landscape and exteriors that adjust to or contrast with both the interior and the surroundings.

Also part of the context of any building is its particular intellectual and cultural setting. The designer and the owner have their own particular backgrounds, values, and prejudices. A concern with patronage has been one of the most interesting recent emphases, since it recognizes that the client not only pays for the structure, but frequently has a particular set of demands and values that might be met. On a larger scale, politics are part of the context, from minute building regulations to the process that builds and controls cities. In his essay, Theodore Turak of American University tells the fascinating story of the Mrs. Avery Coonley whose house in Riverside, Ill., was one of Frank Lloyd Wright's most accomplished and lavish Prairie houses. Professor Turak's interview with Mrs. Coonley's daughter brings important details to light. Walter Leedy of Cleveland State University relates how Cleveland sought an image for the city in the late nineteenth and early twentieth centuries. The Mall, proposed by Daniel Burnham in 1903, its supporters, and subsequent history demonstrate the efforts of citizens to express their aspirations for themselves and their city.

The coming of modernism is now subject to new interpretations as various strains of progressivism are identified. As the egalitarian ideal of culture took hold in America, the status of architecture was the subject of widespread consideration. Shelter magazines, garden suburbs, and influences from abroad all had changing impacts on America's perceptions of architecture. Mary Corbin Sies, from the University of Maryland, describes the development of selected American suburban communities around the turn of the century and brings to light the wide range of contributors to a new vision of the American house. A stratum of society much concerned with making it in the new world of managing and disseminating goods and culture sought to create an ideal living situation for families away from the noisy, crowded cities.

The liberation from a predetermined evolution of architectural style allows a whole new level of detail to appear. Buildings are not merely vehicles for stylistic study, but are part of the study of typology. Kenneth Breisch, from the Southern California Institute of Architecture, demonstrates the impact that the new profession of librarians had on the new, nineteenth-century building type. William Frederick Poole's contribution to library design as a founder of the American Library Association and as combatant in a running battle with H. H. Richardson casts the architect's response to clients' requests in a new light.

Architectural history, as all fields, is filled with prejudices: some architects, movements, or buildings are worthy of study at a particular time, others are not. Frank Furness for years was treated as simply a brief stop on Louis Sullivan's inevitable journey to modernism. Victorian architectural studies had as heroes only those who escaped its stifling embrace, as had Sullivan. A remarkable transformation in Victorian studies has taken place; now it has its own great men irrespective of their contribution to what came later. Mark Mumford of Iowa State University identifies important resources contributing to Frank Furness's design for the Pennsylvania Academy of the Fine Arts. The social stratum that initiated the structure and the influence of John Ruskin on that group and on the architect helped inform Furness's powerful forms.

Similarly, American architecture in the 1920s and 1930s was considered to be a fallow field after the fall of Wright and the Prairie School around World War I. All the activity and interest had gone to Europe, and not until the emigration of the European masters, Mies van der Rohe and Walter Gropius, and the isolated reemergence of Wright in the mid-thirties did American architecture gain importance. This prejudice, rooted in an American tradition of deferring to Europe in cultural matters, has slowly diminished in its effect on historical scholarship.

Some critics might claim that much of recent American architectural history is concerned with the edges, with filling in what was left out, including the Victorians, the patrons, and the 1920s and 1930s. Alternatively one can discern that the power of the unitary mainstream has been displaced by a recognition of an equally powerful variety. The emergence of "context" not only strengthens the landmarks' claims to preeminence, it includes fascinating alternative architecture with its own claim to attention.

Richard Guy Wilson of the University of Virginia reminds us that, just because architectural historians stopped writing about the work of the Prairie School after Wright's departure from the scene, people like Elmslie did not lay down their pencils. Finding a place for work that is transitional, according to established "schools," is part of the new orientation in American architectural history. Grant Hildebrand from the University of Washington draws attention to Frank Lloyd Wright's houses and gives them a new relation to each other. By approaching them with the guidance of current theorists, he finds ways of identifying the typical elements in the early domestic work.

Current academic fads and interests have also found their way into architectural history. The impact of structuralism, deconstructionism, and Marxism has brought to the fore areas of architectural history not previously considered important. Equally, the application of methods from other fields leads to a certain indecisiveness, with the result that final judgments are often avoided. Of course such experiments in cross-disciplinary borrowing will generate their own, yet-to-be-determined successes and failures.

The status of architecture as a language or text and the ways that architects attempt to associate words, in the guise of explanations, with their buildings are of increasing importance in the current climate. Not all buildings are simply the result of an earlier lineage of buildings and drawings. They are also the result of the architect's perception of self in relation to history. Books not by architects can have an impact on an architect's work. As Sidney Robinson from the University of Illinois at Chicago points out, Victor Hugo's chapters on the history of architecture included in *Notre Dame de Paris* affected Frank Lloyd Wright for his whole adult life. Hugo's estimation that architecture had been replaced by the printed word may explain many of the curious twists evolving in architectural history.

The multilayered reality that is now acknowledged to constitute architectural history includes those who write history as well as the place where it appears. The role of journalism and publicity in the creation of reputations of architects and buildings is increasingly important. Philip Johnson has claimed that his buildings do not exist until they are photographed. A building's impact is so circumscribed as to have only a tenuous grip on existence until it is known to a wider audience through publication. Although vernacular studies and a concern with the elements overlooked have attempted to surmount this problem, the fact remains that what is chosen to be written about and published virtually defines its worth. Hence studies of critics and early historians have made an important contribution to American architectural history. Robert Benson of Ohio University brings attention to the work of Douglas Haskell and the criticism of "International" modernism. By setting out the evolution of modernism in America, Haskell's crucial interpretation and advocacy of the new style, beginning in the architectural criticism column for the *Nation* from 1930 to 1942, are made clear.

The essays collected in this volume were written by students of Leonard K. Eaton. They aspire to reflect Professor Eaton's probing scholarship and fascination with subjects that have received little or no previous study. By opening up areas of architectural history, Leonard Eaton set an example for his students that guided but did not confine. Watching him turn over new subjects provided the liberation to discover similar subjects for ourselves. Although both Professor Eaton and his students built upon and respected more traditional architectural scholarship, the following essays by their range and their approach, draw attention to American subjects that would have been outside conventional consideration thirty years ago. Certainly the growth of the Midwest as an architectural force was important to Professor Eaton and has continued to be for his students. But the lessons learned from that initial exposure to exploratory scholarship have been expanded into new areas by all these contributors.

This book also stands as a tribute to Leonard K. Eaton upon his retirement from the University of Michigan. For thirty-eight years he has taught literally thousands of students in the College of Architecture and Urban Planning, along with courses offered in the Department of the History of Art and the Program in American Studies. His many articles and essays and his books, *New England Hospitals, 1790–1833* (1956), *Landscape Artist in America: The Life and Work of Jens Jensen* (1964), *Two Chicago Architects and Their Clients: Frank Lloyd Wright and Howard Van Doren Shaw* (1969), *American Architecture Comes of Age: European Reaction to H. H. Richardson and Louis Sullivan* (1972), and *Gateway Cities and Other Essays* (1989), have helped to define the parameters of architectural history in America. While he will be gone from the "bully pulpit" of the lecture hall, we trust that his voice will not be silent.

RICHARD GUY WILSON
SIDNEY K. ROBINSON

MODERN ARCHITECTURE IN AMERICA

CHAPTER 1

"GOD'S VERY KINGDOM ON THE EARTH"

*The Design Program for the
American Suburban Home, 1877-1917*

MARY CORBIN SIES

> This home of our American people is the flower of all the ages: this sums up all the joy earth has for us: this is our most sacred institution. Through all the enginery of our social order—religion, laws, arts—we should minister to it reverently; striving to foster and extend and adorn such type of fair domestic life—God's very kingdom on the earth.
>
> Albert Winslow Cobb, 1889

When in his introduction to *Examples of American Domestic Architecture* Albert Winslow Cobb characterized the American home as "God's very kingdom on the earth," he merely stated what clients and architects alike believed to be true as they commissioned or designed the new suburban homes of the late nineteenth and early twentieth centuries. They believed that the American home was the repository of moral purpose, the register of the character of the American people, the expression of America's most righteous democratic ideals. More than aesthetic and professional considerations influenced the shape of the new suburban house type. The architect-designed suburban home of the period 1877 to 1917 can only be fully appreciated when we understand the social and cultural aims that influenced those persons who decided in each instance upon its form. It was both a repository of the social ambitions, anxieties, and cultural ideals of those who designed and consumed it and a model, a vehicle of reform, expected to benefit the urban populace as a whole.[1]

Until recently, historical analysis of the American suburban home was not a fashionable topic. But the few intrepid pioneers in the subject, architectural historians all, have greatly influenced the ways that subsequent scholars think about the home. We are used to regarding turn-of-the-century domestic architecture as the product of aesthetic considerations influenced by regional and philosophic rivalries between two camps of professionalizing architects. Leonard K. Eaton advanced this interpretation in *Two Chicago Architects and Their Clients* (1969), his now-classic study of the clientele that sponsored architectural innovation in Chicago's pre–World War I suburban homes. He suggested that domestic architecture there exhibited the pattern of the mounting and failure of a siege by a very progressive group of architects—known as the Prairie School—against their more conservative and socially well-connected colleagues.[2]

In *The Prairie School: Frank Lloyd Wright and His Midwest Contemporaries* (1972), H. Allen Brooks enlarged upon Eaton's thesis by turning it around and suggesting that the siege was mounted in the other direction and that it was a success, not a failure. He argued that the domestic architecture of the period reflected a regional professional conflict between academically trained architects from the eastern United States who advocated conservative styles of houses based upon European precedents and a revolutionary group of midwestern architects who drew upon indigenous sources and aspired to create an original school of architectural design. In Brooks's view, the eastern profession successfully besieged the midwesterners, discrediting their design solutions with the suburban clientele and imposing a conservative, more classical mode of expression upon the new suburban houses. The radicals' capitulation, around 1915, according to this theory, deprived modern architecture of its most promising school of domestic designers.[3]

Although subsequent scholarly treatments have qualified the "Siege Theory," they have continued to rely upon its conservative versus radical interpretation of turn-of-the-century American architecture. Alan Gowans, for example, outlined several points of agreement between the two warring camps in *Images of American Living* (1976), but still reinforced the notion of an aesthetic rivalry between the "Beaux Arts men" and the midwestern "Rebels." His recent study of middle-class mail-order housing, *The Comfortable House* (1986), questions the Siege Theory but continues to invoke the basic "academic" versus "progressive" dichotomy to describe early twentieth-century domestic design. Richard Guy Wilson, in a recent essay on the American Arts and Crafts movement in *The Art That Is Life* (1987), also employs the conservative versus radical model, this time labeling the two mentalities "American Renaissance" and "Arts and Crafts." But Wilson emphasizes that neither camp can be identified with a specific region, that architects from both camps shared many common principles, and that, in particular, Arts and Crafts designs contained many historical references, a characteristic usually associated with the work of the conservatives.[4]

Wilson's careful observations underscore the Siege Theory's limitations as an aid in understanding the turn-of-the-century American home. In focusing upon a few pure examples of "conservative" or "revolutionary" designs—McKim, Mead, and White's H. A. C. Taylor residence (Newport, 1886) or Charles Platt's J. J. Chapman house (Barrytown, N.Y., 1904–1909) versus Frank Lloyd Wright's Robie house (Chicago, 1909) or Purcell and Elmslie's William Purcell residence (Lake of the Isles, 1913–1914), for example—we misrepresent the majority of architect-designed suburban houses from the period that do not fall neatly into one category or the other. When one examines the larger body of suburban domestic architecture, one finds little evidence to document a steady movement toward the adoption of any single style or conservative mode of expression.

The Siege Theory's preoccupation with matters of style—and mostly with exterior characteristics of houses, at that—focuses too little attention on function, on the precise uses that the occupants planned to make of each building's spaces. The nearly exclusive emphasis on aesthetic issues is not peculiar to the Siege theorists but derives from basic assumptions widely held by art historians who center their studies upon the artist and seek to understand and appreciate his creative acts through formal analysis of his works of art. When applied to home design—the most practical of building types—this perspective emphasizes the formal and stylistic decisions made by professional architects at the expense of the client's role in the domestic design process and the equally important contextual factors that contributed to the executed design. The greatest limitation of the Siege Theory, then, is that it fails to analyze the emergence of the new suburban house type as the complex cultural phenomenon that it was. We need to examine *all* of the factors—social, economic, political, moral, as well as professional and aesthetic—that constrained those persons who created the turn-of-the-century suburban domestic environment.[5]

We need, in other words, to study the design of the suburban home in its many-faceted historic context. In the next few pages, I shall discuss the design consensus embodied in the new architect-designed suburban houses that emerged around the turn of the century in a unique set of communities: the planned, exclusive suburbs of major American metropolises. In communities like these across the nation, architects and clients belonging to a new social stratum in urban America gave the suburban house its characteristic twentieth-century form. My argument is based upon an analysis of *all* the houses constructed between 1877 and 1917 in four such communities: Short Hills, N.J.; St. Martin's in Philadelphia, Pa.; Kenilworth, Ill.; and Lake of the Isles in Minneapolis, Minn. For each of these planned, exclusive suburbs, I (1) compiled a profile of the architects, community leaders, and clientele; (2) summarized the local preferences and construction circumstances that influenced design; (3) chronicled the local and developmental history; and (4) reconstructed the domestic design program that emerged in each community.[6]

From this research I discovered that in planned, exclusive suburbs across the nation, communities consisting of the architects, developers, upper middle-class residents, and others interested in the housing question vigorously debated and experimented with the design of the new American suburban home. By 1917, when construction virtually ceased for the duration of the war, members of these communities had worked out a firm consensus regarding the program for the ideal American home. In defining that program, they evinced a dual aim that was both personal and reform-oriented. They sought (1) to accommodate and formalize their own life-style and social position in a suitable setting and (2) to devise a model environment that would address the worst housing and social conditions of the cities. To accomplish their purposes, they created a domestic design program of at least seven principles—efficiency, technology, nature, family, individuality, community, and beauty—which they incorporated into their own houses and, in turn, disseminated as a general formula for ordering the residential environment of the city. Their program of scientifically appointed and artistically designed one-family suburban houses with plenty of outdoor space remains the most prominent American residential ideal of the twentieth century.[7]

Studying the domestic design process as it occurred in actual suburbs brings fresh insight to our understanding of the logic of the design of the new suburban home. We find, for example, that the design program that emerged during the period was more concerned with content than with style. It did not advocate a unified style of expression, conservative or otherwise. Instead, it called for designs that embodied a unified set of assumptions concerning the purpose of the American home and promoted a unified set of principles for achieving that purpose. The most consistent influences on the design program were not aesthetic, professional, or regional issues at all but a set of cultural and prescriptive assumptions about the home that were truly national in their scope. Regardless of whether the new houses were built in suburban New York or Chicago, whether they were conservative or progressive in ornamentation and executed in the colonial revival or the Prairie style, they embodied the same essential design principles and rationale.

I would like to expand upon these conclusions by analyzing the domestic design program that emerged contemporaneously in the four historic suburbs of Short Hills, St. Martin's, Kenilworth, and Lake of the Isles. I will begin with a portrait of the communities of discourse that participated in the design process in each location and an account of the issues and assumptions that constrained their design decisions. Next, I will reconstruct the design program itself as exemplified in the consensus represented by the actual houses constructed between 1877 and 1917. I will conclude by suggesting a few ways in which thorough contextual analysis can broaden and revise our understanding of the logic governing the design of the new American suburban homes.

It may help to clarify the domestic design process if we think of those persons who participated in it in a given suburb as constituting a "community of discourse." This was a set of persons engaged in a continuous discussion concerning, in this instance, the proper design of the ideal home environment. Whether in Short Hills, Kenilworth, or any similar planned, exclusive suburb, the community of discourse included many persons besides the architects who designed the residents' homes. It is important to remember, as Dell Upton pointed out recently, that "throughout American history, clients have always been unwilling to grant architects control over such an important aspect of everyday life as the design and furnishing of their houses." But there were other participants besides clients and their architects in each suburb's debate: developers, housing reformers and other civic leaders, domestic scientists and clubwomen, neighbors and social critics. Although each community's ideas took shape in the form of new suburban houses—and they remain our most articulate evidence about the content of the debate—its members were also listening and contributing to a larger discussion nationwide on the meaning of the American home. That debate took place on the pages of popular magazines and domestic design manuals, in architectural journals, in lectures sponsored by women's clubs, and in thousands of architect-client transactions occurring in such suburbs across America.[8]

In Short Hills, St. Martin's, Kenilworth, and Lake of the Isles, the overwhelming majority of participants in the design process belonged, as Leonard Eaton observed, to a secondary stratum of society, a group I will call the professional-managerial stratum of the urban upper middle class. This distinctive population cohort emerged in major cities after the Civil War as a result of the coalescence of three historic trends: the administrative restructuring of business enterprise, the new respect accorded professional and technical expertise, and the organization of a national mass market for consumer goods. These factors created the three categories of occupation that defined members of the stratum: they were either businessmen, professionals, or the producers or transmitters of culture. Besides similarities in occupation and in professional or technical training, these individuals shared similar social origins and affiliations, and pursued similar life-styles, social practices, and consumption patterns. The vast majority were native-born Americans of northern European descent who possessed high school and often college educations and hailed from privileged, Protestant backgrounds. Keenly ambitious, they were eager to create a market for their services and opportunities for social and economic advancement. As the first nonwealthy group of citizens in American history anxious and able to afford to have an architect design the family home, they were the dominant sponsors of suburban residential building prior to World War I.[9]

The shared experiences and mutual interests of those belonging to the professional-managerial stratum fostered a common belief system among them, a common way of defining the world and their place in it. That belief system, the product of a group emerging during a period of profound change, was bifurcated—split between the old mid-century, middle-class values of family, domesticity, and republicanism and the new values of cost efficiency, career ambition, and the urban marketplace. These individuals, in other words, characteristically embraced both traditional and modern values without acknowledging that they perceived any inherent contradictions between them. For example, they continued to view home and family as a moral haven and the Christian values learned there a guarantor of social stability. At the same time, they recognized that home and family must also supply children with the aptitudes that would bring them success in the occupational realm. While parents reinforced beliefs in the spiritual rewards of hard work, frugality, virtue, and dedication, they also emphasized the financial rewards of efficiency, aggressive self-confidence, opportunism, and cunning. Although most members of the professional-managerial stratum genuinely believed in democratic idealism and equality of opportunity, they simultaneously promoted their own families' social exclusivity.[10]

The new suburban clientele endowed the novel act of commissioning the family home with tremendous personal and so-

cial meaning. They brought an ambitious program of domestic assumptions to the task, but they did so with confidence that their architects, themselves members of the professional-managerial stratum, shared their most precious values. Architects and clients alike hoped to create an environment that would embody all of the values from their belief system and bring order and cleanliness to their everyday lives and the lives of those around them. Most contemporary urban observers recognized the difficulty of accomplishing these goals within the existing residential sections of cities. The residents who founded these planned, exclusive suburbs had experienced at firsthand the toll that periodic epidemics, soot, foul odors, neighborhood saloons, noise, and crime could exact on the quality of urban dwellers' daily lives. The most reasonable solution to their own housing needs, it seemed to them, was one that would simultaneously address these pressing urban residential problems, problems that threatened the well-being of all who, like themselves, were tied by occupation and inclination to the city. They would create a home environment that, since it was designed to accommodate their own wholesome family life-style, could serve as a model for housing reform for all the members of the urban community.[11]

Thus, the professional-managerial stratum's ardent participation in the debate concerning the design of the ideal home environment was driven by their desire to satisfy their own residential needs while devising a strategy for positive environmental reform. Both aims were based on a fundamental belief in the power of the environment to influence human behavior and stimulate social change. By transforming that most basic social unit, the family home, professional-managerial stewards would engineer an environment that would subtly but effectively evoke in the urban populace character traits of morally upstanding and socially responsible citizens. As one well-known writer of domestic design manuals put it, "A well-ordered home . . . is a tremendous missionary society. The light streaming from its windows is an ever-burning beacon of safety to our most cherished social institutions." Those belonging to the new stratum took it for granted that their own life-style would form an appropriate model for upgrading the domestic and moral standards of any family or neighborhood in the city. The editors of *Western Architect,* for example, praised the suburban housing movement because of its potential to "establish those conditions that will reduce disease, immorality, and degeneracy to a minimum." The new American suburban home would provide citizens of any class with privacy, moral well-being, cleanliness, fresh air, family harmony, and beauty—everything needed to conduct a wholesome domestic existence.[12]

Several anxieties and deeply held convictions focused the debate on the American home and influenced the design program that emerged by consensus from that nationwide discussion. Whether offering one's professional design services, campaigning for housing reform, or simply contemplating the commissioning of one's own home, participants in the debate agreed, first of all, on the gravity of the domestic design problem. Between 1877 and 1917, no other reform strategy seemed so promising, so capable of promoting public health, of stimulating virtue and industry in the urban populace, and fulfilling America's democratic goal "of the lodging of all citizens in good, wholesome habitations." Architect George Maher spoke for many of his colleagues when he declared that "it is in the home that the heart of the nation is most responsive and therefore naturally subject to the most advancement." Stewart Hartshorn, the founder of Short Hills, intended that the careful and original design of suburban houses there would bring about "a moral, social, and intellectual, as well as aesthetic betterment of condition" for residents. In 1904, sociologist Samuel Warren Hue argued that the creation of a better home life offered "the greatest single aid to the relief of society from the burdens of crime." Eugene Gardner, a well-known author of domestic design manuals, was more blunt on this point. In his opinion, "half the money spent upon jails, and poorhouses, reform schools, and hospitals would make these institutions needless if it were wisely used in preparing homes for the poor." "Homebuilding," he said, with all the drama and fervor typical of his social stratum's attitude of the time, "is not the mere spending of money, . . . it is the shaping of human destiny."[13]

The promotion of home ownership, particularly among the urban lower classes, was an important component of the professional-managerial stratum's positive environmental reform campaign. Widespread suburban home ownership, or as historian Adna Weber phrased it in 1898—the goal of "every man residing in a cottage of his own"—symbolized the essence of the American egalitarian dream. But many individuals also advocated home ownership as a practical means of quelling social unrest

and labor agitation in the cities. It could be harnessed, as one Progressive sociologist put it, using the jargon of the day, as "a force in promoting personal and social efficiency."[14] In his 1912 domestic design manual, architect Charles E. White, Jr., summarized several factors that made home ownership a "worthy ambition" and a "lofty ideal": "The houseowner is a broader-minded individual than the tenant. His credit is better. . . . The houseowner makes a better citizen for he abides more strictly by the law; he is temperate in all things because of his added responsibility. He is more frugal, more thrifty, more likely to seize an opportunity when it comes his way, because he knows from experience the value and power of money."[15]

The strong advocacy of social change through home design and home ownership placed several crucial constraints upon the design program for the suburban home. For example, the ideal home environment had to be articulated in the form of a model—a general formula adaptable to a variety of domestic and local circumstances. It also had to be economical to build so that it would be suitable for families with limited financial resources. The location of the model home was important as well. If professional-managerial stewards were to create an environment capable of transforming human character, then they had to select a location that allowed them to control all of the factors that they had considered detrimental to family life in the city. Thus, the ideal home environment was conceived as *suburban,* combining "the culture and conveniences of the city with the domestic advantages and natural scenery of the country." Only in such a "middle landscape" could design professionals command both "the primal art of nature and the latest interpretations of science" and technology—the two forces with which they expected to effect a real behavioral transformation.[16]

Most members of the new suburban communities believed that technology, in the hands of experts, possessed nearly limitless potential for bringing continued social and material progress. They viewed the engineering of the ideal home environment, in fact, as a broadly technological process that they promoted, essentially uncritically, as a social panacea. Their infatuation with technology was also revealed in their inclusion of all the latest modern conveniences in the specifications for the model suburban home.[17]

At the same time, these individuals retained the conviction that nature's beauty and goodness could inspire the spiritual and moral regeneration that they hoped would take place in the urban populace. By designing a home so as to place its occupants in daily contact with "fresh air, sunlight, green foliage, and God's blue sky," one might rescue urban commuters from the physically and morally debilitating effects of their contact with the city.[18] The new suburbanites considered the civilizing influence of nature an especially important ingredient in the upbringing of children. In Kenilworth, for example, the Kenilworth Company urged prospective residents to think of the impact of the home environment on the child's character and physical constitution: "Almost imperative becomes the necessity of such a home to parents, where their children, freed from the confinements and frequently undesirable influences of city life, can revel and thrive physically as well as morally in pure air." But many adults also experienced dramatic improvements in health after moving to suburban homes and engaging in the kinds of domestic activities that forged a kinship with nature, such as gardening, strolling, porch-sitting, and the more active forms of outdoor recreation. Their assumption "that the healthiest and happiest life is that which maintains the closest relationship with out-of-doors" remained one of the strongest influences on the design program for the new suburban home.[19]

The model behavior that those belonging to the professional-managerial stratum wished through a carefully engineered home environment to educe in others was based, of course, on their own mode of living. Thus, they tailored the new design program to accommodate and demonstrate their own suburban life-style, which was, first and foremost, family-centered. The new suburbanites, much like conservative civic leaders today, worried that the traditional home and family were falling victim to rampant individualism and the moral decay characteristic of contemporary urban life. Their insistence on the building of "one-family house[s] with private garden and plenty of open space" was premised on their belief that those conditions would best provide parents with the resources for reestablishing moral authority and nourishing familial bonds. Especially important was an environment that in every detail would contribute to the proper upbringing of children, upon which the social future of the stratum's families depended. Fathers and mothers were cautioned that "in constructing their houses they [were] educating their children, teaching them the most lasting lessons in honesty or deceit, as well as in true

artistic taste."[20]

The safeguarding of family members' health—"the first essential of good homemaking"—was perhaps the most acute necessity of the family-centered suburban life-style. A home designed to secure a clean water supply, proper drainage, and fresh air offered obvious advantages over residential alternatives in the city. Many individuals were persuaded that a clean and hygienic home environment offered moral benefits, too. As Albert Winslow Cobb put it, "Noisome, corrupt surroundings stupef[ied] human beings and ke[pt] them powerless to break away to something better."[21]

One of the strongest needs of the professional-managerial stratum community was to develop a life-style that sheltered residents from the stresses and temptations of urban life without repudiating the social and economic values that underlay their occupational achievements. The new suburbanites craved an orderly home environment, one designed to organize daily household activities and provide them with a reassuring feeling of control over their increasingly complex lives. To contrast with the formal manner in which they conducted business and social relations in the city, individuals sought an informal and relaxed atmosphere at home. They wanted a comfortable and practical dwelling—"a spot of quiet and rest, doubly home-like after the tumult of the great city." Parents also hoped to create a repository of those values, so threatened by urban culture, that inspired each person's noblest instincts. Thus, the cultivation of beauty in the design of the home was, to them, a domestic imperative. As far back as 1869, Catharine Beecher and Harriet Beecher Stowe called for the artistic furnishing of the home: "While the aesthetic element must be subordinate to the requirements of physical existence, . . . it yet holds a place of great significance among the influences which make home happy and attractive, which give it a constant and wholesome power over the young, and contribute much to the education of the entire household in refinement, intellectual development, and moral sensibility."[22]

Although they practiced a family-centered life-style, the new suburbanites did not turn their backs on membership in the larger community. Nor did they relinquish a sense of responsibility for addressing the social problems of the nearby city. We can characterize their life-style most accurately as one that sought to balance family, individuality, and community to include both privacy and social stewardship. To compensate for the loss of individual expression that seemed endemic to urban mass society, members of suburban design communities believed that the home environment ought to strengthen the character and individuality of each household member. Although they occasionally decried the selfish individualism that drove commerce and industry, they recognized that strong personal qualities correlated positively with occupational and social success.[23]

Placing the family in a friendly community of homogeneous, like-minded neighbors was an equally important goal. The loss of community that members of the professional-managerial stratum had experienced in the city—their inability to trust their neighbors or to control their social contacts—was remedied with their removal to planned, exclusive suburbs where community spirit and social interaction prevailed. In Short Hills, St. Martin's, Kenilworth, and Lake of the Isles, residents reported keeping busy with a strenuous round of musical entertainments, card parties, lectures, amateur theatricals, club meetings, and informal dining in each others' homes. They needed dwellings that were hospitable, designed to accommodate the frequent informal gatherings of suburban social life.[24]

Beyond the home and local community, the new suburbanites directed their attention to the alleviation of some of the more challenging social problems in the city. Many of their social reform activities were the special purview of women whose leisure to engage in them depended upon their efficient management of household responsibilities. A majority of the female residents of the four communities devoted considerable time to educational reform, charity, social settlements, public health reform, and other "social housekeeping" and public policy concerns. Although most could count upon at least part-time domestic assistance, they demanded efficiently designed homes equipped with rationally planned service and storage spaces, labor-saving appliances, and easily cleaned and maintained surfaces that minimized the housekeeper's daily workload.[25]

Over the period 1877 to 1917, the debate on the proper design of the home reached a climax and a consensus emerged regarding the program for the model suburban home. The new design program was an ingenious if difficult creation; it reconciled most of the special concerns of those participating in the debate—balanced their potentially conflicting values, accommodated the new suburban life-style, and assuaged their uneasiness about urban social problems. Contributors to the consensus in communities like Short Hills, St. Martin's, and Kenilworth thought of the home in a fundamentally different way than had their mid-century predecessors. To them, a dwelling was no longer just a private family retreat; it was also a powerful agent of social progress, one that would induce prescribed patterns of behavior in the inhabitants. They believed that only a professionally trained architect could be entrusted with the challenge of applying the new design program to the actual construction of suburban homes. It required the "technical and artistic knowledge" of the architect to "prepar[e] a proper and correct background for family life." Or, as one professional in Lake of the Isles noted with sage self-interest, "No intelligent person would think of expending any considerable sum of money in the erection of private or public buildings without the services of the architect, which, indeed, are now generally acknowledged to be indispensable."[26]

The tenets of the new design program—efficiency, technology, nature, family, individuality, community, and beauty—specified the elements that had to be present in any proper dwelling, but left architects free to decide how those elements might be embodied in a given commission. Efficiency was the first principle exhibited in the majority of houses. Members of the four communities defined efficiency in the broad social sense characteristic of Progressive Era thinking: the achievement of the greatest possible social and moral good through the systematic efforts of human beings acting in accordance with rational principles. An efficient home environment, then, was one designed by experts according to scientific principles and presumed to engender healthy, well-adjusted, productive human beings. Clients and their architects could produce efficient domiciles by systematically cultivating the qualities of simplicity, utility, structural rationalism, and economy in their designs.[27]

The application of simplicity began in the earliest stages of the design process as those concerned assessed the family's spatial needs and developed a floor plan to accommodate those needs in the simplest, most efficient manner. The new suburbanites agreed that the proper family life-style for persons of their stratum required a 2- or 2½-story residence containing seven to twelve rooms and costing from $5,000 to $12,000. The majority of houses featured an individual arrangement of a standard set of rooms. The typical first floor contained five basic spaces: a living room, hall (often just for circulation), dining room, kitchen, and piazza. On the second floor were a bath and three or four bedrooms; the third floor usually included a servant's room(s) and trunkroom. In addition, many houses contained a den or similar private space for the heads of household, budget permitting. We can see the consistency with which houses in all four suburbs recapitulated this consensus when we compare dwellings of various costs, sizes, styles, and dates of construction. For example, the tiny, twin houses on West Springfield in St. Martin's (Duhring, Okie, and Ziegler, 1910) included the same combination of spaces as the modest Sunset Cottage in Short Hills (Lamb and Rich, 1882) and the more sumptuous Chapman residence in Kenilworth (Nimmons and Fellows, 1910). (See figs. 1.1–1.3.) Although streamlined, each twin provided every feature deemed necessary for domestic comfort or function, right down to the vestibule, rear "mudroom," bedroom fireplaces, serving and storage pantries, rear staircases, and multiple bathrooms.[28]

Because they sought a home that worked—that was comfortable, convenient, and designed to enhance the lives of the inhabitants—members of suburban communities valued utility in design; common sense prevailed over fashion. Many residents of planned suburbs thought utility carried connotations of morality as well. According to George Bertrand, a Lake of the Isles resident and the architect of several houses there, "Interior decoration is the intellectual and moral manifestation of the individuals it surrounds." The strict application of utility to the design, furnishing, and ornamentation of the home was considered a moral good, a positive reflection, and a positive influence on the character of the residents. Thus, there was no room in the model suburban home for disorder, excess, or conspicuous display. Each piece of furniture was selected to perform a practical function, and the interior decoration was simple, restrained, and unobtrusive. As Bertrand succinctly articulated the preferred design approach, "Great art is commonsense idealized."[29]

PORCH DETAIL AND FLOOR PLANS

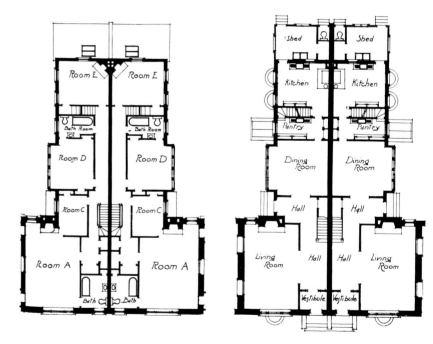

Fig. 1.1. Duhring, Okie, and Ziegler, double house at 305–307 W. Springfield, St. Martin's, Philadelphia, Pa., 1910, first- and second-floor plans, photograph of sideporch. (*American Architect* 102 [1912])

Fig. 1.2. Lamb and Rich, "Sunset Cottage," A. B. Rich residence, Short Hills, N.J., 1882, plan and exterior perspective. (*American Architect and Building News*, 1882)

Fig. 1.3. Nimmons and Fellows, residence of James Chapman, Kenilworth, Ill., 1910, first- and second-floor plans, exterior photographs. (*Brickbuilder* 22 [1913], pl. 174)

"Rosecote," the residence of Jane Jeder in Lake of the Isles (Harry W. Jones, 1905), provides a good example of the cultivation of simplicity and utility in the home (fig. 1.4). The living room was sparsely furnished with Mission-style pieces chosen for comfort and function on the assumption that "whatever . . . is nobly and enduringly useful, thoroughly adapted to its uses, cannot be uncomely." No applied ornament or knickknacks interfered with the rooms' architectural lines. Throughout the house, many furnishings—bookcases, settees, sideboard, and storage dressers—were built-in, a mode of furnishing popular with clients and architects alike for its efficiency and its capacity to organize space and contribute to the quality of interior decoration. The charm of Rosecote's rooms came from their simple utilitarian design—from the warmth of the central hearth, the beauty and craftsmanship of the woodwork, and the decorative flourishes provided by everyday objects, for example, window glass, built-in furnishings, and lighting fixtures.[30]

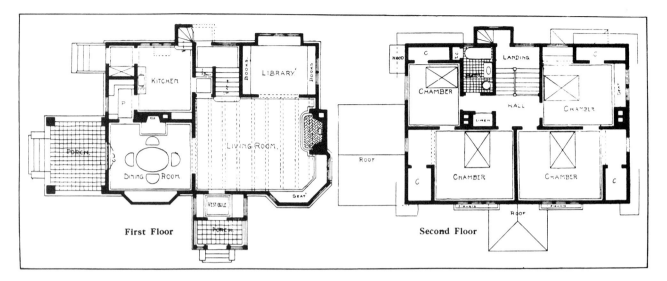

First Floor   Second Floor

Fig. 1.4. Harry W. Jones, "Rosecote," Jane Jeder residence, Lake of the
Isles, Minneapolis, Minn., 1905, first- and second-floor plans.
(*Western Architect* 14 [1909])

Fig. 1.5. Purcell and Elmslie, William Gray Purcell residence, Lake of
the Isles, Minneapolis, Minn., 1913, exterior photograph.
(*Western Architect* 21 [1915])

The majority of homes in the four suburbs achieved efficiency in their exterior design and construction through the application of structural rationalism and economy. C. V. Stravs, architect of several homes in and around Lake of the Isles, stated three requirements for achieving structural rationalism in a building: it must accurately portray its purpose, its form of construction, and the materials used in its construction. Regardless of style, the model exterior revealed its domestic purpose in a straightforward manner. Chimneys, porches, eaves, window placement, and landscaping formed the principal and unmistakably domestic exterior points of interest (figs. 1.2, 1.5, 1.6). Many dwellings honestly conveyed the nature of their structure and materials as well. St. Martin's numerous greystone masonry dwellings, for example, were praised as "embodying livableness, a dignified architectural treatment and perfect sincerity of design." Lamb and Rich's Sunset Cottage—with shingles graded in colors reflecting the sunset—captured the sensuous nature of a skin stretched to contain a volume of space that characterized the best work of the Shingle style[31] (fig. 1.2).

Fig. 1.6. Edmund Gilchrist, Jr., W. W. Gilchrist residence, St. Martin's, Philadelphia, Pa., 1909, first- and second-floor plans, photograph of garden elevation showing paved terrace. (*Brickbuilder* 22, no. 2 [1913], pl. 112)

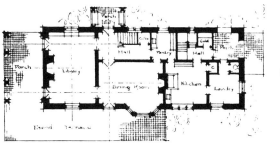

HOUSE AT
ST. MARTINS. PA.
(EXTERIOR WALLS OF TERRA COTTA
HOLLOW TILE)

EDMUND B. GILCHRIST,
ARCHITECT

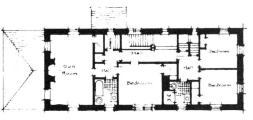

Fig. 1.7. George Maher, F. W. Sutton residence, Kenilworth, Ill., 1908, exterior photograph. (Courtesy, Kenilworth Historical Society, Kenilworth, Ill.)

The need for the new suburban clientele – a group chronically anxious about finances – to economize when building a home stimulated more efficient management of design, construction method, materials, and labor. Architects counseled several strategies for reducing costs: Harry Jones, a prominent Minneapolis architect, reminded potential clients to consider the commissioning of a home a proper commercial transaction in which one could achieve "economy of outlay" by demanding an efficient plan, a substantial structure, but an unostentatious amount of artistic dressing. Thomas Tallmadge's economical construction strategy for suburban Chicago was widely adopted in Kenilworth: "The enormous price of dressed lumber and recurrent expense of painting invites the architect to substitute rough lumber, stained, for his trim and plaster or concrete for his wall spaces. . . . High price [sic] labor calls for simplicity in design and speed in erection" (fig. 1.7). Residents in all four suburbs also kept expenses down by choosing local building materials, for example, the blue traprock, locally made brick, and abundant chestnut trees of Short Hills, and the Wissahickon schist that could often be quarried right on site in St. Martin's.[32]

Because members of the professional-managerial stratum believed that technology and nature could transform the domestic environment, they made both forces central components of the new domestic design program. Their emphasis on technology, for example, was manifested in new construction materials, advances in heating, ventilating, and sanitary technology, and in the proliferation of household appliances and gadgets. Many individuals from Short Hills and the other three suburbs favored the new methods of fireproof construction using hollow tile, metal lath, or reinforced concrete covered with a finish of stucco, brick, or roughcast. One of the most innovative examples was the William DeLanoy residence in Short Hills (William Gurd, 1909). Its steel-reinforced concrete structure enabled the

Fig. 1.8. John A. Gurd, residence of William C. DeLanoy, Esq., Short Hills, N.J., 1909, first- and second-floor plans, exterior photograph. (*Architectural Record* 25 [1909])

architect to achieve several unique design features besides its fireproof quality (fig. 1.8). Because the reinforced beams could span large spaces unobstructed by pillars, the architect could design first-floor rooms that were especially large. Similarly, he could cut out large expanses of window on the lower stories without jeopardizing the dwelling's structural integrity. But neither the spacious rooms nor large openings in the DeLanoy house would have been feasible without advances in central heating technology. The architect's recently acquired ability to regulate temperature, ventilation, light, and water and to offer labor-saving appliances enabled him to provide a comfortable interior environment all year long. All of the dwellings in Short Hills, St. Martin's, Kenilworth, and Lake of the Isles were equipped with furnaces that delivered heat to each room, gas or electrical lighting fixtures (depending upon which service was available), gas cooking ranges, flush water closets, and any number of new-fangled gadgets like electric doorbells, central vacuum systems, and speaking tubes.[33]

Technology increased suburban design communities' ability to build homes that placed residents in close daily contact with nature. In the DeLanoy residence, for example, the reinforced concrete construction enabled the architect to design a flat roof that would withstand snow-loads without buckling or leaking. Gurd took advantage of this feature to provide his client with a

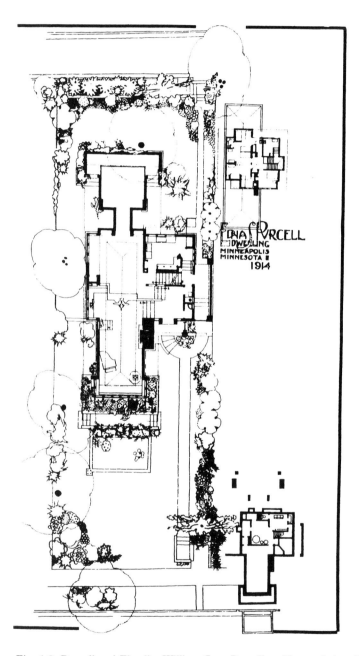

Fig. 1.9. Purcell and Elmslie, William Gray Purcell residence, Lake of the Isles, Minneapolis, Minn., 1914, first-floor, second-floor, and basement plans. (Coll. David Gebhard)

spacious roof loggia that commanded lovely views and sat well above the mosquito line. Nearly every suburban dwelling had a substantial living porch, many of which could be glazed and heated to provide winter sunrooms (figs. 1.1, 1.4, 1.7, 1.9, 1.10). Even in Lake of the Isles with its severe winter weather, residents "expect[ed] to live mainly outside" and demanded houses that would let them "commune with nature." Purcell, Feick, and Elmslie's dwelling for E. L. Powers (1911) allowed the interpenetration of interior and exterior spaces by means of a glazed sunporch, large living room and den window seats, a breakfast porch, a sleeping porch, and a balcony (fig. 1.11). But even the smallest houses offered an abundance of indoor-outdoor spaces: patios, eating terraces, loggias, sleeping porches, and rear porches for the servants[34] (figs. 1.2, 1.3, 1.6, 1.12, 1.13).

Members of all four suburban communities also designed their homes to harmonize with and take advantage of their natural surroundings. Houses were sited so that they would appear to be a part of the landscape. "Charlecote," in Short Hills (Parish and Schroeder, 1902), for example, crowned a hill in the midst of a woodland and was half-timbered with members taken from chestnut trees hewn right on site[35] (fig. 1.14). Architects oriented dwellings very carefully to capture views and increase the amount of sunlight and breezes that would penetrate the living quarters. In Rosecote, Harry Jones placed large grouped windows on the southern exposure of the living and dining rooms but designed the northern exposure to protect occupants against drafts (fig. 1.4). In the St. Martin's residence that he designed for his father (1909), Edmund Gilchrist reversed the floor plan so that the most heavily used rooms and master bedroom faced the garden, which overlooked the scenic Cresheim valley (fig. 1.6). For sites that did not offer felicitous natural features, architects and clients created a landscape design and planted what nature had not furnished. George Maher's house for F. W. Sutton in Kenilworth (1908) was embellished with elaborate plantings to soften the contrast between the home and the landscape (fig. 1.7).

At the heart of the new suburban design program was a careful balance between the values of family, individuality, and community. Most of the houses reflected this delicate balance in a few characteristic ways. To create an environment that would foster family unity, the new suburbanites replaced the formal Victorian room arrangements—arrangements that had segre-

Severely Georgian in type is this house of red brick laid in Flemish bond and trimmed with white Vermont marble. Note the well-arranged planting

An interesting innovation is the provision made for abundant light to the central hall by a window placed at the left of the main door

Green wicker furniture, embellished with cushions of green and white chintz, is used in this cheerful apartment. The window hangings are green sunfast material

The windows on this floor are uniform in size, whether they open off bedroom or bath, thus maintaining the symmetry of the front façade

THE
RESIDENCE OF THOMAS
G. STOCKHAUSEN, ESQ.,
AT CHESTNUT HILL,
PENNA.

*Architects: De Armond,
Ashmead & Bickley*

Fig. 1.10. DeArmond, Ashmead, and Bickley, residence of Thomas G. Stockhausen, St. Martin's, Philadelphia, Pa., 1913, first-floor and second-floor plans, exterior photograph, photograph of sunporch interior. (*House and Garden* 28 [1915]:18)

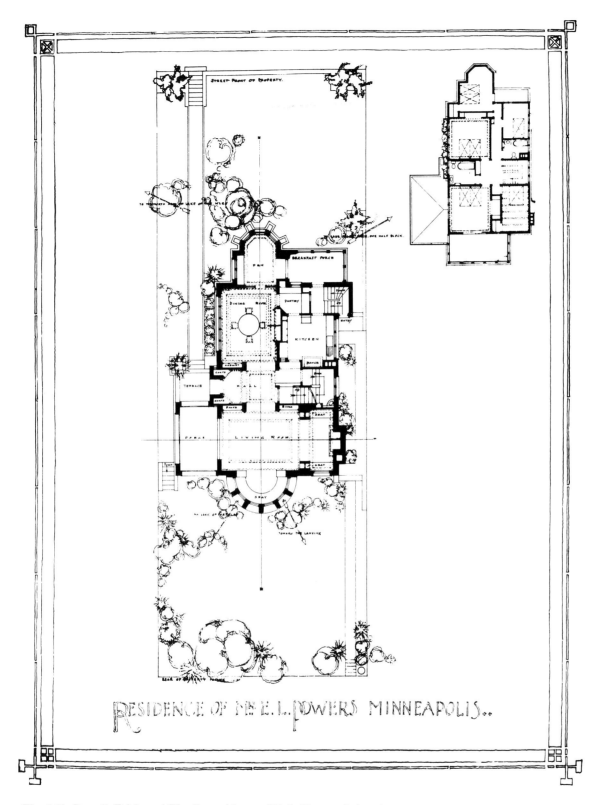

Fig. 1.11. Purcell, Feick, and Elmslie, residence of E. L. Powers, Lake of
the Isles, Minneapolis, Minn., 1911, first- and second-floor plans.
(*Western Architect* 19 [1913])

Fig. 1.12. Lawrence V. Boyd, Henry F. Nell residence, St. Martin's, Philadelphia, Pa., 1898–1899, first- and second-floor plans, exterior photograph. (*American Homes and Gardens* 3 [1906]:366)

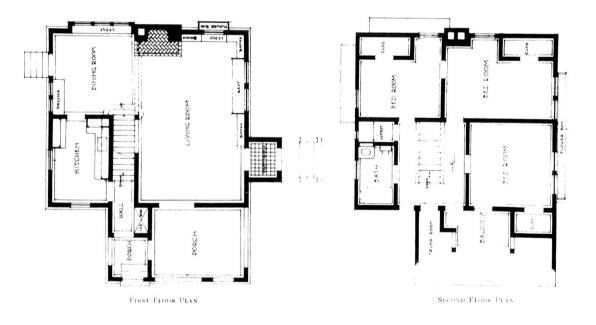

FIRST FLOOR PLAN

SECOND FLOOR PLAN

Fig. 1.13. A. R. VanDyck, Jay C. Vincent residence, Lake of the Isles, Minneapolis, Minn., 1910, first- and second-floor plans, exterior photograph. (*Western Architect,* 1910)

Fig. 1.14. Parish and Schroeder, "Charlecote," residence of C. S. Stout, Esq., Short Hills, N.J., 1902, exterior photograph. (*American Homes and Gardens* 2 [1906]:310)

Fig. 1.15. Parish and Schroeder, "Charlecote," Short Hills, N.J., 1902, first- and second-floor plans. (*American Homes and Gardens* 2 [1906]:310)

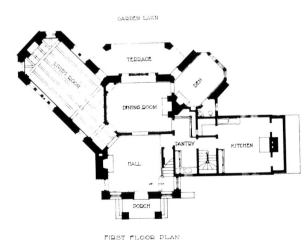

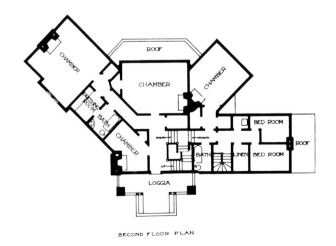

gated household members by age, gender, and activity – with an informal floor plan designed to bring the family together. The hub of the new plan was the living room; "the most commodious room in the house," it was meant to accommodate all of the activities of common family life in a central space (figs. 1.1, 1.3, 1.4, 1.6, 1.10). In the words of Arthur Clausen, the architect of several Lake of the Isles dwellings, "The day of small parlors is past and we now have the large living room, in which are combined the old-time parlor, sitting room, and sometimes the library."[36] An architectural critic, writing in 1910, described the representative St. Martin's interior as

> everywhere instinct with the spirit of home. Every inch of the house is meant to be used and lived in, and is. There is, heaven be praised, neither parlor nor drawing room, but a *living*-room. Here is complete emancipation from the frightful domestic ideals of a period now happily past, that prescribed parlor, a region of starched gloom and perverted furniture, followed by the oftentimes no less dreadful drawing-room, where one's coffee after dinner would be chilled by the marrow-piercing frigidity of the surroundings.

To ensure an "atmosphere of genial cheer [that] gives one the feeling of settling down into a comfortable family nest," architects routinely placed a prominent fireplace, sometimes surrounded by an inglenook, at the living room's center[37] (figs. 1.11, 1.12).

The houses of Short Hills, St. Martin's, Kenilworth, and Lake of the Isles also possessed features aimed at strengthening the character of each household member. Architect Charles Rich articulated the principle of individuality in the new design program quite clearly: "Now, since every man has . . . his own distinct character, so it seems to us that his home should reflect somewhat of this character, . . . so that the man will fit into the house, and his desires and modes of life find expression in the general arrangement of the parts." One of the chief means of reinforcing the client's uniqueness lay in the creation of a floor plan especially suited to individual as well as family needs. According to architect Harrie T. Lindeberg, there was for the new suburban home "no ideal plan, for what would meet the requirements of one family would be entirely inadequate for another. Every site, every difference in personal need, every vagary and individual fancy, set up new conditions, so that each house, no matter how small or unpretentious, is a new and distinct problem." Many houses in Kenilworth where there was abundant

musical talent, for example, featured music rooms, and several Lake of the Isles dwellings built during the height of the Minneapolis bicycle craze had bicycle storage spaces. Other homes provided conservatories, photographic darkrooms, libraries, or observatories according to the special interests or customs of the commissioning family.[38]

Suburbanites also insisted that private space be set aside in each dwelling to encourage the development of moral responsibility, personal identity, and self-discipline in each household member. Ideally, each child was assigned his own bedroom and, if possible, this privilege was extended to servants as well (figs. 1.3, 1.8, 1.10). When the budget allowed, either or both heads of household would have a private preserve – a den, boudoir, sewing room, or, perhaps, a converted nursery after the children grew past infancy. (See, for example, room C in fig. 1.1 and figs. 1.8, 1.11, 1.15.) Most houses also contained semiprivate spaces where family members might retreat without removing themselves entirely from the larger life of the home: window seats, nooks, built-in hall benches, porches, servants' halls, or bedroom alcoves[39] (figs. 1.3, 1.4, 1.8, 1.13).

While preserving the family's privacy and its members' personalized expression, the dwellings conveyed a spirit of hospitality toward neighbors. Most houses projected a thoroughly friendly visage by means of cheerful flower gardens, inviting front porches, and the absence of fences or other barrier devices. A surprising degree of architectural harmony prevailed, reflecting residents' compliance with local housing conventions and their willingness to refrain from conspicuous display or ornamental one-up-manship. But the celebration of community was most evident in suburbanites' preference for informal room arrangements in their first-floor plans. Instead of the strict division between public and private space characteristic of Victorian city homes, the new suburban floor plans welcomed guests directly into the living room or into a stairhall from which the family rooms were accessible through wide openings. Arthur Clausen explained the function of the nondefensive room arrangements:

> In large country houses, bungalows, or houses of craftsman style the living room is also the reception hall. This change of affairs has developed out of the fact that there is a feeling prevalent throughout the nation that homes should be built on a more informal, simpler, and homelike plan. We always feel more at home and

more honored upon entering a home for the first time to be taken into the family living room, where a more homelike atmosphere prevails than is to be found in the formal parlor or reception hall.[40]

Three dwellings of contrasting styles, designed at widely spaced intervals, illustrate the balance between family, individuality, and community that prevailed in the new suburban house type. "Sunset Cottage," which Lamb and Rich built for Rich's father in Short Hills, has been characterized by latter-day critics as "spatially undistinguished"; contemporary critics, however, understood how aptly its "matter-of-fact planning" suited the suburban life-style of the Rich family. The first-floor plan efficiently accommodated family and social needs in just two primary spaces: the living room and an adjoining dining room (fig. 1.2). Both rooms were spacious and warmly outfitted to provide the convivial atmosphere desired just as much for family gatherings as when entertaining guests. The room arrangement was nondefensive so that visitors entered through the family living porch and stepped into a stairhall that gave ready access to the "inner sanctum." On the second floor, each family member had a private bedroom, and even on the first floor, the octagonal alcove and the porches provided semiprivate places of retreat. The most highly individualized part of the dwelling, however, was the custom third-floor studio that Rich designed for himself. A very masculine room with exposed beams and rustic brick fireplace, it housed all the architect's treasures: his drafting table, telescope, telegraphic apparatus, billiard table, and a photographic darkroom placed under the roof of the tower.[41]

The floor plan of the Henry F. Nell residence in St. Martin's (Lawrence V. Boyd, 1898) bore a close resemblance to that of Sunset Cottage, and it embodied the values of family, community, and individuality in essentially similar ways (fig. 1.12). The ingeniously efficient first floor was entirely open, symbolizing the warmest hospitality to callers and increasing the chances for family interaction in the home's primary spaces. Throughout the dwelling, Boyd provided cozy nooks to encourage intimate family tête-à-têtes, spaces that doubled as spots for solitary contemplation under less crowded conditions. William Gray Purcell's own home in Lake of the Isles (Purcell and Elmslie, 1913–1914) boasts one of the most delightful and spatially imaginative first floors of any suburban dwelling of the pre–World War I period (fig. 1.9). Using changes in level and spatial volume rather than interior walls to define basic functional areas, the architects created "a new space . . . within the house, all free and open, filled with soft light, . . . invit[ing] one to exercise the various functions of everyday living." Although Purcell and Elmslie's mode of defining space was truly novel, the spaces defined and the values that they embodied duplicated those in Sunset Cottage and the Nell residence. From the entry, one stepped into a hall from which there was ready visual access to both primary living spaces: (1) the sunken living room that sheltered both family activities and neighborly entertainments, and (2) the raised dining room with its adjoining eating porch. In place of nooks or window seats, the architects tucked a clever denlike alcove between the living and dining spaces to provide a semiprivate spot of quiet on the primary floor. On the second floor, each family member's bedroom was custom-designed to satisfy individual needs and preferences.[42]

The culminating element in the design program that emerged in these four suburbs was "the desire to build with beauty," to make the American home "at least as fair to the aesthetic eye as to the examination of the utilitarian." Believing that "there is no influence so potent upon life as harmonious surroundings," the new suburbanites considered the "possess[ion of] a home which is harmonious in a simple and inexpensive way" a basic democratic right—"the privilege of all but the wretchedly poor." Members of suburban design communities cultivated artistry in at least five ways, with most houses exhibiting some combination of approaches.

The first approach, favored by all those "striv[ing] to raise the standard of our native domestic architecture," defined beauty as the observation of "simplicity, harmony of outline, and proper proportions." Many, though by no means all, proponents of this classical understanding of beauty advocated houses designed in time-honored styles like the Georgian of the Stockhausen residence in St. Martin's (DeArmond, Ashmead, and Bickley, 1913). (See fig. 1.10.)

The beauty of harmonizing the dwelling with its natural surroundings was also practiced widely, whether the home was blessed with an especially felicitous site, like Charlecote in Short Hills, or embellished with new plantings, like the Sutton residence in Kenilworth[43] (figs. 1.14, 1.7).

The third means for incorporating beauty was through fine craftsmanship manifested in a variety of skills and materials.

The beauty of craftsmanship was exhibited, for example, in the remarkable masonry of St. Martin's Italian stonecutters working with the local Chestnut Hill greystone. It was evident, as well, in the polychrome, terra-cotta mantel ornament, decorative glasswork, "highly enriched built-in furniture, and flush veneer inlaid doors" of Purcell, Feick, and Elmslie's Powers residence, and in the sensuous woodwork of the stairhall in the Jeder dwelling.

The most widely espoused but least satisfactorily realized form of beauty from the architect's point of view was architectural unity — the coordination of every aspect of composition, ornamentation, furnishing, and landscape design. A chronic source of tension between architects and clients reluctant to relinquish control over interior design, artistic unity was probably best exemplified in Purcell and Elmslie's domestic masterpiece for the Purcell family — where architect and client had a perfect meeting of minds.

The most common kind of beauty cultivated in the new house type was the beauty of domesticity — the "spiritual element emanating from utilitarian forms" that imparted a "vastly important" value to everyday living. The straightforward celebration of domesticity, whether expressed in the delightful service provided by one of Purcell and Elmslie's raised hearths, a well-planned kitchen, or a cheerfully furnished sunporch, remains the most remarkable achievement of the new suburban homes[44] (fig. 1.10).

The Siege Theory — an interpretation that argues that architects played the decisive role and that aesthetic issues the decisive influence in domestic design — provides us with only a partial understanding of the new suburban home. Suburban communities like those in Short Hills, St. Martin's, Kenilworth, and Lake of the Isles carefully and cleverly integrated all seven of the foregoing principles — efficiency, technology, nature, family, individuality, community, and beauty — into the design of most of the houses they constructed prior to World War I. The ubiquity of the suburban design program suggests the strength of the consensus then emerging nationwide concerning the proper form of the ideal American home. That consensus — the product of extensive debate and experiment — embodied a whole range of issues and anxieties facing urban Americans of the professional-managerial stratum around the turn of the century.

Among these issues, professional and aesthetic matters figured prominently, but they did not, alone, account for the shapes that suburban houses assumed.

There were many more similarities than differences in the designs of houses built in Short Hills and the other three suburbs. In examining not only the few progressive or conservative architectural gems in each community but also the houses next door and across the street, I found insufficient evidence to support a conservative versus progressive or East versus Midwest model of suburban domestic architecture. Few of the houses could be called pure examples of either conservative or progressive architectural principles as they were defined at the time.[45] But even upon deliberate examination of the extremes, their similarities overshadowed their differences because they were products of the same basic suburban design program. Let us compare four roughly contemporary dwellings of contrasting styles from four suburbs: the Georgian revival Stockhausen residence of St. Martin's (fig. 1.10), the Prairie style Purcell residence of Lake of the Isles (figs. 1.5, 1.9), the Tudor revival Charlecote of Short Hills (figs. 1.14, 1.15), and the Tudor revival/Prairie style Chapman residence of Kenilworth (fig. 1.3). Although differing in the degree of conservatism or progressivism in their exterior expression, all four dwellings accommodated and evoked the new suburban life-style in essentially similar ways.

The stately classical symmetry of the Stockhausen residence and the patterned, geometric, modern visage of the Purcell house represented the extremes of approach to the problem of style in suburban domestic architecture. The contrast was only a superficial one, however; it began and ended with the question of style. Upon entering the Stockhausen residence, one left historical associations behind for the most part and simply encountered the same kinds of functional family living spaces that made up the floor plan of the Purcell residence. All four houses, in fact, could be said to have met Purcell's conscious purpose in designing his own home: "to first establish a real modern American family life, and then give it expression in real forms." Each first-floor plan, while different from the others, arranged the same basic spaces in an informal manner that allowed free circulation and visual penetration among the principal rooms. Each dwelling was sensibly but sensitively decorated and comfortably furnished to provide the creature comforts —

mental, physical, and emotional—presumed to ensure domestic well-being. Whether seated in the plain and homey Stockhausen living room, amidst the rustic family clutter of Charlecote, in the refined and learned atmosphere of the Chapman living room, or before the golden glow of Purcell's raised living room hearth, one was immersed in an environment carefully calculated to stimulate the human mind, nourish the family spirit, and welcome the society of neighbors.[46]

The similarities extended to the ways in which technology and nature were employed in each dwelling to enhance the lives of inhabitants. All four houses featured sophisticated domestic technology and multiple bathrooms, although Purcell's home held a technological edge with its all-season system for controlling temperature and humidity. Each floor plan provided thoroughly, even imaginatively, for the practical details of housekeeping and storage. Kitchens were carefully organized with built-in workstations and storage dressers to save worry and steps. Butler's pantries (in the three larger dwellings), storage larders, and laundry rooms increased the functional efficiency of service areas and promoted cleanliness. Each kitchen was gaily decorated and oriented to secure adequate light, cross-ventilation, and pleasant views to cheer and uplift those required to labor there.[47]

In all of the dwellings, the designers made the experiencing of nature an integral part of inhabitants' daily lives by providing indoor-outdoor living opportunities and harmonizing each home with its natural surroundings. On this point, suburban houses differed only in adapting to the details of the site and the limitations of imagination. Since Charlecote was blessed with a beautiful wooded site offering panoramic views, Parish and Schroeder devised a bent floor plan that captured views for every principal first-floor room and second-floor chamber. The Chapman residence featured the greatest variety of indoor-outdoor spaces: a glazed sunporch, open-air terrace, servant's porch, and a sleeping porch and roof deck adjoining the master bedroom. Purcell and Elmslie made the best of a narrow lot by creating a delightful water garden in the Purcell house front yard and lowering the living room below grade to bring family members in intimate proximity to it:

> Below the living room group of windows is a pool that catches and reflects the color notes cast by plaster, wood, and leaded glass. This is a paddling place for all the babies in the neighborhood. It is

two inches deep and accidental "wet all over" averages one a week. The house has been provided with landscape setting, of which this pool is the feature. The morning sun reflects upward from the water through the tall windows and dances on the tinted ceiling until the maple begins to shade it.

In the "conservative" Stockhausen residence, however, the architects did the most with the least generous site of the four—a barren stretch of land cleared previously for farming. In addition to ringing the dwelling with shrubbery to soften its profile, DeArmond, Ashmead, and Bickley flanked the main block with spacious sunporches. These conservatory-like spaces, filled with greenery year-round and glazed from floor to ceiling with windows designed in a delightful Palladian motif, epitomized the pleasures of suburban indoor-outdoor living.[48]

The most striking differences among the four dwellings came from their contrasting approaches to aesthetic expression, especially toward the use of historical sources of design inspiration. In recreating a specific historic precedent, the architects of the Stockhausen residence, for example, presented the conservative argument favoring the adoption of traditional design sources. Purcell and Elmslie, on the other hand, shunned historic elements and sought to create a wholly original, American mode of expression. Occupying intermediate positions were Charlecote, whose designers created an original composition that relied upon a traditional timbering technique for its primary stylistic motif, and the Chapman residence, whose architects quoted frequently and at length from medieval design sources, creating in an ostensibly Prairie style dwelling an unmistakably medieval effect. Despite the different ways in which these architects resolved the central aesthetic controversy of their era, they were of one mind in (1) calling for the cultivation of beauty and (2) making the archetypal domestic trappings of the home the focus of ornamental or compositional attention. Thus, the delicately patterned leaded glass windows of the Purcell residence and the towering chimneys and flanking sunporches of the Stockhausen dwelling became primary symbols of the domestic mission within. All four homes, in other words, achieved visual delight by bringing to expression the simple tenets of the new suburban domestic program.

Among houses in the four suburbs, similarities in form and function outweighed differences in style; in addition, dwellings in the eastern locations were no more nor less conservative than their counterparts in the Midwest. Since several principles from the new design program were inherently progressive, there was a good deal of progressive architecture in each suburb, regardless of region. This becomes evident when we compare the dwellings in Kenilworth—a midwestern suburb renowned for its architects' progressivism—and those in St. Martin's—famous for its presumed Philadelphia conservatism in matters both social and architectural. Prior to World War I, both suburbs sponsored an identical percentage (60 percent) of dwellings embodying design principles that were predominantly progressive. One might still argue that Kenilworth contained a greater number of strikingly innovative designs in the Prairie style houses of George Maher, Tallmadge and Watson, and Frank Lloyd Wright. But in the Pastorius Park development, St. Martin's boasted one of the most innovative and comprehensive examples of the successful integration of architecture and planning anywhere in the country.[49] Architects from both regions discussed the problem of achieving originality in domestic architecture in strikingly similar terms. According to Frank Miles Day of Philadelphia,

> If the plan be a simple and direct expression of the needs and life of the people who are to live in the house, and if the elevations are a logical outgrowth from a reasonable expression of that plan, and if the whole be made beautiful and vocal of its time and place, then the building will have style in the best sense and will need none of that exotic archaeological style that is the bane of so much of our work today.

Day was no less adamant in his condemnation of historic reproduction than Prairie School architects like George Maher: "Our democratic architect must know his client's habits, the climate in which he lives, the location, possibilities of his site and its other relations, . . . to work out a solution that is both practical, sensible, and which, without effort, will possess beauty. With such an understanding there need be no struggle for originality in style."[50]

As defined by members of the profession in the pre–World War I era, progressive design encompassed a wide range of domestic form, principles, and expression; it was not the exclusive property of the Prairie School. Architectural innovation could manifest itself, for example, in the dazzling structural achievements of reinforced concrete construction displayed in the DeLanoy residence (fig. 1.8). A simple but uninspiring domestic exterior might surround a brilliant floor plan—a wholly

original arrangement perfectly suited to the commissioning family—like that of the Nell residence in St. Martin's (fig. 1.12). The rational composition of Charlecote—in which the exterior directly and appropriately revealed the interior arrangement—compared favorably with the simple and functional midwestern compositions of George Maher (figs. 1.14, 1.7). Edmund Gilchrist's reversed-plan dwellings in St. Martin's (1909, 1912) were no less significant an innovation than Purcell, Feick, and Elmslie's reversed-plan composition for E. L. Powers in Lake of the Isles (1911).[51] (See figs. 1.6, 1.11.)

There was no marked difference in the amount of progressive domestic architecture built in the eastern and midwestern suburbs between 1877 and 1917, nor did they provide evidence of a strong movement toward conservatism. Some of the most dramatic evidence for a conservative trend issued from the statements of self-styled rebels associated with the midwestern Prairie or Chicago schools of architects. At various times, Maher, Purcell, Tallmadge, and, certainly, Sullivan and Wright portrayed themselves as embattled geniuses struggling to advance the cause of American architecture against an entrenched and unimaginative profession. During the 1880s and 1890s, in addition, prominent architects from the Midwest and South—progressives and conservatives alike—formed a separate professional association to redress what they felt was an eastern-based prejudice against their accomplishments and their regional conditions of professional practice.[52] There is no reason to consider their sentiments and sense of rivalry as anything but genuine; but neither should we accept their observations uncritically. The houses of Short Hills, St. Martin's, Kenilworth, and Lake of the Isles furnish little evidence that substantiates a movement after 1900 toward the adoption of one style or conservative mode of expression.

Within these suburbs, in fact, design communities thought less about style than about how well their houses satisfied the manner in which they wished to live and exemplified how they thought others ought to live. The range of regional and stylistic expression exhibited was simply the logical result of adapting the general suburban design consensus to local aesthetic preferences and local circumstances of construction. Community members achieved distinctive variations of expression in four principal ways: (1) They used to advantage the most local, economical building materials—like the chestnut timbers felled right on the site for Charlecote—incorporating the special qualities of those materials into their designs. (2) They adapted local building or craft traditions, as in St. Martin's frequent revival of the colonial Pennsylvania farmhouse vernacular style so well-suited for houses built of the local stone. (3) In some suburbs, one style or the work of a single architect set the dominant aesthetic tone, like George Maher's Prairie style dwellings established the architectural character of early Kenilworth. (4) Sometimes a principal developer imposed his own aesthetic preferences on architects and their clients, imparting a unity of expression to a substantial number of the community's houses. But ultimately, the chief source of inspiration in the new dwellings was the communal suburban design program itself. Its ambitious agenda prompted suburbanites to create beauty in their domestic environments and to strive to convey the individuality of their residents and the uniqueness of their suburban adventure.

The crucial part each suburban community played in determining the design program that emerged there cannot be overemphasized. Only when we have analyzed the full context of the design process—when we have identified the participants and reconstructed the issues that guided their design decisions—can we fully understand the logic of suburban houses. Advocates of the Siege Theory have often based their conservative versus progressive model of domestic architecture on a comparison between midwestern suburban houses designed for members of the professional-managerial stratum and eastern country houses designed for members of America's exclusive upper class. The failure to discern, for example, that Wright's Hiram Baldwin residence (Kenilworth, 1905) and Platt's John Jay Chapman residence (Barrytown, N.Y., 1904–1909) derive from entirely different design contexts has resulted in the proverbial comparison between oranges and apples. Each of these domestic subtypes was commissioned by a distinctive clientele to meet a different set of needs and purposes. Upper-class country houses may,

indeed, have embodied more conservative design principles than the smaller, more informal dwellings commissioned by the professional-managerial stratum. The contrasting design preferences of upper-class clients and those deriving from a secondary level of society was noted long ago by Leonard Eaton in his study of the domestic practices of Wright and Howard Van Doren Shaw.[53] By concentrating on the aesthetic characteristics of domestic architecture, many historians have overlooked the rich texture of meaning that both housing subtypes held for their creators and consumers.

Those who contributed to the design of houses in suburbs like Short Hills, St. Martin's, Kenilworth, and Lake of the Isles fashioned a domestic environment that precisely represented how they wished to structure their daily lives. During the initial design process, each community also seemed intent upon creating a model—an ideal home environment that might inspire moral and physical improvement in other urban residential communities. Numerous testimonials suggest that the residents of planned, exclusive suburbs did, indeed, liken life in their new suburban houses to "God's very kingdom on the earth." And although their model houses failed to transform the rest of the urban populace, they did inspire the postwar housing that raised the quality of living for thousands of new suburban home owners from the middle reaches of society. The distinctive qualities of the new suburban house type—and, no doubt, of many suburban tract houses modeled on them—did not issue simply from aesthetic considerations, from the architect's desire to make an original or traditional stylistic statement. They were the result of a design community's effort to give real form to the suburban ideal of living in the most straightforward, economical, and artistic manner possible. Despite the constraints imposed on the local design process, the new suburban houses embodied many progressive principles and practices. As Kenilworth's resident architect, George Maher, understood, "originality in design arises from obvious local reasons."[54]

Notes

The author gratefully acknowledges the Horace H. Rackham School of Graduate Studies of the University of Michigan and the American Institute of Architects Foundation for their generous support for the research on which this article is based. Special thanks are due Sidney K. Robinson and Donald Hoffmann for their insightful comments on earlier drafts.

1. Albert Winslow Cobb, "Introduction," in John Calvin Stevens and Albert Winslow Cobb, *Examples of American Domestic Architecture* (New York, 1889), 40.

2. Leonard K. Eaton, *Two Chicago Architects and Their Clients* (Cambridge, Mass., 1969). Two other important works that presaged Eaton's hypothesis of the Siege Theory are Lewis Mumford, "A Backward Glance," in Mumford, ed., *Roots of Contemporary American Architecture* (1952; reprint, New York, 1972), 1–30, and Vincent J. Scully, Jr., *The Shingle Style and the Stick Style* (New Haven, Conn., 1955). Alan Gowans makes a strong case for the importance of the subject matter of American suburban housing in *The Comfortable House: North American Suburban Architecture, 1890-1930* (Cambridge, Mass., 1986).

3. H. Allen Brooks, *The Prairie School: Frank Lloyd Wright and His Midwest Contemporaries* (New York, 1972), especially chs. 1 and 9. Brooks's version of the Siege Theory is not without support; both Sullivan and Wright encouraged the view that progressive architecture was under siege from conservative Beaux Arts–trained architects, and the *Western Architect* echoed this position in its editorials during the second decade of the twentieth century. For a sample of these, see "Professional Coldness in the East Detrimental to the West," *Western Architect* 19 (1913): 24–25; "Narrow Views Concerning Western Progressives," *Western Architect* 19 (1913): 33–34; "*Western Architect* Illustration for 1915," *Western Architect* 20 (1914): 1; "Do Architects of Taste Cross the Alleghenies?" *Western Architect* 20 (1914): 1–2; "Rebels in Architecture Discovered by Daily Press," *Western Architect* 20 (1914): 85.

4. Alan Gowans, *Images of American Living* (New York, 1976), 372–386, 389–413; Gowans, *The Comfortable House,* 102–104, 203–206; Richard Guy Wilson, "American Arts and Crafts Architecture: Radical 'though Dedicated to the Cause Conservative," in Wendy Kaplan, ed., *The Art That Is Life* (Boston, 1987), 101–131. Among the recent spate of books treating the domestic architecture of the period are a number that do not invoke the conservative versus radical model for their interpretations. See, for example, David Handlin, *The American Home* (Boston, 1979); Gwendolyn Wright, *Moralism and the Model Home* (Chicago, 1980) and *Building the Dream* (New York, 1981); Clifford Edward Clark, Jr., *The American Family Home* (Chapel Hill, N.C., 1986); Colleen McDannell, *The Christian Home in Victorian America, 1840-1900* (Bloomington, Ill., 1986); Simon J. Bronner, "Manner Books and Suburban Houses: The Structure of Tradition and Aesthetics," *Winterthur Portfolio* 18 (1983): 61–68; and Margaret S. Marsh, "The Suburban House: The Social Implications of Environmental Choice" (paper presented at Annual Meeting of the Organization of American Historians, New York City, 1986).

5. Richard W. Longstreth argues strongly that the academic tendency in pre–World War I American architecture was eclectic in character rather than an effort to impose a unified mode of classical expression, in "Academic Eclecticism in American Architecture," *Winterthur Portfolio* 17 (1982): 55–82. Reyner Banham has for years been inveighing against architectural historians' tendencies to direct too much attention to building exteriors; see his *Architecture of the Well-Tempered Environment* (Chicago, 1969). The practical result of the Siege Theory's overemphasis on aesthetic and professional matters—a deemphasis on the role of the client in architectural decision-making—runs counter to Eaton's original intentions in his study of architect-client relations in *Two Chicago Architects and Their Clients.*

6. The planned, exclusive suburb was a post–Civil War community type created to house upper middle-class families of the professional-managerial stratum who wished to live in a controlled suburban environment close enough to allow commutation to the city. Riverside, Ill., (1869) may be considered the prototypic planned, exclusive suburb of the pre–World War I period although most such communities were founded between the late 1870s and the turn of the century. Although a formal, written community plan may not have been prepared for each "planned" suburb, they were, nevertheless, carefully and comprehensively designed and their development closely guided by one or a small group of founder(s). Since they were intended for a homogeneous and privileged group of residents, access was controlled by a variety of ordinances, restrictions, and strategies. For a complete account of the history of design and development in the four planned, exclusive suburbs discussed in this article, see Mary Corbin Sies, "American Country House Architecture in Context: The Suburban Ideal of Living in the East and Midwest, 1877–1917" (Ph.D. diss., University of Michigan, 1987). Three important histories of planned, exclusive suburbs are Walter J. Creese's account of Riverside, Ill., in *The Crowning of the American Landscape* (Princeton, 1985); Carol A. O'Connor, *A Sort of Utopia: Scarsdale, 1891-1981* (Albany, 1983); and Michael Ebner's *Creating Chicago's North Shore: A Suburban History* (Chicago, 1988).

7. For a more full analysis of the "suburban ideal" developed in planned, exclusive suburbs—one that examines planning and social organization as well as domestic architecture—see Sies, "American Country House Architecture in Context." Marc Weiss details how the suburban residential ideal was perpetuated after World War I in Marc A. Weiss, *The Rise of the Community Builders: The American Real Estate Industry and Urban Land Planning* (New York, 1987). The best general history of American suburbanization is Kenneth Jackson's *Crabgrass Frontier* (New York, 1985). The strongest treatment of the origin of the Anglo-American suburban ideal is Robert Fishman, *Bourgeois Utopias: The Rise and Fall of Suburbia* (New York, 1987).

8. I use *community of discourse* as intellectual historian David A. Hollinger has defined it to refer to "any population that has left a record of having addressed 'shared questions,' regardless of the nature of the questions and of the educational level and mental capabilities of those who shared the questions." See Hollinger, "Historians and the Discourse of Intellectuals," in John Higham and Paul Conkin, eds., *New Directions in American Intellectual History* (Baltimore, 1979), 42–63. I am quoting from pages 54–55. Dell Upton, "Pattern Books and Professionalism: Aspects of the Transformation of Domestic Architecture in America, 1800–1860," *Winterthur Portfolio* 19 (1984): 114. For information about various venues in which the debate concerning the ideal home environment took place, see Wright, *Moralism and the Model Home;* Karen Blair, *The Clubwoman as Feminist* (New York, 1980); Mary C. Sies, "The Shelter Magazines and Standards of American Domestic Architectural Taste in the East and Midwest, 1897–1917" (paper presented at American Studies Association convention, Philadelphia, 1983).

9. Eaton, *Two Chicago Architects and Their Clients,* ch. 1. I base my concept of a professional-managerial stratum on Barbara and John Ehrenreich's description. See Barbara Ehrenreich and John Ehrenreich, "The Professional-Managerial Class," *Radical America* 11, no. 2 (1977): 7–31. Sources helpful in providing background on this population cohort and its historical circumstances include Alfred Chandler, Jr., *The Visible Hand: The Managerial Revolution in American Business* (Cambridge, Mass., 1977); Robert Wiebe, *The Search for Order, 1877-1920* (New York, 1967); Alan Trachtenberg, *The Incorporation of*

America (New York, 1982). I classified as businessmen such occupations as managers or executives in business or industrial concerns, accountants, bankers, and brokers but not entrepreneurs, industrialists, or financiers. Among professionals I included physicians, attorneys, and members of the design professions – engineers, architects, and landscape architects. Producers or transmitters of culture included educators, ministers, artists, musicians, advertisers, writers, editors, or museum administrators.

10. I refer to the concept of "belief system" developed by Murray Murphey and described in his essay, "The Place of Beliefs in Modern Culture," in Higham and Conkin, *New Directions in American Intellectual History,* 151–165. I use *bifurcated* in the sense intended by Thomas Bender to describe the "competing patterns of order" of local community and trans-local market that affected Americans after 1870. See Bender, *Community and Social Change in America* (New Brunswick, N.J., 1978), 114. For sources concerning the values themselves, see especially Karen Halttunen, *Confidence Men and Painted Women* (New Haven, Conn., 1982); Steven Mintz, *A Prison of Expectations: The Family in Victorian Culture* (New York, 1983); Wiebe, *The Search for Order, 1877–1920;* Trachtenberg, *The Incorporation of America;* Clark, Jr., *The American Family Home;* Burton J. Bledstein, *The Culture of Professionalism* (New York, 1976); and Ehrenreich and Ehrenreich, "The Professional-Managerial Class."

11. The developers and early residents of Short Hills, St. Martin's, Kenilworth, Lake of the Isles, and other similar suburbs were quite direct in stating that they intended their homes and communities to serve as models. See, for example, Cora Hartshorn, *A Little History of Short Hills* (Millburn, N.J., 1979), 4–6; Alfred Mathews, "Short Hills, New Jersey," in Everts and Peck, *History of Essex and Hudson Counties* (Philadelphia, 1890); William I. Russell, *The Romance and Tragedy of a Widely Known Business Man of New York* (Baltimore, 1913), 78; George Woodward, "Landlord and Tenant," *The Survey* 45 (1920): 389–391; Colleen Browne Kilner, *Joseph Sears and His Kenilworth* (Kenilworth, Ill., 1969), 325–331; Theodore Wirth, *The Minneapolis Park System* (Minneapolis, 1945), 31–36; O'Connor, *A Sort of Utopia,* viii.

On previous urban residential experiences, Joseph Sears, developer of Kenilworth, lost a child and a nephew to a diphtheria epidemic that swept through Chicago; his family also assisted Chicagoans who lost their homes during the Great Fire. Sears, Stewart Hartshorn, founder of Short Hills, and William I. Russell, a prominent resident of Short Hills, all suffered from serious urban pollution-related health problems that improved dramatically when they relocated to the suburbs. During the latter half of the nineteenth century, St. Martin's was a haven during the summer for Philadelphians fleeing the yellow fever epidemics and polluted water sources of the city. See Kilner, *Joseph Sears,* 103; Hartshorn, *A Little History,* 5–6; Russell, *Romance and Tragedy,* 76; Willard S. Detweiler, Jr., *Chestnut Hill: An Architectural History* (Philadelphia, 1969), 18.

12. E. C. Gardner, *Homes and All About Them* (Boston, 1885), 220; *Western Architect* 21 (1915): 43. The best analysis of positive environmental reform strategies can be found in Paul Boyer's *Urban Masses and Moral Order in America, 1820–1920* (Cambridge, Mass., 1978), chs. 12–19. That social reform (and not just architectural reform) impulses strongly influenced the design of the home has been well documented, especially by Gwendolyn Wright in *Moralism and the Model Home* and by Clifford E. Clark, Jr., in *The American Family Home.*

13. Albert Winslow Cobb, in Stevens and Cobb, *Examples of American Domestic Architecture,* 10–11; George W. Maher, "The Western Spirit," *Inland Architect* 47 (1906): 39; Mathews, "Short Hills, New Jersey," 9; Samuel Warren Hue, "The Problem of the Family," in Howard J. Rogers, ed., *St. Louis, Missouri, Universal Exposition, Congress of Arts and Sciences* 7 (1904): 715; Gardner, *Homes and All About Them,* 696, 441.

14. Adna F. Weber, "Suburban Annexations," *North American Review* 166 (1898): 616; Carol Aronovici, "Housing and the Housing Problem," *Annals of the American Academy* 51 (1914): 3.

15. Charles E. White, Jr., *Successful Houses and How to Build Them* (1912; reprint, New York, 1927), 1, 6. See also William B. Patterson, "The Religious Value of Proper Housing," *Annals of the American Academy* 51 (1914): 41–47; Hue, "The Problem of the Family." Margaret Marsh notes higher home ownership rates among blue-collar than white-collar workers in "The Suburban House," 13–15; it is possible that her counter-intuitive statistics reflect the success of positive environmental campaigns among members of the working class. In *Shaky Palaces* (New York, 1984), Matthew Edel, Elliott Sclar, and Daniel Luria note that home ownership may have been a negative force for upward mobility among working-class Americans in Boston. In his book-in-progress, *Own Your Own Home: The American Real Estate Industry and National Housing Policy,* Marc A. Weiss looks at the interaction between private and public interests in promoting home ownership among Americans.

16. Dorothy Sears, quoted in Kilner, *Joseph Sears,* 119; E. P. Powell, *The Country Home* (New York, 1904), 9. On the prescriptive importance of "model" homes, see Wright, *Moralism and the Model Home.* The importance of suburban location was stressed continually during the period; see, for example, Olmsted, Vaux and Company, "Riverside," Riverside, Ill., 1869, *Landscape Architecture* 21 (1931): 283; M. G. Van Rensselaer, "A Suburban Country Place," *Century* 43 (1897): 3; Eugene Clancy, "The Car and the Country Home," *Harper's Weekly* 55 (1911): 30. For a discussion of the presumed role of nature and technology in transforming the urban residential environment, see Mary Corbin Sies, "The City Transformed: Nature, Technology, and the Suburban Ideal, 1877–1917," *Journal of Urban History* 14 (1987): 81–111. Although I focus on the home in this essay, it is important to note that in the view of the new suburbanites, home and community could not be separated in designing the ideal home environment.

17. The best examination of American attitudes toward technology and the use of technology to achieve social and material progress is Howard Segal's *Technological Utopianism in American Culture* (Chicago, 1985). See especially ch. 6 for a discussion of technology and positive environmental reform with reference to suburbia.

18. Weber, "Suburban Annexations," 616. See also, Powell, *The Country Home,* 374; A. H. G., "Lake Forest: The Beautiful Suburb of Chicago," *House and Garden* 5 (1904): 275; Peter J. Schmitt, *Back to Nature: The Arcadian Myth in Urban America* (New York, 1969).

19. Kenilworth Company, "The Model Suburban Home" (1890), and "Kenilworth: The Model Suburban Home" (n.d.), promotional booklets in Kenilworth Historical Society Collection, Kenilworth, Ill.; Gustav Stickley, "The Craftsman Idea . . . ," in Stickley, ed., *Craftsman Homes* (1909; reprint, New York, 1979), 196. See also Gardner, *Homes and All About Them,* 67; J. C. Nichols, quoted in Bill Worley, "Origins of the Twentieth Century Suburb" (paper presented at Annual Meeting of Popular Culture Association, Toronto, 1984), 12.

20. Aronovici, "Housing and the Housing Problem," 3; Ella S. Babbitt, "Ultra Practical and Ultra Theoretical Architecture," *Inland Architect* 7 (1886): 21. See also Patterson, "The Religious Value of Proper Housing"; Hue, "The Problem of the Family," 710–713.

21. Mabel Tuke Priestman, *Art and Economy in Home Decoration* (New York, 1908), 105; Cobb, "Introduction," 39; Catharine Beecher and Harriet Beecher Stowe, *The American Woman's Home* (1869; reprint, Watkins Glen, N.Y., 1979), 150.

22. "Residence of Mr. Charles Roe, Kenilworth, Ill.," *Architectural Review*

14 (1907): 52; Beecher and Stowe, *The American Woman's Home,* 94; Harold D. Eberlein, "A House at St. Martin's," *American Homes and Gardens* 8 (1911): 430.

23. Mintz, *A Prison of Expectations,* 20, 39, 197.

24. See, for example, Celeste Penney, "Historical Perspective," in *Sticks, Shingles, and Stones: The History and Architecture of Stewart Hartshorn's Ideal Community at Short Hills, New Jersey, 1878-1937* (Millburn, N.J., 1980), 4-6; Russell, *The Romance and Tragedy,* 84-85, 124-127, 143-145; Kilner, *Joseph Sears,* chs. 28-29, 31-33.

25. For a summary of the social reform and charity activities engaged in by the women of Short Hills, St. Martin's, Kenilworth, and Lake of the Isles, see Mary Corbin Sies, "The Domestic Mission of the Privileged American Suburban Homemaker, 1877-1917: A Reassessment," in Pat Browne and Marilyn Ferris Motz, eds., *Making the American Home: Middle Class Women and Domestic Material Culture, 1840-1940* (Bowling Green, Ky., 1988), 192-209. Gwendolyn Wright provides a concise summary of the efficiently designed modern home in ch. 9 of *Building the Dream* (New York, 1981).

26. Candace Wheeler, *Principles of Home Decoration* (New York, 1908), 17; Isaac Hodgson, "Hints on a National Style of Architecture," *Inland Architect* 8 (1886): 71. On the meaning that the mid-century American home held for its inhabitants, see Kirk Jeffrey, "The Family as Utopian Retreat from the City: The Nineteenth Century Contribution," *Soundings* 55 (1972): 21-41; Clifford Clark, Jr., "Domestic Architecture as an Index to Social History: The Romantic Revival and the Cult of Domesticity in America, 1840-1870," *Journal of Interdisciplinary History* 7 (1976): 33-56; and, of course, Andrew Jackson Downing, *The Architecture of Country Houses* (1850; reprint, New York, 1969).

27. For a discussion of the meaning of the term *efficiency* at the turn of the century, see Samuel Haber's *Efficiency and Uplift: Scientific Management in the Progressive Era, 1890-1920* (Chicago, 1964). See Mary Corbin Sies, "American Country House Architecture in Context," for a detailed analysis of the seven design principles discussed below as manifested in the houses of Short Hills, St. Martin's, Kenilworth, and Lake of the Isles.

28. These and subsequent observations are based upon my field survey of every house constructed between 1877 and 1917 in Short Hills, St. Martin's, Kenilworth, and Lake of the Isles. See also *Millburn–Short Hills Historic Structures Survey* (Millburn, N.J., 1979); Jefferson M. Moak, "Inventory of Buildings Within the Chestnut Hill Historic District: An Appendix to the Chestnut Hill Historic District Nomination for the National Register" (Chestnut Hill, Philadelphia, Pa., 1985); "Record Book of the Kenilworth Company," Kenilworth, Ill.; Building Permits, City of Minneapolis, Minn. Larger and costlier dwellings differed from more modest suburban houses chiefly in their more elaborate master bedroom and service areas, in the number of bathrooms, and, of course, in the quality of their interior appointments.

29. George Bertrand, "The Decoration of an Inexpensive House," *Western Architect* 2, no. 3 (1903): 14, and "Architecture," *Western Architect* 2, no. 2 (1903): 14. Authors of domestic design manuals were nearly unanimous in advancing the merits of utility. See, for example, Priestman, *Art and Economy in Home Decoration,* 14-18; Elsie DeWolfe, *The House in Good Taste* (1911; reprint, New York, 1975), especially ch. 2; Gardner, *Homes and All About Them;* White, *Successful Houses and How to Build Them,* especially ch. 28; Beecher and Stowe, *The American Woman's Home;* Wheeler, *Principles of Home Decoration,* ch. 13.

30. Gardner, *Homes and All About Them,* 25. Although built-in furnishings have been associated especially with Craftsman Enterprises and the Prairie School architects, their use was much wider, having reached the status of a craze between 1900 and World War I. For the widest illustration of built-in furnishings, see Stickley, *Craftsman Homes.*

31. C. V. Stravs, "Some Contributions to the Theme 'Modern Architecture'," *Western Architect* 20 (1913): 74-75; John Lynne Grey, "The Country Home of a Composer," *House and Garden* 18 (1910): 339. In the houses of Short Hills, St. Martin's, Kenilworth, and Lake of the Isles, the honest representation of the nature of construction materials was not nearly so universally achieved as the direct expression of domestic purpose.

32. Harry W. Jones, "The Architect and the Public," *Western Architect* 2, no. 1 (1902): 19; Thomas Tallmadge, "The Chicago School," *Architectural Review* 15 (1908): 72. See also Bertrand, "Architecture," 14. For an introduction to the changes in the construction industry occurring between 1870 and 1920 and how they affected the suburban residential construction boom, see Michael J. Doucet and John C. Weaver, "Material Culture and the North American House: The Era of the Common Man, 1870-1920," *Journal of American History* 72 (1985): 560-587.

33. Fireproof construction became a serious preference in Kenilworth, for example, after 1903 when an entire class of boys from Rugby School perished in the fire at the Iroquois Theatre in Chicago. On suburban fireproof construction, see Benjamin A. Howes, "Architectural Development in the Reinforced Concrete House," *Architectural Record* 25 (1909): 341-358; White, *Successful Houses and How to Build Them,* ch. 13. On the general impact of technology on suburban design, see Wright, *Moralism and the Model Home,* ch. 8, and *Building the Dream,* ch. 9; Banham, *The Architecture of the Well-Tempered Environment,* ch. 6; Handlin, *The American Home,* ch. 7; Beecher and Stowe, *The American Woman's Home.*

34. Florence E. Parker, "The Ideal Country House," *Western Architect* 1, no. 1 (1902): 15.

35. " 'Charlecote', the Residence of C. H. Stout, Esq.," *American Homes and Gardens* 2 (1906): 309-311.

36. Parker, "The Ideal Country Home," 14; Arthur Clausen, *The Art, Science, and Sentiment of Homebuilding* (Minneapolis, n.d.), 75.

37. Harold D. Eberlein, "A House at St. Martin's," *American Homes and Gardens* 8 (1911): 428, 430. See also, for example, Clausen, *The Art;* Stickley, "The Craftsman Idea" and "The Living Room," in *Craftsman Homes,* 196-197, 129-136; Priestman, *Art and Economy in Home Decoration,* ch. 11; and DeWolfe, *The House in Good Taste,* ch. 11.

38. Charles A. Rich, "Suburban Residence Built of Brick," *Brickbuilder* 7 (1898): 157; Harrie T. Lindeberg, "The Design and Plan of the Country House," *American Architect* 99 (1911): 136.

39. On the need for dens or other private spaces in the home, see, for example, Stickley, "The Craftsman Idea," 196; Aymar Embury III, *One Hundred Country Houses,* 180; Rich, "Suburban Residence Built of Brick," 157-158; Russell, *The Romance and Tragedy,* 106, 109; Edith Louise Allen, *American Housing* (Peoria, Ill., 1930), 137-138.

40. Clausen, *The Art, Science, and Sentiment of Homebuilding,* 75. See also Stickley, "The Craftsman Idea," 196. Both Stewart Hartshorn and Joseph Sears, founders of Short Hills and Kenilworth, strongly discouraged conspicuous display in the design of homes in their communities. In St. Martin's, the few elaborate houses that departed from the more modest suburban design program detailed here were commissioned by the handful of upper-class residents that moved to St. Martin's prior to World War I. On the supercession of the parlor by the living room during this period, one should note that rooms in suburban houses that were labeled parlor on floor plans nevertheless functioned as living rooms—i.e., they were the primary family dayroom and not just a formal room reserved for the receiving and entertaining of guests. In the few instances where suburban homes retained a parlor or receiving room in addition to the living

room, the parlor was generally pushed to the side of the plan, obviating its function as a formal barrier to the family living spaces. Sally McMurry's article on the American parlor is an interesting discussion but one that lacks the illumination that a consideration of suburban living rooms would have provided her treatment of rural and urban floor plans; see McMurry, "City Parlor, Country Sitting Room: Rural Vernacular Design and the American Parlor, 1840–1900," *Winterthur Portfolio* 20 (1985): 261–280.

41. Compare, for example, two relatively recent criticisms of the Sunset Cottage floor plan–Arnold Lewis, ed., *American Country Houses of the Gilded Age* (New York, 1982), plate 86, and Scully, *The Shingle Style and the Stick Style,* 101–and two contemporary accounts–George William Sheldon, *Artistic Country Seats* (New York, 1886–1887), and Bruce Price, "The Suburban House," *Scribner's Magazine* 8 (1890): 3–19. I rely on Sheldon for my description of the upper floors of the interior.

42. Francis Durando Nichols, "A Small Country House," *American Homes and Gardens* 3 (1906): 365–369; William Gray Purcell, "Parabiography," unpublished typescript, Minneapolis, Minn,, Northwest Architectural Archives, Purcell Collection, #197; William Gray Purcell, "Where Other People Live," undated clipping, Minneapolis, Minn., Minneapolis History Collection, File: "Mpls. Houses: Purcell, Wm."

43. Mathews, "Short Hills, New Jersey," 3; Wheeler, *Principles of Home Decoration,* 227; Harrie T. Lindeberg, "Some Observations on Domestic Architecture," *House Beautiful* 33 (1913): 34; Rich, "Suburban Residence Built of Brick," 157.

44. Purcell, "Parabiography," 39. On architectural unity, see, for example, Lindeberg, "Some Observations on Domestic Architecture," 38; Clausen, *The Art, Science, and Sentiment of Homebuilding,* 75; Wilson Eyre, Jr., "American Country Homes of Today," *Craftsman* (1905): 23; George Maher, "Art Democracy," *Western Architect* 15 (1910): 30.

45. In Short Hills, only 7 of the 102 residences constructed by 1917 could be considered "pure" examples of progressive architecture, and only 5 were "pure" examples of conservative design. In St. Martin's, there were 17 progressive and 8 conservative residences among 187 commissions. In Kenilworth, there were 14 progressive and only 1 conservative residence among the 135 designed before 1917, and in Lake of the Isles, there were 11 progressive and 4 conservative designs among 433 dwellings. Those interested in the criteria that I used in making these classifications should refer to Mary Corbin Sies, "American Country House Architecture in Context," where I discuss this matter in some detail in the introduction. I based my classifications on progressive and conservative design criteria gleaned from professional journals and architectural publications from the period 1877 to 1917. Conservative criteria included such matters as the use of historical precedents as the basis for design, period furnishing, applied ornament of historical details, pretension, large numbers of rooms with specific functions, and formal order to the plan. Progressive criteria included, for example, the use of local materials, building traditions or vernacular sources of design, structural rationalism, harmony with landscape, efficiency of floor plan, spatial flow, and absence of pretension.

46. William Gray Purcell, quoted in Alan Lathrop, "Architectural Tour of the Prairie School" (unpublished pamphlet prepared for seventh Biennial Convention of American Studies Association, Minneapolis, 1979), 10. Both Charlecote and the Purcell residence show the common addition of a den (or denlike space, in the case of the latter) to the first-floor plan of the suburban home. Purcell used an ornamented partition to close off his alcove from the larger living room.

47. For a detailed description of the technological improvements in the Purcell residence, see Purcell's "Parabiography," 203B–203G. Laundries were located in the basements of the Purcell, Chapman, and Stout (Charlecote) residences; Purcell provided a spacious walk-in larder in the basement as well.

48. Purcell, "Where Other People Live," 3. In addition to its careful orientation, Charlecote was constructed of hand-adzed chestnut timbers felled on the site; only those trees within the footprint of the building were removed during the construction and landscaping process. The Chapman residence devoted a greater square footage to indoor-outdoor spaces than the other three dwellings in the comparison.

49. In both St. Martin's and Kenilworth, 60 percent of the houses designed prior to World War I exhibited predominately progressive design characteristics, as opposed to predominately conservative or a relatively equal balance of progressive and conservative characteristics. The figures for Short Hills and Lake of the Isles were considerably lower–40 percent and 39 percent, respectively. On the Pastorius Park development in St. Martin's, see Harold D. Eberlein, "Pastorius Park, Philadelphia, and Its Residential Development," *Architectural Record* 39 (1916): 25–40, and C. A. Ziegler, "Developing a Suburban Community," *American Architect* 112 (1917): 78–80.

50. Frank Miles Day, "Choosing a Style for a House," in Charles Osborn, ed., *Country Houses and Gardens of Moderate Cost* (Philadelphia, 1907), 27; George W. Maher, "a *democrat* in Architecture," *Western Architect,* 20, no. 3 (March 1914): 25. See also, Eyre, "American Country Houses of Today," 21; Purcell, "Where Other People Live," 3.

51. Howes, "Architectural Development in the Reinforced Concrete House"; Nichols, "A Small Country House"; " 'Charlecote,' the Residence of C. H. Stout, Esq."; Grey, "The Country Home of a Composer." Robert McGoodwin's Cotswold Court houses for George Woodward's Pastorius Park development in St. Martin's also featured a reversed plan so that the primary living spaces looked out onto the landscaped courtyard; see Eberlein, "Pastorius Park, Philadelphia, and Its Residential Development."

52. Purcell, "Parabiography," 35, 39, 203L; Maher, "The Western Spirit," *Inland Architect* 47 (1906): 38–41, and "Art Democracy," *Western Architect* 15 (1910): 28–30; Frank Lloyd Wright, "Prairie Architecture," in Edgar Kaufmann and Ben Raeburn, eds., *Frank Lloyd Wright, Writings and Buildings* (New York, 1960), 37–55; Louis H. Sullivan, "The Young Man in Architecture," in Sullivan, *Kindergarten Chats and Other Writings* (New York, 1979), 214–223 (paper read before Architectural League of America, 1900); Tallmadge, "The Chicago School." On the establishment of the Western Association of Architects, see "Western Association of Architects," *American Architect and Building News* (1884): 255–256.

53. This was the argument of Eaton in *Two Chicago Architects and Their Clients.*

54. George Maher, "Originality in American Architecture," *Inland Architect* 10 (1887): 34. Perhaps the most straightforward (but not untypical) statement of intention that the planned, exclusive suburb should function as a model came from Mrs. Russell Sage in her description of the purpose of Forest Hills Gardens; she said that she intended "to create something of permanent value to the country; a practical investment, perhaps, but also a means of education to all those of moderate means seeking the peace and comfort of a model village." She was quoted in Edward Hale Brush, "A Garden City for the Man of Moderate Means," *Craftsman* 19 (1911): 446–447. For examples of testimonials concerning the quality of life in turn-of-the-century planned, exclusive suburbs, see Kilner, *Joseph Sears,* 326–331. On the extension of suburban home ownership to the middle and working classes, see Gowans, *The Comfortable House,* and Edel et al., *Shaky Palaces.*

CHAPTER 2

THE RUSKINIAN GOTHIC

Architecture as Social Ideology

MARK MUMFORD

Leonard Eaton has significantly contributed to a revision of the history of modern American architecture. He is among a number of historians who have influenced a renewed interest in the study of the history of art and architecture as a record of cultural change and an expression of class structure. Eaton has argued that the historian cannot isolate the work of art from the cultural milieu in which it was made. The study of art must take into account the psychological and sociological forces that motivate the artist, client, and critic. In his book *Two Chicago Architects and Their Clients: Frank Lloyd Wright and Howard Van Doren Shaw* (1969), Eaton demonstrated that the radical shift in style, which marked the emergence of the modern movement in America in the architecture of Frank Lloyd Wright, was based on a change in the structure of American society. At the same time artistic and theoretical influences formed Wright's thinking, the new architectural development was furthered by the rise of a new social stratum with new artistic interests.

This essay was significantly affected by Eaton's work. It investigates how nineteenth-century American architects and their clients were influenced by the ideas of John Ruskin in conceiving buildings as tools of cultural development and social reform. The study focuses on Philadelphia's Pennsylvania Academy of the Fine Arts (1876) as an expression of the changing class structure in nineteenth-century industrial America.

Since its founding in 1805, the Pennsylvania Academy of the Fine Arts (PAFA) has been a major social and artistic institution in Philadelphia. It was organized by a group of the city's most prominent upper-class gentlemen. Among the founders were representatives of Philadelphia's best families: Peale, Tilgham, Rawle, McKean, Meredith, Rush, and Cox. The first president of the board of directors was George Clymer, a signer of the Declaration of Independence. His successor, Joseph Hopkins, a prominent lawyer, was the son of a signer of the Declaration. The tradition of birth and achievement was carried on by succeeding presidents who were all members of Philadelphia first-families: Joseph Ingersall, Henry Gilpin, George Pepper, and Edward Coates.[1]

The founders of the Academy were for the most part eighteenth-century gentlemen, descendants of British families and heirs to the tradition of British classical culture. The first Academy, designed by John Dorsey in 1805, reflected that society (fig. 2.1). In 1847, Richard Gilpin designed the second Academy building after a fire destroyed the original structure (fig. 2.2). The new Academy was considerably larger and more monumental in effect. It was also more sophisticated stylistically, designed in the Classical mode of Latrobe and Mills, and stood as a noble and monumental symbol of the classical culture of Philadelphia. Its abstract form emphasized a geometric purity, logic, and proportional precision, presenting an image of immutable order, stability, and clarity.

Built on the western edge of the city at Tenth and Chestnut streets, the pristine Academy sat on stately park grounds separated and secluded from the rough tumult of the industrial city. It was a haven of solitude visited by studious artists and connoisseurs who came to contemplate great works of art in the midst of idyllic tranquillity. During the 1850s the expanding city had encroached upon the Academy property so that by 1860 the museum was almost hidden from view by city structures (fig. 2.3). Neglected during the Civil War and obscured by commercial and residential structures on its site, the old Academy fell into dilapidation.

Fig. 2.1. John Dorsey, Pennsylvania Academy of the Fine Arts (PAFA), Philadelphia, Pa., 1805. (Courtesy of the Pennsylvania Academy of the Fine Arts)

I.J.Barralet del.   The PENNSYLVANIA ACADEMY of the FINE ARTS.   B. Tanner f.

ERECTED 1806.— PARTIALLY BURNED AND REBUILT 1845-6.— FINALLY DEMOLISHED 1870

Fig. 2.2. Richard Gilpin, PAFA, Philadelphia, Pa., 1847. (Courtesy of the Pennsylvania Academy of the Fine Arts, Dr. Paul J. Sartain Bequest)

In 1870 a severe storm damaged the building to such an extent that its rehabilitation became impractical. In 1871, board member John Sartain was asked to "draw up a plan for the arrangement of rooms and galleries adapted to the wants of the institution [which] would serve as a starting point for further development by an architect" to build a new academy. A committee consisting of Sartain, James L. Claghorn, Henry Gibson, Henry G. Morris, and Fairman Rogers invited Philadelphia architects John McArthur, Jr., James Windrim, Thomas Richards, Addison Hutton, Henry Sims, and the firms of Collins and Hudenreid and of Fraser, Furness, and Hewitt to submit drawings for a new building. After much deliberation and disagreement, the committee awarded the commission to architects Furness and Hewitt.[2]

Fig. 2.3. PAFA, Philadelphia, Pa., 1869. (Courtesy of Free Library of Philadelphia)

The Academy was relocated to a site on Broad and Cherry streets. Situated in the center of Philadelphia, the institution assumed a prominent position among the most important civic and commercial structures in the city. Across Broad Street, Addison Hutton built the Arch Street Episcopal Church (1870), and one block south on Broad, James Windrim built the Masonic Temple (1868–1873). John McArthur, Jr.'s, magnificent new city hall (1871–1901) was being constructed two blocks south on Broad and Chestnut streets at the geographic center of Penn's city. Two blocks south of city hall, still on Broad Street, John Fraser designed the Union League Club (1864). With city hall at the political and civic center of the city, the Pennsylvania Academy on north Broad exactly balanced the Union League on south Broad. Certainly, the Academy board of directors knew the symbolic implications of this urban configuration when they chose the site for the new museum.

Fig. 2.4. Frank Furness, PAFA, Philadelphia, Pa., 1872–1876.
(Courtesy of the Pennsylvania Academy of the Fine Arts)

Furness's design contrasted sharply with its predecessors (fig. 2.4). Opposed to Gilpin's restrained Classical structure, the new Academy was a wild mixture of Gothic, Byzantine, Moorish, and other forms. The elegant simplicity, lightness, and geometric purity of the old Academy was replaced by the massive, elaborately decorated, and wildly polychromatic new museum. Furness's stridently monumental and vigorously expressive edifice presents an image of power. The building is characterized by a massive solidity, weight, and giant scale. The complex configuration of limestone, brick, and granite is charged with an energy and tension. The parts of the composition seem capable of movement as lines and surfaces, masses and voids compress and expand, abut and overlap. The action of the parts seems mechanical and systematic. The energy in the massive movements that animate the composition recalls the sublime strength of magnificent machines. Hard, rigid blocks of brick, stone, and granite fit together with a machined precision. Furness's brutally severe, energetic, and tough forms forcefully embody the character of the industrial age. In this sense, the Pennsylvania Academy might be compared to such machine-marvels as the Corliss engine that powered Machinery Hall in Philadelphia's Centennial Exposition of 1876. The building and the machine were focal points of the Centennial that celebrated America as an industrial empire. They symbolized power, largeness, grandeur, and wealth.

The period after the Civil War was an age of enormous economic and industrial expansion. In Philadelphia's industrial districts, such as Passyunk, Kensington, Manayunk, Southwark, and along the Delaware and Schuylkill rivers giant manufacturing plants developed. Philadelphia profited enormously from the Civil War by maintaining economic ties with both Northern and Southern states, supplying the war efforts of both. As a result, while other Northern city economies stagnated during the war, Philadelphia's expanded. The city was one of the nation's largest shipbuilding centers. Its manufacturers supplied railroad equipment, engines, and cars throughout the world. Philadelphia was also a center for machine and tool production, textile and milling, mining, banking, warehousing, transportation, and other industries. Rapid urbanization accompanied industrial expansion. The city's population multiplied from approximately 200,000 in 1840 to nearly 600,000 in 1860 and to more than 800,000 in 1880.[3]

The industrial revolution stimulated a restructuring of Philadelphia's society. After the Civil War the dominance of the traditional upper class, the descendants of colonial Philadelphia first-families, gave way to members of the industrial elite that emerged during the 1850s and 1860s. The industrial elite were successful businessmen, industrialists, capitalists, entrepreneurs, inventors, and organizers. For the most part, they were self-made men. Most were from the middle classes. They were well-educated, though few had college or professional training. Beginning work in their teens, they worked their way up and established their own businesses. The expanding economy of the early industrial revolution allowed them to consolidate economic and social positions during the decades before the Civil War. The war produced trade and manufacturing opportunities that allowed many of these men to accumulate great fortunes. Wealth and business success eventually paved the way for the new industrial elite to enter the upper class.[4]

Before the Civil War almost all of the Academy directors were members of the traditional colonial upper class. After the war the composition of the Academy board changed considerably. Of the twenty-one directors who served between 1871 and 1876, only five were descendants of the traditional upper class. All the other directors belonged to the new industrial elite. Compared to the descendants of the colonial upper class, the industrial aristocracy was enormously wealthy. A study of the incomes of the two groups, made on the basis of a pamphlet titled "Rich Men of Philadelphia" published in 1865, dramatically illustrates the differences.[5] The richest directors—all industrialists, bankers, and businessmen—show incomes many times those of the hereditary aristocracy.

On the basis of wealth, the industrial aristocracy aspired to the highest positions of power and preeminence. However, wealth alone was not sufficient to elevate them to upper-class status. Oliver Wendell Holmes enunciated the prevailing attitude toward the industrial elite held by many members of the traditional upper class. Let us admire a "self-made man whittled into shape with his own jack-knife, but other things being equal, in most relations of life, I prefer a man of family," wrote Holmes. " 'Self-made' is imperfectly made." It takes "the union of exceptional native gifts and generations of training to bring the 'natural man' " to completeness. Upper-class status required "the cumulative humanities of at least four or five generations."[6] In order to assert a claim as leaders of society, the industrial elite needed a moral ideology on the basis of which they could assume a place at the head of the social hierarchy. Such an ideology was found in the writing of John Ruskin.

John Ruskin (1819–1900) was a prominent English art historian and social critic. His first book, *Modern Painters,* published in England in 1843 and in America in 1847, was "one of the sensation-books of the time," wrote an American observer. In 1849 Ruskin's *Seven Lamps of Architecture* and in 1851 the first volume of *Stones of Venice* were published in England and America. Americans read Ruskin's works with great interest and studied his ideas with intensity. Excerpts from Ruskin's books and articles were regularly reprinted in American art journals and the popular press. His ideas penetrated American thinking to such an extent that in 1855 Ruskin conceded to the editors of *The Crayon* that his American readers had a "heartier appreciation and better understanding of what I am and what I mean, than I have ever met in England."[7]

Ruskin's philosophy of art, nature, and morality appealed to Americans for whom aesthetic and religious values were inseparably bound. He maintained that God was immanent in nature and that art was spirit in nature transformed. Perception of beauty in art was related to perception of nature, and these were similar to religious insight. The ability to discern the beautiful was not sensuous but depended on the observer's competence to make moral distinctions. Just as all moral human beings could know God in their souls, every individual could perceive essential truth in nature and in art. However, for most individuals this perception was incomplete. If one lacked the moral faculty of imagination, nature and art would remain forever dismal, inert, and meaningless. Only those with a highly developed "imaginative" faculty could apprehend completely the moral and aesthetic ideals that art and nature taught. This high endowment was bestowed by God upon the "elect."[8]

Ruskin's philosophy of art and culture was derived from conservative Protestant doctrine. He believed that society was hierarchically organized and that each person's place in the hierarchy was the ordinance of God. Ruskin maintained that the hierarchy that organized society established each member in the social structure according to the moral capacity of the individual, and moral capacity was determined and measured by the individual's response to beauty in art and in nature. Taste was

"an analogy to, and in harmony with, the whole spirit of the Christian moral system, . . . based on the relations [individuals] hold to their Creator," Ruskin wrote. "It is only by music, literature, and painting, that cultivation can be given. The faculties thus received are hereditary; so that the child of an educated race has an innate instinct for beauty, derived from the arts practiced hundreds of years before its birth." Taste was the ultimate test of moral character, Ruskin believed. "The first, and last, the closest trial question to any living creature is, 'What do you like? Tell me what you like and I'll tell you what you are'." "We are born to like and dislike certain aspects of things; nor could I, by any arguments, alter the defined tastes which you receive at your birth, and which the surrounding circumstances of life have enforced."[9]

Finally, Ruskin's philosophy provided the industrial elite with a way of legitimizing their claim to upper-class status. His ideas became politically useful because they offered a way of proving moral and social superiority on the basis of aesthetic sensitivity. After the Civil War, families of newly made wealth and ambitious culture replaced those of ancient lineage as the chief patrons of art. "The great manufacturing community [has become] the chief friend of art," Earl Shinn wrote in his *Art Treasures of America* (1879). "A Phidias who makes a god may go abegging in the nineteenth century unless there is a weaver to buy it. This ideal sense which the medieval knight would have satisfied by building a chapel, and the Roman council by maintaining a poet, our merchants of . . . Philadelphia gratify by buying dear pictures."[10]

Shinn produced a compendium of America's most important art collections, which he intended as an "estimate of the country's civilization," measured by the "love of art, the most obvious test of enlightenment for any nation." Shinn sought to prove that "there is a great modern art, which is the development of this century, . . . an art plainly modified by the industrial and practical spirit of the age, but modified just as plainly by its intelligence, and by the application of that scientific treatment which is changing history, physics and creeds beneath our eyes."[11] Among America's great art collectors, Shinn identified Pennsylvania Academy directors Fairman Rogers, Thomas Dolan, Joseph Bates, J. Gillingham Fell, George Whitney, William Bement, Clarence Clark, James Claghorn, and Henry Gibson.

Henry Gibson's collection of 102 paintings was displayed in

specially designed galleries built in his house. These galleries were like "little chapels," Shinn explained, each in a different style, each containing works of art that together with the architectural setting produced a mood of dreamlike contemplation. "The general impression of the Gibson gallery," Shinn wrote, "is that it is the most fastidiously chosen, in a taste at once catholic and careful." Furness designed Gibson's house and galleries in 1871, modeled on the Pennsylvania Academy. Shinn described Fairman Rogers's gallery as "the solace and delight of a man of science. . . . [It] is an interesting test to see philosophical acumen brought up to the judgment of the fine arts, and found after all to be the same thing as acumen of taste." Rogers's gallery, also designed by Furness, contained some 54 canvases, according to Shinn's record. Joseph Bates collected 36 canvases; William Bement possessed 64; among Clarence Clark's holdings were 6 valuable works of art; Thomas Dolan had 19 canvases; J. Gillingham Fell's collection numbered 18 works; and George Whitney collected 21 paintings. James Claghorn, president of the Academy board, amassed more than 300 canvases and some 50,000 engravings—a staggering personal holding.[12] Possession of art was an outward sign of inner cultivation and moral development. It was as though these men were answering Ruskin's demand for proof of taste and moral aptitude. The more pictures, the larger the capacity for beauty and the more diverse and all-encompassing the taste.

Taste, as Ruskin defined it, was not a matter of intellectual acumen or sensuous appreciation but the comprehensive grasp of spirit in beauty, which was a reflection of divinity. Those who possessed such highly developed moral ability assumed the highest position in society, and such high "calling" exacted a reciprocal responsibility. The "elect" were required to serve society as guides, to determine standards of beauty, taste, and truth. The industrial elite saw a duty to elevate culture to counter what some observers of American society saw as a general moral and spiritual degradation brought about by industrialization, urbanization, and materialism. "That is the fatal quality which we discover in our pursuit of wealth," wrote Ralph Waldo Emerson, "that it is treacherous and is bought by the breaking or weakening of the sentiments." Emerson believed that a true aristocracy is "constituted of those persons in whom heroic dispositions are native, with the love of beauty, the delight in society and the power to embellish the passing day." In

the industrial society, only art could "raise to a divine use the railroad, the insurance office, the joint-stock company" and improve "the moral nature" of the American people through a developed sense of beauty, wrote Charles Eliot Norton.[13]

Conscious of their moral responsibility, during the years after the Civil War, enlightened reformers sought to redirect society by sponsoring quasi-religious organizations to educate and spiritually elevate the masses. Although religious values remained essential in American life, the influence of the church had declined. To bolster the work of the church, nineteenth-century reformers established educational institutions. They founded libraries, athenaea, and historical societies. Musical societies were established to promote orchestras and operas, and artistic foundations were formed to support the arts and literature. American reformers placed a heavy emphasis on the moral appeal of art as instructor of the masses. The arts became a counterforce to the materialism that threatened the nation's character. The function of American museums changed significantly. They were no longer isolated havens for artists and art connoisseurs. Museums became major cultural institutions and the principal agents of moral reform. By diffusing the knowledge of art, the founders of museums sought to humanize, educate, and refine the people. "The first function of a Museum," wrote Ruskin, "is to give example of perfect order and perfect elegance . . . to the disorderly and rude populace."[14]

During the 1870s and 1880s most of the major American museums and academies of art were founded or enlarged in a great expansion of museum building. In 1874 the Corcoran Gallery was completed in Washington, D.C.; it had been designed by James Renwick, Jr., in 1859. In New York, Peter Bonnett Wight designed the National Academy of Design (1862–1865). The Brooklyn Academy of Design was designed by J. Cleveland Cady and Henry M. Congdon between 1871 and 1876. Henry J. Schwarzmann designed Memorial Hall for the Centennial Exposition in Philadelphia in 1876. The first wing of the Metropolitan Museum in New York was built by Calvert Vaux and Jacob Wrey Mould between 1874 and 1880. In Boston, John H. Sturgis and Charles Brigham designed the Museum of Fine Art between 1872 and 1879. Furness's Pennsylvania Academy was part of this building boom. With the exception of the Corcoran Gallery and Memorial Hall, all of these museums were designed in the Modern Gothic mode.[15]

The Gothic was at the center of Ruskin's ideology. He believed that the revival of medieval art and Gothic architecture would contribute to a renewal of the spirit of the Middle Ages and that the restoration of these ancient feelings and sentiments would revolutionize the industrial world. Ruskin made architecture an instrument for reforming and humanizing the nation's values. He believed that among the arts, architecture had the closest relationship to the life of the people, to its wants, habits, and culture. The history of a great people is recorded not only in the triumphs of battle, in the advances of intellect, science, and industry, but most of all is measured by its art and architecture. And religious art is the truest measure of human greatness. As one American critic put it: "Religion and art cannot be separated. Religion is the mother of architecture, and Christianity invented the Gothic."[16]

Influenced by Ruskin, Americans believed that if modern society were to be saved from moral degradation it would have to undergo a spiritual awakening similar to the enlightenment that Christianity brought about during the Middle Ages. A number of American authors made analogies between medieval and post–Civil War culture. Charles Eliot Norton wrote *Historical Studies of Church Building in the Middle Ages* (1880) as a history of medieval civilization and a criticism of American society. Norton described how Christianity held civilization together after the decline of the Roman Empire, uniting the people with the "indissoluble ties of common faith and a common rule of conduct." This faith was expressed most significantly in church buildings.

> It was especially in the building of churches that the impulse for expression in architecture displayed itself, for it was in the church that the faith of the community took visible form.
>
> In the midst of darkness and confusion and dread, the ideal church . . . presented herself as a harbor of refuge from the storms of the world, as the image of the city of God, whose walls were sure defense. While all else was unstable and changeful, she, with her unbroken tradition and her uninterrupted services, vindicated the principles of order and the moral continuity of the race.[17]

In medieval times, the Christian church tamed the barbarian hordes by the grandeur, wisdom, and authority of religion. In the nineteenth century, art became the civilizer of the masses. During the Middle Ages religious sentiment led Christian patriarchs to build magnificent churches. In post–Civil War society the industrial aristocracy built vast museums. For centu-ries the church had been the principal protector of culture and the arts. As the church declined in modern times, the function of upholding the arts fell upon the enlightened elite and the public institutions they controlled. In the midst of the upheaval produced by the industrial revolution, the museum as an "ideal church" became a refuge from the vulgarity of the material world.

The belief that art offered man religious benefit, widely held by Americans, had been in large part influenced by Ruskin. He maintained that beauty in art was not an abstract concept or esoteric ideal. The perception of beauty was emotional and, Ruskin argued, all emotions were aspects of the moral faculty. "The arts and the morality of men are founded on the same primal order," he wrote, and this order is expressed "through the higher forms of all lovely literature and art." Through art, the viewer or reader "held communion with a new mind" and beheld the "keen perception and the impetuous emotions of a nobler and more penetrating intelligence." "In art, there is caught by the [senses] . . . a perception . . . of the immediate operation of the intelligence which so formed us and so feeds us."[18]

Furness used the concept of ideal church as the basis for his design. The museum became a spiritual sanctuary and, like a church, a place for moral revitalization. The association between museum and church is made explicit in the exterior form of the Academy. Furness rejected the standard prototypes for museum buildings that were usually based on classical temple or palace structures. He modeled the Academy on the Christian basilica. The Broad Street elevation is composed of three elements: a tall, central block flanked by shorter wings. The center block contains a large Gothic window that corresponds to the navelike central gallery of the museum. Smaller Gothic windows in the flanking wings mark the presence of smaller galleries that flank the central "nave" like "aisles" (fig. 2.5). The three-part basilican form extends longitudinally along Cherry Street. A crossing arm divides the Cherry Street elevation, similar to the basilican transept. A secondary entrance located in the crossing arm provides access to the Academy school.

Stylistic elements, architectural details, and materials reinforce the connection between museum and church. Furness used pointed arches, banded columns with carved foliated capitals, trefoils, and other Gothic elements. The vigorously polychromatic composition is Ruskinian, associated stylistically

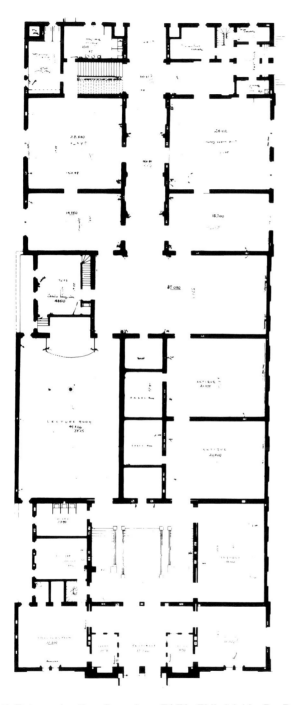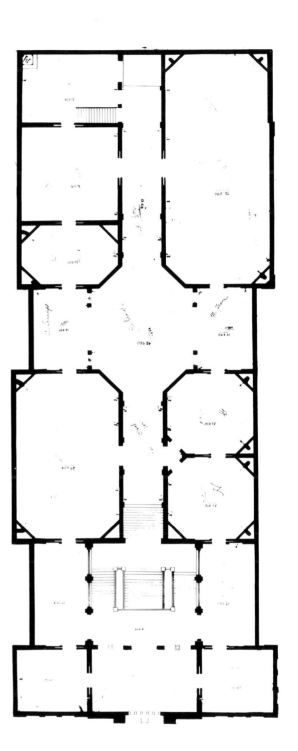

Fig. 2.5. Entry and gallery floor plans, PAFA, Philadelphia, Pa. Drawn by Furness and Hewitt. (Courtesy of the Pennsylvania Academy of the Fine Arts)

with designs produced by such Ruskin-inspired architects as William Butterfield, George Edmund Street, or William Burges. Furness's use of colored brick laid in complex geometric patterns and the use of brilliantly colored masonry and tiles might be compared to Butterfield's All Saints Margaret Street (London, 1850–1859) or to the work of Street or Burges. The thick, massive forms that characterize Furness's style are also comparable to the works of English Ruskinians. Although to the modern eye the Pennsylvania Academy is not Gothic, in fact the complexly eclectic composition is not easy to categorize stylistically. To the nineteenth-century observer—whose perception of architecture was conditioned by association—pointed arches, rose windows, banded columns, polychromatic brickwork, natural carved ornament, and other related elements firmly established Furness's design in the Ruskinian tradition of architecture and, by extension, associated the Academy with the Ruskinian ideology.

The exterior mass of the Academy expresses directly the plan configuration. Furness divided the plan into three parts that roughly correspond to the basilican form consisting of a central nave with flanking aisles. The nave contains the entrance, grand stair, and a tall central gallery, and the aisles contain smaller galleries on either side. A crossing arm divides the central gallery, forming a large octagonal gallery similar to spaces under the domes or towers that span the crossing arms of basilican plans. Although the plan functions well—Furness was known for producing well-functioning buildings—the plan-type was unusual for museum buildings. Typically, small museums were planned as a series of galleries connected by broad doorways. Larger museums were most often designed after the Paris Louvre, which is composed of a series of gallery wings organized about courtyards. Furness's basilican plan was unprecedented.

Furness's Academy functions like a church. He designed the museum interior as a ceremonial transformation. Within the space, the visitor enacts a ritual that is essentially similar to a religious ceremony. The spatial arrangement, decoration, and style of the building, combined with the works of art, form an iconographic program, an architectural script that determines a ceremonial performance. The Academy interior was conceived as a dramatic set, a "tableau," in which the visitor enacts and internalizes the values and beliefs written into the

Fig. 2.6. Entry detail, PAFA, Philadelphia, Pa. (Mark Mumford)

architectural script.[19]

In the space, the viewer is elevated from the material world into the transcendent domain of art. The spatial process develops axially. It begins in darkness and compression and ends in light and openness. From the exterior, entrance into the Academy is up a short flight of steps that spills out of the cavity in the center block. The entrance is set deep under a heavy flattened arch that is compressed by an enormous weight (fig. 2.6). The squat segmental arch is compressed by the crushing weight of the massive canopy that looms above the entrance like a craggy cliff. The arch over the door seems on the verge of fracture, supported precariously by a thin metallic column that holds its center. Entry is from openness and light into a dark, compressed interior. The sudden juxtaposition of light and darkness, openness and enclosure, accentuates the act of passage. Furness's entrance is unlike the usual form for monumental public buildings such as museums. Instead of an open, receptive doorway, Furness's entrance is closed and psychologically uncomfortable. It is a hurried escape from under the compressing arch and the great weight of stone that looms precariously above the entrance. Furness provided virtually no landing at the door. There is no place to pause for respite, no easy transition from outside to inside. The effect of uneasiness was intended. The entry is a symbolic cathartic purging. Once through the door, beyond the collapsing arch, the visitor is in another world.

From the entrance, the process continues through a dark foyer (fig. 2.7). The view ahead is through a double arch into a large, light-filled space. Like the arch over the entrance, the double arch that separates the vestibule from the further space is heavy and compressed. It too is held by a center pier that stands directly on the axis. The downward press of the arch and the darkness of the vestibule are suddenly relieved by a great rush of light and explosion of space. Similar to the entrance, the sudden juxtaposition of light and darkness, openness and enclosure, heightens the emotional sense of transition.

Having passed through the vestibule, under the arch, the visitor is confronted by a monumental stair (fig. 2.8). The stair is the most important moment in the process. It symbolizes the transition from the earthly to the spiritual. The stair lifts the visitor from the material world to the heavenly world. It represents the ascent of the spirit. Furness's stair rises within a light-filled space under a great, sky-lit dome (fig. 2.9). The dome

symbolizes the spiritual world toward which the visitor rises. Light pours through a large skylight in Furness's square dome. Around the skylight the dome is painted blue, with silver stars on the blue field. The sky image reinforces the connection between light, the heavens, and the spiritual ascent.

The effect within the Academy's grand stair space is electric, ethereal. Furness covered every surface with richly colored and textured ornament. He separated the spiritual dome from the material ground by decorating all things that belong to the earth with plant forms. The stone at the base of the stair land-

Fig. 2.7. View from vestibule, PAFA, Philadelphia, Pa. (Mark Mumford)

Fig. 2.8. Main stair, PAFA, Philadelphia, Pa. (Mark Mumford)   Fig. 2.9. Main stair, PAFA, Philadelphia, Pa. (Mark Mumford)

ing, the brass stair rail, the stone stanchions on which treelike brass lamps stand, and the stone column capitals that unfold with luxuriant foliage are all decorated with plant forms. These all belong to the earthly domain (figs. 2.10, 2.11). Above, only stars decorate the celestial dome. The area between the ground and the heavens is richly patterned with abstract plantlike medallions in gold leaf set on raised diamond bases on a field of reddish purple. The gold leaf medallions vibrate and shimmer in a dance of light and color. Architectural surfaces seem to dematerialize, creating an illusion of ascent into the incorporeal.

Furness's use of decorative motifs, form, and light in the Academy was not arbitrary. He conceived the Academy interior as an interpretation of Ruskin's ideas. Art was nature transformed, Ruskin believed. The artist took his inspiration from nature. The poetry of nature entered his vision, and God's order became manifest. The artist penetrated the sacred mystery of nature to apprehend the unseen order behind visible things and then converted his vision into the forms of his painting or poem. Art mediated between the natural and the spiritual world. In accord with Ruskin's idea, like the work of art, the museum represented a conversion from the earthly to the spiritual. Thus, the material world—represented by the abstract plant forms that decorate the space where the human walks—is transformed in the vertical space, through shimmering light, into a spiritual domain. As the visitor ascends the center flight of stairs, the vista opens gradually into the central gallery (fig. 2.12). Another arch divides the stair from the gallery. Unlike the previous arches in the sequence, this arch is held high by a pair of columns attached to the wall. The transition from the stair to the gallery is a triumphal ascent into light.

Fig. 2.10. Detail, main stair, PAFA, Philadelphia, Pa. (Mark Mumford)

Fig. 2.11. Main stair, PAFA, Philadelphia, Pa. (Mark Mumford)   Fig. 2.12. Main gallery, PAFA, Philadelphia, Pa. (Mark Mumford)

Notes

1. For a history of the Academy see N. Burt, *Palaces for the People: A Social History of the American Art Museum* (Boston, 1977), 137–138; H. Henderson, *The Pennsylvania Academy of the Fine Arts and Other Collections of Philadelphia* (Boston, 1911); and R. Boyle, "The Pennsylvania Academy of the Fine Arts," *The Magazine of Antiques* 121(1982): 672–678.

2. J. Sartain, *The Reminiscences of a Very Old Man, 1808–1897* (New York, 1899), 20.

The building committee's selection of Furness was in part politically motivated. The Furness family was well known in Philadelphia. Frank Furness's father, the Reverend William Henry Furness, was a prominent Unitarian minister. He gave the oration at the opening of the Academy. An older brother, William Henry Furness, Jr., was a respected painter and was elected an Academician in 1860. Another brother, Horace Howard Furness, was a noted Shakespearean scholar and professor at the University of Pennsylvania. John Sartain was a close family friend and a member of Furness's congregation. Fairman Rogers knew Frank Furness from early childhood. Rogers's sister, Helen Kate, was Horace Howard Furness's wife.

The invitation to submit a design for the Pennsylvania Academy competition came to the firm of Fraser, Furness, and Hewitt. However, only Furness and Hewitt submitted drawings. Fraser had at the time moved to Washington, D.C.

3. See R. Weigley, ed., *Philadelphia: A 300-Year History* (New York, 1982).

4. My description of Philadelphia's social structure is based on E. D. Baltzell's *Philadelphia Gentlemen: The Making of a National Upper Class* (Chicago, 1971) and *Puritan Boston and Quaker Philadelphia: Two Protestant Ethics and the Spirit of Class Authority and Leadership* (New York, 1979).

5. The directors of the Pennsylvania Academy and their dates of service were

Matthew Baird (1872–1877)	Joseph Harrison (1855–1876)
Joseph W. Bates	Alfred D. Jessup (1866–1876)
William B. Bement (1872–1877)	Francis W. Lewis (1869–1871)
Edwin N. Benson (1872–1873)	William H. Merrick (1876–1879)
John Bohlen	Henry G. Morris (1870–1875)
James L. Claghorn (1862–1884)	George S. Pepper (1850–1884)
Clarence H. Clark (1871–1905)	Fairman Rogers (1871–1883)
Edward S. Clark (1872–1877)	John Sartain (1855–1877)
Caleb Cope (1842–1872)	William Sellers (1866–1876)
Thomas Dolan	A. May Stevenson
J. Gillingham Fell (1865–1878)	William Struthers
Henry C. Gibson (1870–1891)	George Whitney (1864–1879)

Matthew Baird (1817–1877). Baird came to the United States from Ireland in 1821. At the age of five, he went to work in a brick yard; at seventeen, he became an apprentice to the New Castle Manufacturing Company in Delaware. In 1838 he was made foreman of the sheet iron and boiler department of Baldwin Locomotive Works. In 1854 he bought an interest in the company from Matthias Baldwin, and the firm became a partnership under the name of M. W. Baldwin and Company. On Baldwin's death, Baird became sole proprietor of the largest locomotive works in the world. In 1873 he retired from the company, closing his interest of $1,660,000. He was a director of several railroad and

manufacturing firms and of the Central National Bank and an incorporator of the American Steamship Company.

Joseph W. Bates (1821–1886). Bates came to the United States in 1841 to represent his father's worsted wool goods manufactured in Halifax, England. In 1844 he established Bates and Coates. He was a member of the Union League, a director of the Commercial Bank, and a member of the Fairmont Park Association.

William Barnes Bement (1817–1897). Son of a New Hampshire farmer, and formally uneducated, Bement became an apprentice in a machine shop in 1834 and two years later bought interest in the firm. While working for the St. Joseph Iron Company, he designed and constructed the first engine lathe and gear-cutting machine in America. He produced cotton and woolen machinery for the Lowell Machine Shops. In 1851 he established Marshall, Bement and Company, manufacturers of machine tools. In 1870 the firm became William Bement and Sons; Clarence S. Bement joined him that year, and another son, William P., in 1879. Bement was director of the National Bank of the Republic (for which Furness designed a building in 1878), director of the School of Design for Women, and a member of the Union League.

Edwin North Benson was the son of Alexander Benson, a prominent banker in Philadelphia. He entered the firm, retiring in 1870 with a considerable fortune. He joined the Seventh Pennsylvania Regiment at the outbreak of the Civil War and retired from the army in 1868 at the rank of major. He devoted the rest of his life to philanthropic activities. He was a founder of the Union League, its vice president from 1879 to 1884, and its president from 1885 to 1888. He was a member of the Philadelphia Club, Rittenhouse Club, Penn Club, New York's University Club, and New York's Union Club.

James L. Claghorn (1816–1884). He began work at the age of fourteen for Jennings, Thomas, Gill and Company, merchants, in which his father was a partner. He formed his own concern with Altemus and Meyers, retiring in 1861. The firm did $10 million annual business in 1861. He was a charter member and treasurer of the Union League. In 1867 he was elected president of the Commercial National Bank. He was director of the Philadelphia Bank and Girard Trust. From 1871 to 1880 he served as president of the Academy board.

Clarence H. Clark (1833–1906). Clark was the son of Enoch Clark, who in 1837, with his brother-in-law Edward Dodge, started E. W. Clark and Company. In 1844 the firm opened offices in St. Louis, New Orleans, and New York. With branch offices in all the major American ports, Clark cornered the financial market. In 1854 Clarence Clark became a partner in the firm, which was largely responsible for settling the debt incurred by the United States in the Mexican War. Clarence Clark was a founder of the Fidelity Trust, a trustee of the Free Library, and a member of the Union League and Rittenhouse clubs.

Caleb Cope (1797–1888). At age twelve, Cope began work for John Wells, a storekeeper. He came to Philadelphia in 1815 amd worked for his uncles Jasper and Israel Cope, merchants. In 1820 he acquired the concern that became Caleb Cope and Company, dealing principally in silks, and became one of the wealthiest men in the nation. In 1861 he opened the Continental Hotel. In 1864 he was elected president of the Philadelphia Savings Fund Society, having been a director since 1841. He was one of the original trustees of the Lehigh Coal and Navigation Company. He was president of the Academy board between 1859 and 1871.

Thomas Dolan (1834–1912). While a young man Dolan went to work in a knitting goods and hosiery factory. In 1861 he had established his own knitting factory, which became the basis for the Keystone Knitting Mills, the largest producer of menswear in the United States. One of the greatest nineteenth-century business tycoons, Dolan reinvested his fortune in traction and in Philadelphia's gas works at the time when the entire city was to become equipped with gas lighting. He was president of the United Gas Works when that firm contracted to provide the lighting for thirty years. Dolan was one of the organizers and the first president of the Manufacturer's Club of Philadelphia, the president of the National Association of Manufacturers, a member and vice president of the Union League, and a member of the Rittenhouse Club.

J. Gillingham Fell (1816-1878). Fell was born in Buck's County, Pennsylvania, and educated in Friends' School. He joined the engineering corps for the Beaver Meadow Railroad Company in 1833. He learned about engineering and mining and in 1839 became associated with Arlo Pardee in A. Pardee and Company. Also in 1839 he became director of the Hazelton Coal Company, which was sold to the Lehigh Valley Railroad Company in 1868. Fell, who had been director of Lehigh between 1857 and 1862, became its president in 1868. He was director of Allenton Rolling Mills, Glendon Iron Company, and Andover Iron Company, Fidelity Trust, and the Philadelphia Bank. He was a founder of the Union League and its second president.

Henry C. Gibson (1830-1891). Gibson was the son of John Gibson, who emigrated from Belfast, Ireland, and eventually founded the Gibsonton Mills Distillery on the Monongahela River in western Pennsylvania. Henry Gibson graduated from high school and joined his father's firm. In 1856 the elder Gibson retired, leaving the firm to Henry; the company became John Gibson Son and Company, and Gibson retired in 1884. He was one of the founders of the Fidelity Insurance Trust and Safe Deposit Box Company, a director of the First National Bank, and a manager of the Philadelphia and Reading Railroad. He was a director of the Real Estate Post Company of Philadelphia and the Philadelphia Ware House Company (for which Furness designed a building in 1875). Gibson was a member of the Penn Club and the Rittenhouse Club.

Alfred D. Jessup was the son of Augustus E. Jessup, who formed a partnership with Bloomfield H. Moore in 1843 to manufacture paper goods. Alfred and his brother Edward A. Jessup joined the firm, and in 1859 Alfred Jessup and Bloomfield Moore remained sole partners. Jessup retired in 1870 with a considerable fortune.

Henry G. Morris was born into prominent Philadelphia family. In 1835 he became a partner in Pascal Iron Works, which his father, Stephen Morris, had organized. The firm began making gas pipe by hand. By 1838 it was producing sixty thousand lineal feet, and by the end of the Civil War, five million lineal feet of pipe per year. It became a nucleus for the gas-fitting and tool industry, which supplied the material for the gasification of Philadelphia. At the time, Philadelphia became the supplier of gas-making machinery to the entire United States, and the Pascal foundry was one of the biggest in the nation. Morris was a member of the Philadelphia Club, the Union League, and a number of civic organizations.

George S. Pepper (1808-1890). Pepper represented a distinguished family of Philadelphia who traced its history to Penn's founding. Pepper inherited a considerable family fortune, becoming one of the city's richest men. He trained for the bar but never practiced, devoting his entire life to philanthropic activities and the promotion of Philadelphia's cultural development. He was director of the Academy for thirty-four years, serving as its president from 1880 to 1890. He was instrumental in the organization of the American Academy of Music. Upon his death, his estate of $2 million went to public benefactions.

Fairman Rogers (1833-1900). Rogers was a son of Evans Rogers, who was a self-made millionaire in the hardware trade. Rogers graduated from the University of Pennsylvania in 1853. Between 1855 and 1871 he was professor of civil engineering at the University of Pennsylvania. In 1880 he was offered the provostship of the university, but declined. He was a member of the American Philosophical Society, the First City Troop, a founder of the Union League, and one of the original members of the National Academy of Sciences.

John Sartain (1808-1897). At age twelve, Sartain began work as a scene-painter in his native England. At fifteen he became apprentice to engraver John Swain. In 1830 he came to the United States. He became a nationally recognized engraver, working for Thomas Sully, John Neagle, and other well-known Philadelphia painters. He executed plates for *Gentlemen's Magazine, The Casket,* and *Godey's Lady's Magazine.* In 1841 he began a publishing career, becoming associated with *Graham's Magazine.* He bought the *Union Magazine* in 1848. In 1849 he organized *Sartain's Magazine.* He was chief of the Bureau of Art for the Centennial Exposition. He was a director of the Academy for twenty-one years, serving as its director of schools. He was a vice president of the Philadelphia School of Design for Women.

William Sellers (1824-1905). Sellers represented one of the oldest families of the Pennsylvania Colony. Privately educated and a graduate of the University of Pennsylvania, Sellers was a prominent engineer, inventor, and manufacturer. At age twenty-one he joined Fairbanks, Bancroft and Company of Providence, R.I., machine manufacturers. Three years later he began manufacturing tools on his own, first as Sellers and Bancroft and later as Sellers and Company. In 1868, he organized the Edgmoor Iron Company, which furnished all the structural material for the Centennial Exposition and the Brooklyn Bridge. He was president of the Franklin Institute, a charter member of the Union League, vice president of the board of the Centennial, trustee of the University of Pennsylvania, and commissioner of Fairmont Park. In 1864 he became a member of the Philosophical Society and in 1873 of the Academy of Natural Sciences. He was a member of the Rittenhouse Club, elected in 1875, and vice president of the Union League from 1870 to 1874.

George Whitney (1819-1895). Whitney was a son of Asa Whitney, a partner with Matthias Baldwin. Asa Whitney resigned from the Baldwin Works in 1846 to start manufacturing steel railroad car wheels. In 1847 George Whitney joined his father in the firm of Asa Whitney and Sons. The firm became the largest manufacturer of railroad wheels in the country. George was a member of the Union League and the University Club and was director of several corporations.

The incomes of some Pennsylvania directors, reported in "Rich Men of Philadelphia" (1865), were

J. Gillingham Fell	$389,550	William Bement	$36,933
Matthew Baird	208,049	James Bohlen	31,453
William Sellers	177,915	George S. Pepper	18,735
Thomas Dolan	109,207	Henry G. Morris	13,600
William Merrick	82,704	A. May Stevenson	12,779
Clarence H. Clark	69,400	Joseph W. Bates	11,720
Alfred D. Jessup	59,400	Fairman Rogers	7,308
Henry G. Gibson	41,255	Edwin Benson	2,160
George Whitney	39,197		

Another means of assessing a man's position in the upper class is through the clubs to which he belonged. Established members of the traditional upper class typically belonged to the most exclusive clubs, while men of lesser standing belonged to less prestigious ones. In order of exclusivity, the Philadelphia men's clubs were the Schuylkill Fishing Club, the oldest in the city (no Academy directors belonged although members of the Pepper, Morris, and Bohlen families were members); the Philadelphia Club (Merrick, Morris, and Benson were members); the Rittenhouse Club, a notch below the Philadelphia Club in exclusivity (nine Academy directors were members, including Furness); and the Union League Club, a "must" club for the aspiring upper-class member (thirteen directors were members). Among the lesser clubs, two directors were members of the University Club, and three were members of the Penn Club.

A number of sources were consulted for the biographies. Among these, the most important are *Dictionary of American Biography* (New York, 1929–1946); J. Jordan, *Colonial Families of Philadelphia* (New York, 1911); J. T. Scharf and T. Westcott, *History of Philadelphia, 1609–1884* (New York, 1884); J. Young, *Memorial History of Philadelphia* (New York, 1895); E. Freedley, *Philadelphia and its Manufacturers* (Philadelphia, 1867); *Philadelphia and Popular Philadelphians* (Philadelphia, 1865); *The History of the Baldwin Locomotive Works, 1831–1920* (Philadelphia, n.d.); N. Burt, *The Perennial Philadelphians: The Anatomy of an American Aristocracy* (Boston, 1963); J. Jordan, *Encyclopaedia of Pennsylvania Biography* (New York, 1921); and Baltzell, *Philadelphia Gentlemen.*

6. Holmes quoted in E. Cady, *The Gentleman in America: A Literary Study in American Culture* (New York, 1949), 150, 153–154.

7. *North American Review* 66(1848): 110; *The Crayon* 1(1855): 283. For Ruskin in America see R. Stein, *John Ruskin and Aesthetic Thought in America, 1840–1900* (Cambridge, Mass., 1967).

8. See H. Ladd, *The Victorian Morality of Art: An Analysis of Ruskin's Aesthetic* (New York, 1932).

9. J. Ruskin, *The Works of John Ruskin,* ed. E. Cook and A. Wedderburn, 39 vols. (London, 1904), 4:59–62; 20:36; 25:45.

10. E. Shinn, *The Art Treasures of America,* 3 vols. (Philadelphia, 1879), 3:23.

11. Ibid., 1:v, vi.

12. Ibid., 1:80, 83. Furness designed a number of buildings for Rogers, including his homes in Philadelphia and Newport, R.I. For Claghorn's art collection see Scharf and Westcott, *History of Philadelphia,* 1070–1073.

13. R. Emerson, *Journals of Ralph Waldo Emerson,* ed. E. Emerson and W. Forbes (New York, 1912), 3:142–147; 4:223–258. C. Norton, *The North American Review* 107(1868): 371.

14. Ruskin, *Works,* 34:247.

15. For a history of American museums see J. Cantor, "Temples of the Arts: Museum Architecture in Nineteenth-Century America," *New York Metropolitan Museum of Art Bulletin* 28(1970): 331–354.

16. J. Hart, "Unity in Architecture," *The Crayon* 6(1859): 85.

17. C. Norton, *Historical Studies of Church-Building in the Middle Ages* (New York, 1880), 3–35.

18. The art critic James Jackson Jarves commented on the American museum: "America has at last come to the conclusion that museums of art are necessary for the national culture from the fact that considerable attention is now given to their establishment in the chief cities of the union. When one recalls the general indifference to them scarcely one year ago, this is a great step onward. It has been left to our epoch to construct museums proper, forming a part of a system of popular instruction." From "Letter to the Editor," *New York Daily Tribune,* 16 January 1871, quoted in M. Floyd, "A Terra-Cotta Cornerstone for Copley Square: Museum of Fine Arts, Boston, 1870–1876, by Sturgis and Brigham," *Journal of the Society of Architectural Historians* 32(1973): 91; Ruskin, *Works,* "Order," 15:467; "Art," 26:334; 3:134; 4:25–50, 208–218.

19. Architectural space treated as tableaux was the basis of design teaching at the Ecole des Beaux-Arts; Furness was trained in this French method. His teacher, Richard Morris Hunt, was the first American to complete studies at the Ecole. Beaux-Art composition worked dynamically, as a carefully paced series of tableaux arranged along an axis of movement. The tableaux were conceived as an architectural setting, a stage set, which determined the actions and relations of those using the building. The user was considered an actor who performed a predetermined role in the given setting. The architect designed this activity by designing the architectural script that regulated the action. The actor's movements upon the building-stage and the sequence of scenes or spaces through which the action moved were defined in terms of marche. Marche, according to the French definition, was the linked process, similar to the development of plot in literature or to the structure of music, poetic verse, or the composition of a painting. Marche, applied to architectural space, designated the experience of walking through the plan. Thus, it was the sequence of tableaux that was the actual material of a Beaux-Arts architectural composition.

Carl Duncan and Andrew Wallach analyze the Louvre as a spatial sequence, as tableaux, in "The Universal Survey Museum," *Art History* 3(1980): 449–469. My analysis of the Pennsylvania Academy is based on their article.

CHAPTER 3

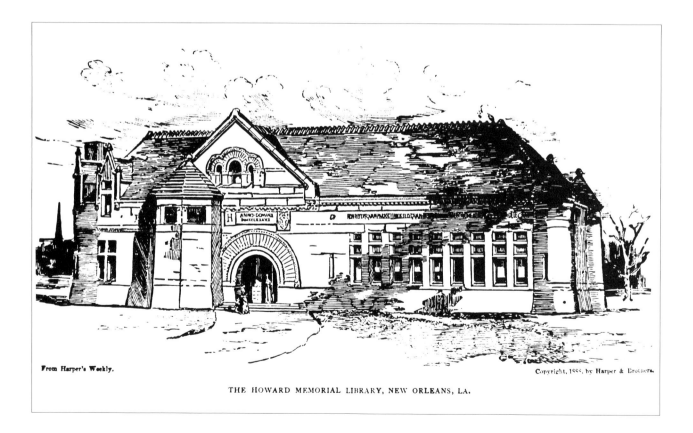

From Harper's Weekly.

Copyright, 1888, by Harper & Brothers.

THE HOWARD MEMORIAL LIBRARY, NEW ORLEANS, LA.

WILLIAM FREDERICK POOLE AND MODERN LIBRARY ARCHITECTURE

KENNETH A. BREISCH

As a result of the leading role that he played in the battle to professionalize the administration, organization, and planning of the American public library, an institution which for the most part was invented during his lifetime, William Frederick Poole is often referred to as one of the fathers of the modern library movement in the United States.[1] Poole was a man of wide-ranging interests and abilities. Between 1852 and his death in 1894, he served consecutively as the director of the Boston Mercantile Library, the Boston Athenaeum, the Cincinnati Public Library, the Chicago Public Library, and, from 1887 on, the Newberry Library in Chicago. He authored *Poole's Guide to Periodical Literature,* the precursor to the well-known *Readers Guide,* and in 1876, became one of the founding members of the American Library Association (ALA), an organization that he would serve as president in 1886 and 1887, years in which he also was elected president of the American Historical Association. Although not a single public library building stood complete in the United States at the beginning of Poole's career in 1852, by 1894 some three hundred libraries had opened their doors. Needless to say, this was a period of great excitement and innovation in the library world. It was also an era of sometimes intense controversy, which William Frederick Poole never

attempted to avoid.

Designed to accommodate an essentially new, nineteenth-century institution, the American library building, like its contemporary the railway depot, was expected to function in a "modern" world as an efficient and modern structure. At the same time, it was also the recipient of a rich historical and architectural tradition that stretched back to the great Baroque libraries of Europe, and before them, to the monastic and university libraries of the Middle Ages. Consequently, in addition to incorporating the latest innovations in lighting, heating, and the most efficient storage of books, it was assumed by many that American public libraries should also embody visible architectural associations from the past. Thus in the late nineteenth century the design of public libraries became the source of much controversy, and a fundamental yet all too common conflict arose between the drive to create a modern institution and a nostalgic yearning for tradition: a classic struggle between romanticism and pragmatism, iconography and function.

Although private and subscription libraries had been common in the seventeenth century, the first substantial library buildings were not erected in the United States until the second quarter of the nineteenth century; and even then, there were

54

only a handful completed before 1850. Among the more prominent of these were Gore Hall at Harvard, constructed between 1837 and 1841, the Yale College Library, which was completed in 1846 – the year in which Poole returned to school there and also became an assistant librarian – and the Boston Athenaeum, erected between 1847 and 1850 – where Poole was to serve as director from 1856 to 1868. The interior arrangement of all of these structures was modeled on the traditional hall and alcove library.

This type of arrangement represented a conflation of the medieval alcove library with the Baroque form of the great European hall libraries, or *Saalbibliotheks,* of the seventeenth and eighteenth centuries, buildings such as the Biblioteca Ambrosiana in Milan of 1603–1609 or J. B. Fischer von Erlach's Vienna Hofbibliothek of 1723–1737.[2] It was this alcoved, hall form, moreover, that served as the model for the first public library buildings in the United States: the Astor Library (1849–1854) in New York and the first Boston Public Library of 1855–1859 (fig.3.1). Though significantly more sophisticated in terms of their aesthetic design and iconography, even the later libraries of Henry Hobson Richardson exhibited little, if any, innovation in respect to the arrangement of their book rooms (figs. 3.2–3.4).

Fig. 3.1. Charles Kirk Kirby, first Boston Public Library, Boston, Mass., 1855–1859, second-floor reading room. (United States Bureau of Education, *Public Libraries in the United States of America: Their History, Condition, and Management,* 1876, part 1, 865)

Fig. 3.2. Henry Hobson Richardson, Crane Memorial Library, Quincy, Mass., 1880–1882, facade. (*American Architect and Building News,* 30 June 1883)

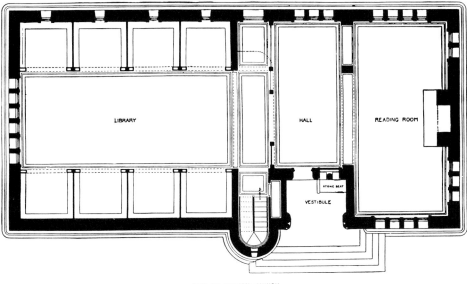

PLAN OF LIBRARY, QUINCY.

Fig. 3.3. Crane Memorial Library, plan. (Mariana Griswold Van Rensselaer, *Henry Hobson Richardson and His Works,* New York, 1888, 79)

Fig. 3.4. Crane Memorial Library, book room. (*Address of Charles Francis Adams, Jr. and Proceedings at the Dedication of the Crane Memorial Hall at Quincy, Massachusetts, May 30, 1882,* Quincy, Mass., 1883, 25)

Within a broad historical context, the form of these American public library buildings as it evolved during the last half of the nineteenth century resulted from the interplay of diverse interests: those of the monied patrons who built them, the public for whom they were being erected, the newly established architectural profession, and the librarians, who, like their counterparts in the building profession, were struggling to establish their own "professional" identity during this period. One reflection of this struggle was the founding of the ALA in 1876; another was that within a decade, American librarians had published some sixteen articles on the planning and arrangement of public library buildings, no fewer than six of which were authored by William Frederick Poole.[3]

One of the first American librarians to write about library planning and to suggest an alternative to the traditional hall library form was Justin Winsor, who as early as 1872 suggested that "the first principle" of library design should consist of "the primary adaption of the building to its uses."[4] Four years later he elaborated on this concept in an article entitled "Library Buildings," which appeared in the United States Bureau of Education's landmark publication *Public Libraries in the United States of America: Their History, Condition, and Management.* Here he stated that the "plan of administration" for a library should first be formulated by the librarian "and in accordance with that its book rooms, public waiting rooms, official and service quarters should be planned to fall into the most convenient relations one to the other." Only then should an architect be employed to "build his edifice around these quarters without disturbing [their] size or relative position."[5]

Most importantly, wrote Winsor, a library should be designed so that the maximum number of books could be stored in the smallest and most economical space—bringing them, as a result, within the shortest possible distance to the delivery area, thus making them quickly and easily accessible to the library staff. In the traditional hall library, he complained, librarians often had to climb many flights of stairs and circle the hall several times in order to retrieve even a handful of books. Winsor's alternative to this arrangement was the stack system of book storage, the first American example of which he and the architect Henry Van Brunt were erecting at that time as an addition to the old Gore Hall Library at Harvard (fig. 3.5).

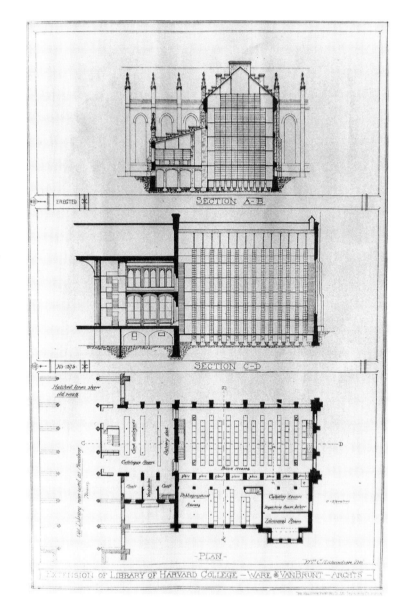

Fig. 3.5. Ware and Van Brunt, addition to Gore Hall, Harvard University, Cambridge, Mass., 1875–1877. (*American Architect and Building News,* 23 November 1887)

This "revolutionary" new form of book storage was described by Van Brunt at the third annual meeting of the American Library Association in Boston in July 1879. Echoing Winsor, Van Brunt began by stating that

> the architect, when called upon to study [library design] cannot but recognize at the onset that there is involved in it one point of construction and design paramount to all others, viz.: how to provide accommodation for the accumulation of books in such a manner that the utmost compactness of storage shall be made consistent with the most convenient classification, with accessibility, equality of temperature, abundance of light, complete security from dampness and from fire, and with provisions for the indefinite enlargement of the collection in any department without unnecessary waste of space.[6]

In order to accomplish this, Van Brunt erected a book room whose walls were composed of a series of brick and stone piers divided by wide expanses of glass. Behind each of these piers lay several stories of metal shelving, arranged in rows and divided by aisles, that were set perpendicular to the windows. Both the shelving and the aisles were hung on a series of "iron skeleton uprights" that extended the full height of the building and also supported an iron and terra-cotta roof and skylight. In respect to its tectonic structure alone, this was revolutionary because the entire metal shelving system was structurally independent of the masonry and glass shell. It was also revolutionary in respect to its completely utilitarian approach to book storage.[7]

"It is to be observed," announced the proud architect, "that in this structure no sacrifice of convenience or economy has been made for the sake of any architectural pretense. The external aspects of the building are a legitimate growth from necessity, and have been adjusted so as to secure a proper and decent harmony of proportions and just significance of detail, no more, and no less."[8] This system represented, he thus felt, "the greatest degree of economy as regards space, material, and cost yet attained in the fire-proof and damp-proof stacking of books for the uses of a public library." And while it would be difficult to evolve any universal design from this example, for this "part of the problem . . . must be governed by local conditions, by the amount of money available, by the character and shape of the ground to be occupied, and by various other circumstances," the Harvard stack, Van Brunt believed, could serve "as a convenient point of departure for further development" of this type of

purely functional book-storage room.[9] In this belief he was strongly defended by his associate, Justin Winsor. If an architect "complains," wrote Winsor, that this type of system does "not give sight of the books, and that he must fail of half his effects if he cannot have handsome bindings and vistas of shelves, tell him to fail; that the public wants books to read, not to look at."[10]

Although Poole, who joined in the discussion that followed Van Brunt's paper, was wholly in favor of a functional approach to book storage, he, unlike Winsor, strongly objected to the use of a stack system for this purpose, proposing instead that the ideal library should be composed of a series of small, subject-oriented rooms arranged in two stories around a central courtyard. These rooms, as Poole was to outline in more detail many times in the future, were to be sixteen feet in height and "would have no galleries, for galleries [were only] a pest and a nuisance."[11] Not only did librarians—as Winsor already had noted—tire of continually climbing up and down stairways, but the volumes in the upper galleries were often ruined by the heat that gathered near the ceiling of the hall. Therefore, Poole suggested that no bookcase should be taller than the reach of the average person; the extra space between the top of the shelves and the ceiling would serve to dissipate this excessive heat.

"In all cases," he added, "I would hold architectural effect subsidiary to the practical uses of the library—in other words, would build around my books."[12] In this respect he believed all earlier libraries, especially the larger ones, had failed, and he made this very clear when he stated: "I know of no better rule to be observed in library architecture of the future, than this: 'Avoid everything that pertains to the plan and arrangement of the conventional American library building'."[13]

Poole's unequivocal indictment of American library architecture and, by implication, the architectural profession did not pass unnoticed. Just three weeks later the editors of *The American Architect and Building News* responded with a lengthy rebuttal that was to touch off a debate between librarians and architects that would last well into the next century. Particularly vexing to the architects was what they saw as an increasingly common tendency to undervalue their services. "This prejudice," they noted,

> found fair expression in the discussion to which we have alluded, where one librarian of eminence gave utterance to a remark which

apparently found acceptance among most of his brethren, that in the building of the ideal library it is necessary to forget all that architects have hitherto done for them, and to begin anew on what he called a practical basis, without any embarrassments from the traditions of architectural practise; as if ideas of beauty and style, which seemed to be considered the whole stock in trade of architecture, could only be expressed at the expense of some practical requirement of convenience and necessity.[14]

Of course, they added, this was not at all the case, for it was the "fundamental basis of all sound building" to combine the two so as to obtain "beauty without any unnecessary sacrifice of fitness and economy."[15]

Unconvinced by this argument, Poole led a second foray against the architects at the 1881 annual meeting of the ALA. Here he read a paper, entitled "The Construction of Library Buildings," in which he reiterated his earlier observations on "conventional" structures, such as the Boston Public Library, the Boston Athenaeum, or the Astor Library in New York. To previous criticisms, he now also noted that in the event of its being filled, this kind of library was very difficult to enlarge. "Shall it be extended heavenward," he asked sarcastically,

> and more galleries be piled on these, with more wasted space in the nave, greater difficulty of access to books, and more extravagance in the heating? Shall the transcepts and chancel be built, so that the plan will represent the true ecclesiastical cross? However pious these improvements and gratifying to the taste of the refined architect, they are expensive, they involve demolishing much that has already been constructed, and they will give but little additional room. Why library architecture should have been yoked to ecclesiatical architecture . . . is not obvious, unless it be that librarians in the past needed this stimulus to their religious emotions. The present state of piety in the profession renders the union no longer necessary and it is time that the bill was filed for a divorce. The same secular common sense and the same adaption of means to ends which have built the modern grain elevator and reaper are needed for the reform of library construction.[16]

Poole's solution to the problem, as he had suggested two years earlier, was to design a building composed of a series of individually compartmentalized rooms, each arranged by subject matter. A later published version of this paper was accompanied by a plan that would serve as the basis for designs he would help to prepare for the Newberry Library in Chicago during the five years preceding his death.

Although in the discussion that followed there was much disagreement over what might be the best system to replace the

gallery arrangement, the general contention of the librarians was expressed in a resolution offered to the meeting by John Edmands of the Mercantile Library of Philadelphia: "That, in the opinion of the Association, the time has come for a radical modification of the prevailing typical style of library building, and the adoption of a style of construction better suited to economy and practical utility."[17] It was adopted unanimously.

The following year, 1882, Poole was assigned by the ALA to report to their annual meeting on the progress of library architecture. Although he reiterated many of the same points that he had raised the previous year, his attention, and that of the other librarians at the convention, was more specifically directed towards plans that had recently been developed by the architectural firm of Smithmeyer and Pelz for the new Library of Congress building that was then being contemplated in Washington.[18] These called for a great rotunda surrounded by six tiers of alcoves and shelving, and, of course, were condemned vociferously by the conference, which resolved "that the plans submitted to this Association at the Washington meeting, by Mr. J. L. Smithmeyer, and adopted by the Joint Committee of Congress, embody principles of construction which are now regarded as faulty by the whole library profession; and, therefore, as members of the A.L.A., we protest against the erection of the building for the Library of Congress upon those principles."[19]

Although Poole himself presented neither a report nor a paper to the 1883 ALA conference, he did use the period of discussion that followed John Edmands's report on library architecture to attack vehemently again the plans for the new Library of Congress and to reaffirm his own views on library design: "The problem of library architecture," he said,

> is not a difficult one to solve if we will abandon conventional and medieval ideas, and apply the same common-sense, practical judgement and good taste which is used in the construction of houses to live in, stores to do business in, and hotels to accommodate transient visitors in. We want buildings for doing the work of a library in; for giving readers the best facilities for study; for storing books in the most convenient manner, where they will be secure from fire, and for doing everything which pertains to the administration of a library. The architect is not qualified to decide what the requirements of a library are, for he knows nothing about the details of its administration. The librarian should study out and design the original plan, and the architect should take these practical suggestions, harmonize them, and give to the structure an artistic effect. It will be well if librarians gave more attention to

library construction. If left to architects alone, the business will run in the old ruts.[20]

In spite of Poole's repeated criticisms, however, opposition to Smithmeyer and Pelz's designs for the new Library of Congress building was beginning to weaken. Ainsworth Spofford, the librarian of Congress, for instance, now stated that "a grand hall, sufficiently impressive in height and proportions to show at once, by its well-lined walls, the wealth of its literary stores" might in fact be appropriate for a National Library in order "to appeal to public taste as something worthy of the country."[21] Surprisingly, several other librarians were beginning to agree with this line of reasoning. In addition, they seemed to have begun to tire of Poole's apparently endless stream of invectives.[22]

Undaunted by the softening of his colleagues' stand against the hall library, Poole had his own remarks published independently in a small booklet in 1884, along with an appendix in which he further attacked a short essay entitled *Suggestions on Library Architecture* that had been published by Smithmeyer the previous year.[23]

"Those who have read any of Mr. Poole's writings," responded the editor of *The American Architect and Building News,*

> will not need to be told that his criticism of Mr. Smithmeyer's book is pretty lively reading—much too lively, in fact, for the taste of those who dislike the use of such words as "fraud," "dishonesty," "ignorance," "falsification," and so on, in the consideration of technical subjects. It is true that Mr. Poole finds some provocation for his violence in expressions contained in the book which he reviews, but he should remember that a world which looks indulgently upon the unskilled brandishing of dangerous weapons by a novice in warfare turns away with terror and repugnance at the sight of the same weapons in the hands of an expert gladiator.[24]

The following year, 1885, Poole turned his attention to the planning of small library buildings, noting in a paper, which he presented at the annual meeting, that since the founding of the ALA in 1876 the discussion of library construction had "been directed almost wholly to the requirements of large libraries," when for every library of the larger class that had been erected in America, "a hundred" small buildings were in fact needed.[25] Here and in an article published in the September 1885 issue of *The Library Journal* Poole thus presented a plan for a library

building that would cost in the neighborhood of fifty thousand dollars and would be capable of storing up to thirty thousand books (fig. 3.6).

Arranged within it were a reference room (C), a periodical reading room (D), a delivery area (E), a ladies' reference room (F), a stairtower (H), and (A), "a room for the storage of books *without alcoves or galleries.*"[26] This latter room was, as Poole had suggested earlier in his scheme for larger libraries, to be fifteen or sixteen feet in height, with five-foot-high wall cases around its periphery and rows of freestanding, double-sided, wooden shelves in between. It was to be illuminated by a row of windows set above the wall cases and was capable, with minor modifications, of being expanded in any of three directions.[27]

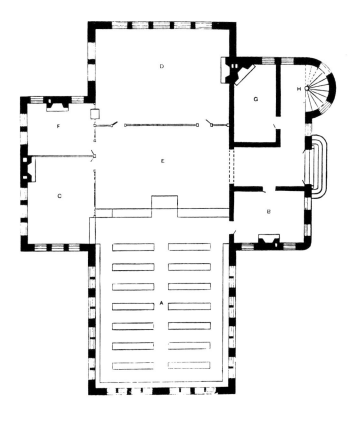

Fig. 3.6. William F. Poole, "Plan for a Public Library," 1885. (*The Library Journal,* Conference No., 1885)

Although Poole's library was cross-axial in plan, he claimed that this form had "not been taken for its medieval and ecclesiastical associations—it being that of the old cathedrals —but for the reason that it gives the most convenient arrangement of the rooms, the most economical subdivision of the space, and the best distribution of the light. It is a form of structure which can be enlarged in several directions without disturbing its architectural symmetry, the convenience of the internal arrangements, or the obstructing of light.[28] As to the style of the exterior elevation," Poole added, he (not surprisingly) had some opinions but would say nothing concerning them in this particular paper. He did note, however, that his plan, "in the breaking of lines in the facade, [would] commend itself to any tasteful architect."[29]

The same year in which Poole presented this new plan to the library association, the trustees of a small bequest that had been left in 1882 by Jesse Hoyt of New York City to the town of East Saginaw, Mich., formally invited five architectural firms to submit designs to a competition for the construction of a new public library building that was to be erected there. This structure, according to the *Invitation to Architects* that they issued—like Poole's ideal small public library—was to be erected at a cost of no more than fifty thousand dollars. It was to include a reading room, lecture hall, work space, and offices for the librarians, as well as a well-lighted, fireproof book room capable of storing up to thirty thousand volumes. It was stated, moreover, that the trustees were specifically committed to the system of book storage advocated by Mr. Poole, who, according to a note that later appeared in *The Library Journal,* was acting as a consultant to the project.[30] Designs for this building were to be submitted no later than 1 February 1886.

Although the identities of two of the five firms that were invited to enter the Hoyt Library competition have been lost, the other three alone comprised an impressive group. They included the firms of McKim, Mead, and White; Henry Hobson Richardson; and Van Brunt and Howe.[31] Richardson and Van Brunt were, of course, among the most prominent designers of library architecture in the country: Van Brunt, through his association with Winsor and the Harvard stack system, and Richardson, because he had already designed four highly acclaimed libraries similar in scale to the proposed Hoyt building.[32] Richardson's Crane Memorial Library in Quincy, Mass. (1880–1882;

figs. 3.2–3.4), in particular, had been lavishly praised in *Harper's Weekly,* which in 1883 had cited it as the most successful of Richardson's libraries to date, and saying this, they continued, "is pretty safely saying it is architecturally the best Village library in the United States."[33]

Symbolically and aesthetically, in fact, they were no doubt correct, for in this building Richardson had completed the evolution of a library iconography with which he had been experimenting since he drew his first design for the Winn Memorial Library in 1875. At the same time, at Quincy, he had also managed to mold the diverse symbolic elements of this iconography into a unified composition, one which reflected both the forms and the functions of his library's parallel interior spaces. With its celebrated entry arch, stair tower, and reading-room window balanced against the brilliantly articulated book wing, Richardson's Quincy facade, like that of the Bibliothèque Ste.-Geneviève in Paris (1832–1840), read as a masterpiece of intelligibility.[34] The book wing, in particular, managed to convey its protective function and yet visually continued to express the syncopation of the gallery and alcove system it housed. Richardson's interior spaces, likewise, were elevated to an equally high level of aesthetic and symbolic meaning: melding the medieval, ecclesiastical and secular forms of the church and the monastic library into both a memorial to the Crane family and a new American institution dedicated to the dispensation of a culture. In short, Richardson had invented not only a new public library building type, but a "democratic" iconography expressive of the aspirations and ideals of America's leading entreprenurial families.

As impressive as this aesthetic and iconographic achievement may have been, it did not, as might be expected, entirely please the library profession. After a visit to the library in 1890, K. A. Linderfelt, the director of the Milwaukee Public Library and a close friend of Poole's, wrote, "The faults of arrangement, common to all Richardson's [library] buildings, [are] still more emphasized in this, one of his latest works. . . . The result is in the highest degree unsatisfactory."[35] Not only was the lighting poor throughout the building, but the books were delivered to the public in the middle of the reading room, which was disturbing to the readers. Furthermore, these books were stored in the librarians' bête noire, a traditional alcove and gallery book room.

Fifteen years later, Charles Francis Adams, Jr., one of the original trustees of the library and a personal friend of the architect, also pronounced the interior arrangement of the Crane Library a failure. Though he accepted part of the blame for this himself, "for one thing," he wrote, he was not responsible, "that is, for the wretchedly inadequate lighting. I well remember telling Mr. Richardson that I thought the supply of light was inadequate. He over-ruled me, insisting that, if anything, there was too much light. Architects are apt to be wrong on this head. The result is that, whereas the interior of a library should be bright and cheerful, in that case it is murky and dismal."[36] Additionally, since the collection had grown from twelve thousand to twenty-six thousand volumes by 1905, Adams also criticized the architect's use of an alcove arrangement, "which now no architect or builder would adopt." It was "dark, inconvenient and suppl[ied] a minimum of shelf space," and even more seriously, it did not allow for a convenient means of expansion.[37]

Given William Poole's role as consultant in East Saginaw and the problems that had already surfaced in his other libraries, it is not surprising that Richardson, even though his exterior elevations were still strongly dependent upon his Quincy building, made significant adjustments in the interior arrangement of his Hoyt library design (figs. 3.7–3.10). According to his *Prospectus* and plans, for example, he proposed to abandon his standard alcove and gallery book room in favor of freestanding, iron book racks with wooden shelving similar to, but not exactly like, those preferred by Poole. The narrow slits with which he still intended to light this space, however, must surely have irritated the librarian, as perhaps did his placement of this room on the west side of the building and not, as Poole had suggested it should be in his article of 1885, on the north.[38] Richardson had also faced his entry south, even though the *Invitation to Architects* specified that it face west. Hence, no doubt, the motivation for a hastily penned letter from Richardson to his designer, George Shepley, dated one month after the close of the competition, which reads in part, "The longer they delay the decision the better for us. You had better see Poole if you can, *not* in Chicago but in Saginaw – I am right about placing and facing the building – the southern sun on the porch and steps alone, all things considered, is enough to decide it. Stand solid on position as it is – I thought all their recommendations were suggestions."[39]

Fig. 3.7. Henry Hobson Richardson, design for the Hoyt Memorial Library, East Saginaw, Mich., ca. 1885, facade. (By permission of the Houghton Library, Harvard University)

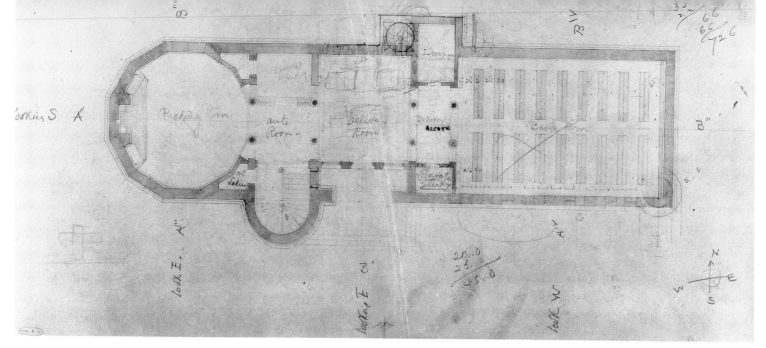

Fig. 3.8. Henry Hobson Richardson, design for the Hoyt Memorial Library, plan of first floor. (By permission of the Houghton Library, Harvard University)

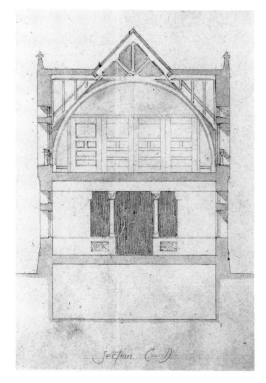

Fig. 3.9. Henry Hobson Richardson, design for the Hoyt Memorial Library, cross section through delivery room. (By permission of the Houghton Library, Harvard University)

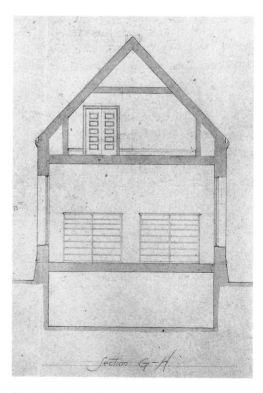

Fig. 3.10. Henry Hobson Richardson, design for the Hoyt Memorial Library, cross section through book room. (By permission of the Houghton Library, Harvard University)

Clearly, Henry Hobson Richardson did not know William Frederick Poole. Richardson's design was not accepted.

Neither, for that matter, was the entry of McKim, Mead, and White—if indeed they ever submitted one. If Charles McKim's design for the Manchester, Mass., Memorial Library, which was executed in 1886, bears any resemblance to what they might have proposed, however, their failure needs little explanation. McKim's interior arrangement, which even he described as "mediaeval," would surely have mortified Poole, especially the ill-lit and tiny book room, which in no way reflected modern library planning theory.[40]

Even a brief examination of Van Brunt and Howe's *Specifications,* on the other hand, explains why their entry was ultimately accepted by the trustees, for Van Brunt, unlike Richardson, appears to have taken both Poole's and the trustees' recommendations seriously (figs. 3.11–3.13).[41] This is not surprising, however, for Van Brunt had a long history of working closely with librarians, a tradition of cooperation that he continued to follow in his designs for the East Saginaw library. Van Brunt's Hoyt reading room, following Poole's suggestions, for instance, is placed on the north side and his entry on the west side of the building. His shelving was freestanding and constructed entirely of wood, as Poole preferred. And most importantly perhaps, the original cross-axial plan of the Hoyt Library appears as a mirror image of the ideal plan that Poole published in *The Library Journal* in 1885: the only major differences being a shifting around of the tower and entry porch and the substitution of an apsidal reading room for Poole's reference and ladies' reference rooms (fig. 3.6).

Fig. 3.11. Van Brunt and Howe, Hoyt Memorial Library, East Saginaw, Mich., 1885–1890, photo ca. 1890. (Eddy Room Collection, Hoyt Memorial Library, East Saginaw, Mich.)

Fig. 3.12. Van Brunt and Howe, Hoyt Memorial Library, delivery room. (American Library Association Archives, University of Illinois at Champaign-Urbana)

Surprisingly, almost nothing of this important confrontation between Richardson; Van Brunt and Howe; McKim, Mead, and White; and William Frederick Poole reached the professional or popular press, and thus until recently has been almost entirely ignored.[42] The controversy that surfaced here, however, did not die with the selection of the Van Brunt and Howe designs, for the rejected Richardson plans were to appear again in New Orleans in the form of the slightly larger Howard Memorial Library. This was begun in 1885 under Richardson's direction but not completed until after his untimely death in April 1886.

This episode in the continuing controversy over library design became especially heated in late September 1888, when the plans and elevations for the Howard Memorial Library were exhibited at the annual conference of the ALA. To fuel the fire, Richardson—or Shepley, Rutan, and Coolidge—had reintroduced a traditional gallery and alcove shelving arrangement in the design for the Howard Library book room (figs. 3.14, 3.15).[43] This feature, as might be expected, did not sit well with the librarians, who, according to a report printed in *The Nation*, "riddled" Richardson's designs "with objections." Not only did they especially dislike this building, but they now pronounced "all of Richardson's designs for libraries . . . , from the library point of view, failures" and further wondered

> whether the famous architect ever gave any thought to the object for which his buildings of this sort were intended: there is little indication that he did in any of them. He appears to have been satisified if he drew a beautiful design, and to have left it to some draftsman to fit in the books and the service. When shall we find an artist who will plan for use first and beauty next; who will see where his book-shelves and his reading-halls and his work-rooms ought to go for the highest efficiency, and then will mould his library building around them? Looking at such plans as this of the Howard Library (where, for instance, an attendent must go 320 feet to get a book within 10 feet of the delivery desk), and scores of others like it, . . . one may say, as did the President of the Association, "The architect is the natural enemy of the librarian."[44]

"The Convention of the American Library Association," returned the editors of *The American Architect and Building News,* who seemed particularly irritated that the librarians had dared criticize their recently deceased and very highly revered colleague,

> amused itself, as usual, by falling foul of the architects, over whose prostrate forms every scientific hobby is made to prance. . . .
>
> Considering that no two librarians appear to be agreed as to where book-shelves and reading halls and work rooms ought to go . . . and that the plan advocated by one is generally laughed to scorn by the rest, it is not surprising that architects have not yet invented an arrangement which suits everybody.[45]

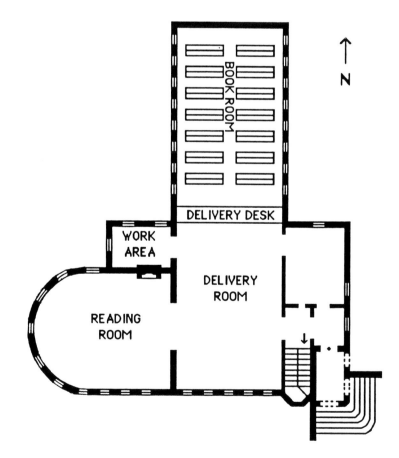

Fig. 3.13. Van Brunt and Howe, Hoyt Memorial Library, reconstructed plan, not to scale. (Kenneth A. Breisch)

Not true, replied *The Library Journal* the following month: "The fact that different librarians prefer different forms of building, some alcoves, some separate rooms, some stacks, is no excuse for architects if they make bad alcoves, rooms and stacks." Even though they might disagree on some points, "all librarians are perfectly agreed" when they say "they want plenty of fresh air, plenty of light, warmth in the winter, coolness in the summer, compact storage, easy access to their books: and these things the architects ought to know how to give them. These things they have often not given them, furnishing them instead with a handsome or imposing or a charming facade."[46]

Not all librarians, of course, were as irritated with architects as the editors of *The Library Journal*. William I. Fletcher, for example, adopted a much more conciliatory stand when he wrote this same year, 1888, to the editors of *The American Architect and Building News* in response to this editorial:

> With the great increase of public libraries and the growth in public taste, the architecture of libraries becomes daily of more importance. It is to be regretted that there should seem to be a sort of irrepressible conflict between librarians and architects, as indicated in a recent editorial, occasioned by the librarians' conference. As a librarian of perhaps a little more than ordinary experience with, and observation of, library buildings of different styles, I feel inclined to attempt to explain this appearance of conflict and say a word for peace and cooperation.[47]

In reference to Richardson, in particular, Fletcher noted that although he presumed "no librarians can be found who will fail to do justice to the excellence of the work of our greatest architect," he was "equally satisfied that no librarian, who could be quoted as authority in the profession, would express approval of the main features of Mr. Richardson's library buildings in so far as the interior is concerned or affected."[48] This was, however, primarily because he had not had the opportunity to work directly with librarians, but rather had been in the employ of trustees and building committees. "I have the best reason for believing," concluded Fletcher,

> that had he lived but a few years longer, he would have come to build libraries no less beautiful and appropriate in general effect than those he left, but far better fitted to meet the wants of the modern public library. For while there may be more or less conflict between "art and use," in this department as elsewhere, I do not believe that any man of genius, alive to the real needs of any institution, will fail in the attempt to meet those necessities, while

still responding to the aesthetic requirements peculiar to this class of work. Fortunately examples of success with this problem are multiplying, and many librarians are ready to point to their architects as friends, not "natural enemies."[49]

As if to point up this fact, Normand S. Patton, the architect of the newly designed Hackley Public Library (fig. 3.16) in Muskegon, Mich. (1888–1890), was invited to exhibit his plans for this building and to speak before the National Conference of Librarians in 1889, the first architect to be so honored since Henry Van Brunt's appearance a decade earlier. Not surprisingly, perhaps, the basic arrangement of this building, like that of Van Brunt's Hoyt, was derived from Poole's plan of 1885 and its books were stored in freestanding wooden shelves in a book room, which conformed closely to Poole's ideal (figs. 3.17, 3.18). Patton's own discussion of the topic of library design seems to reflect the influence of Poole and his colleagues.

Fig. 3.14. Henry Hobson Richardson and Shepley, Rutan, and Coolidge, Howard Memorial Library, New Orleans, La., 1886–1889.
(*The Library Journal* 13 [1888]:317. Originally from *Harper's Weekly;* copyright 1888, by Harper and Brothers.)

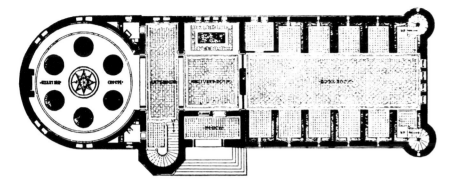

Fig. 3.15. Howard Memorial Library, plan. (*The Library Journal* 13 [1888]:317)

"There are two parties to be provided for in a library building," said Patton at this meeting, "the public who patronizes the institution and the administrators who procure and arrange the books and give them out. No library is perfect that does not provide for the convenience and comfort of both of these parties. In the old-style building the public was cared for, and the librarian and his assistants left to make the best they could out of the premises."[50]

In the past, librarians had not been able to assert themselves, continued Patton, because they were typically brought to the institution to purchase and arrange books only after the trustees or patron had constructed a building. That, reasoned Patton, was why librarians had "had so little influence on library architecture" and also why "so great an architect as Richardson should have gone on designing museums, and calling them libraries."[51]

Fig. 3.16. Patton and Fisher, Hackley Public Library, Muskegon, Mich., 1888–1890. (Postcard in collection of Kenneth A. Breisch)

At the dedication of Hackley Library in 1890, Patton continued this spirit of reconciliation when he argued that there was no reason why the symbolic and the functional had to be mutually exclusive of one another in any building. In point of fact, he continued, good architecture should

> unite beauty and utility. If [it] has been made beautiful at the expense of utility, then it has so far failed of the highest excellence. If on the contrary we find that the wants of every one have been met, so that the librarian will think the building constructed for his special benefit, and at the same time the public will see that none of their rights have been curtailed, and that the design is a natural development of a convenient plan, we will have the only form of beauty that is lasting and satisfactory in architecture, a beauty that is the expression of the character of the building—that can be compared not to the handsome clothes and jewels with which a lady of fashion may adorn herself, but rather to that beauty of countenance which is the reflection of the soul within.[52]

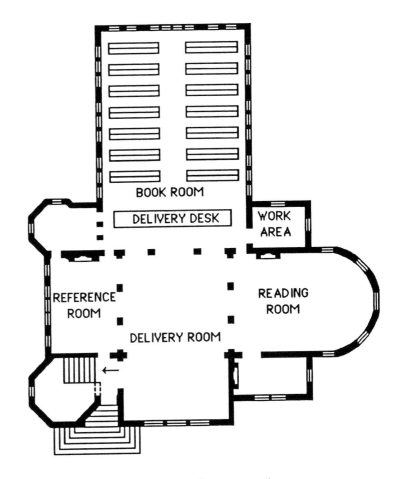

Fig. 3.18. Hackley Public Library, plan, not to scale. (Kenneth A. Breisch)

Fig. 3.17. Hackley Public Library, delivery and book rooms, photo ca. 1890. (With permission of Hackley Public Library, Muskegon, Mich.)

Patton's commitment to the librarian's interests was subsequently acknowledged by the editors of *The Library Journal,* who wrote, paraphrasing Poole: "Mr. Patton, the architect, has the true theory of library construction; he thinks that the shell should be fashioned to accommodate the animal, not that the animal should be squeezed into the shell."[53]

Ironically, at the same time that Patton's "animal" reflected modern concepts of library design promulgated by Poole and the libarians, his "shell" closely reflected the work of Richardson. Because of this, as he himself stated at the dedication of the building in 1890, "you would not need the inscription over the entrance to tell you [that this building] is a library. If no other feature should give the clue, the high windows on the sides of the rear wing would hardly be adapted to any apartment except one for book storage."[54] His tower, likewise, was intended to act as "an appropriate expression of" the main staircase, as well as to serve "as a beacon to guide [the public] by day or night" to "the prominent and inviting" entrance arch.[55]

Although, as can be seen at Muskegon, Richardson's style and iconography would persist as major themes in library design well into the 1890s, by the late 1880s the type of book-room arrangement he had employed in his buildings already had begun to disappear. The Howard Memorial Library in New Orleans, in fact, represents one of the last such buildings to employ a traditional two-story gallery and alcoves. After 1890, these were consistently replaced with freestanding shelving of the type advocated by Poole or the utilitarian metal stacks of Justin Winsor.

Interestingly, too, the plans of more than a dozen small public libraries constructed during the last decade and a half of the nineteenth century in the United States also directly reflect Poole's plan of 1885. These include, in addition to the structures at Muskegon and East Saginaw, libraries in Kalamazoo (1891;

fig. 3.19) and Coldwater (1886), Mich.; Dedham (1886–1887), Cambridge (1888–1889), and Fairhaven (1891), Mass.; Stratford, Conn. (1896; figs. 3.20, 3.21); and Dayton, Ohio (1885–1888; fig. 3.22).[56]

It was in reference to this later building that its director, Robert W. Steele, wrote to Poole in January 1888:

> I sent you the papers relating to the formal opening of our Library Building because I felt that we were largely indebted to you for its success. The plan is substantially the one furnished by you with a few minor changes to adapt it to its location. I congratulate myself that it was at my suggestion you were consulted. But for that the rotunda with its galleries would have been adopted. We now have a practical demonstration of the great superiority of your method of shelving the books. Our librarians are delighted with it.[57]

By the end of the nineteenth century Poole's pragmatic approach to the shelving of books in particular—especially his concept of setting freestanding shelves in an attached and expandable book wing—had become a standard feature in small American libraries and was consequently employed in most of the more than fifteen hundred Carnegie libraries constructed between 1899 and 1915.[58]

His contribution to the modern design of the small library, then, was immense, for it was certainly Poole, along with his colleague, Justin Winsor, who pioneered the idea that the library should be designed as a warehouse for books. And certainly he and his colleagues were correct when they recognized that in a utilitarian sense Richardson's libraries were generally ill-suited for library purposes. What they did not completely understand, however, was that had Richardson not established the type of architectural iconography that was employed, at least in part, by architects like Normand S. Patton, the institution itself would never have attained the recognizability and ultimately the stature that it did in the cultural life of small towns all across the country.

Fig. 3.19. Patton and Fisher, the Kalamazoo Public Library, Kalamazoo, Mich., 1891. (*Inland Architect and Building News* 17 [June 1891])

Fig. 3.20. W. H. Miller, Stratford Public Library, Stratford, Conn., 1896. (*Stratford Public Library, Dedication Exercises,* Bridgeport, Conn., 1896)

Fig. 3.21. Stratford Public Library, plan. (*Scientific American, Building Edition,* June 1893)

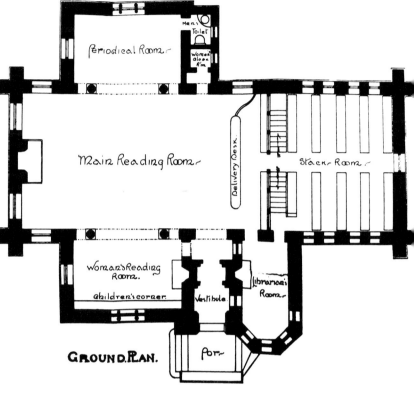

Fig. 3.22. Peters and Burns, Dayton Public Library, Dayton, Ohio, 1885–1888. (*American Architect and Building News* 19 [6 Feb. 1886])

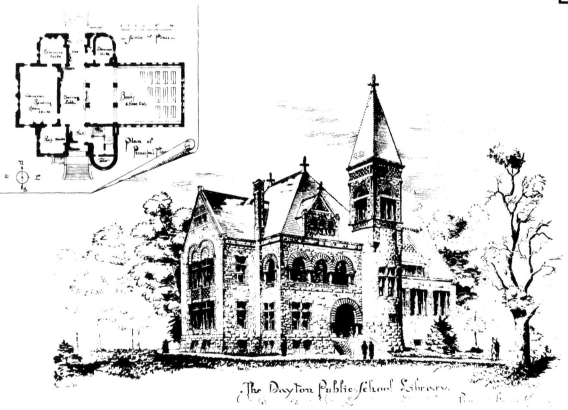

Notes

1. This article is based upon a lecture given at the Newberry Library in Chicago in July 1985. It, in turn, was derived from sections of my dissertation, "Small Public Libraries in America 1805–1890: The Invention Evolution of a Building Type," which was completed in 1982 at the University of Michigan under the direction of Professor Leonard Eaton. I first discovered William Poole while writing a paper on the Hackley Public Library in Muskegon, Mich., for Dr. Eaton in 1975. For more on Poole see William Williamson, *William Frederick Poole and the Modern Library Movement* (New York, 1963).

2. The hall library began to evolve in Southern Europe toward the end of the sixteenth century. The characteristic feature of this arrangement was that books were shelved in cases set around the periphery of a great hall. The halls were often two or more stories in height. In the late seventeenth and early eighteenth centuries, this type was often combined with the stall or alcove library arrangement of the Middle Ages, creating multistory, longitudinal spaces similar in form to the nave of a basilica or cathedral. For more on this see John W. Clark, *The Care of Books: An Essay on the Development of Libraries and Their Fittings, from the Earliest Times to the End of the Eighteenth Century* (Cambridge, England, 1909); Georg Leyh, "Das Haus und Seine Einrichtung," *Handbuch der Bibliothekswissenschaft,* ed. F. Milkau, 2 vols. (Leipzig, 1933), 2: 1–38; and Nikolaus Pevsner, *A History of Building Types* (Washington, D.C., 1976), 91–103. For the influence of these European buildings on early American libraries see Breisch, "Small Public Libraries," 48–115.

3. Although a few were published before 1875, the majority appeared between 1876 and 1885. Many of these will be discussed below. Among the most significant of the earlier discussions were "Hints on Library Buildings," *Norton's Literary Gazette and Publisher's Circular* 3 (15 January 1853): 1–2; Nathaniel Shurtleff, *A Decimal System for the Arrangement and Administration of Libraries* (Boston, 1856); William Rees, *Manual of Public Libraries, Institutions, and Societies in the United States and British Provinces of North America* (Philadelphia, 1859); and S. W. Benjamin, "Libraries," *Harper's New Monthly Magazine* 29 (June–November 1864): 482–484. Many of the ideas expressed in these and later discussions of the topic reflected European theories. For more on this topic see Breisch, "Small Public Libraries," 23–32, 75–83, 91–101.

4. Justin Winsor, "Report of the Superintendent," *Twentieth Annual Report of the Trustees of the Public Library* (Boston, 1872), 15. Winsor was superintendent of the Boston Public Library from 1868 until 1877, when he accepted a new position as librarian at Harvard University. In 1876, he was elected as the first president of the American Library Association. See Breisch, "Small Public Libraries," 126–129; Walter Muir Whitehill, *Boston Public Library: A Centennial History* (Cambridge, Mass., 1956), 75–102; and also W. F. Yust, *A Bibliography of Justin Winsor* (Cambridge, Mass., 1902).

5. Justin Winsor, "Library Buildings," in United States Bureau of Education, *Public Libraries in the United States of America: Their History, Condition, and Management,* 2 vols. (Washington, D.C., 1876), 1:465–466.

6. Henry Van Brunt, "Library Buildings," *The Library Journal* 4 (1879):294–295.

7. For Gore Hall see also *The American Architect and Building News* 3 (1878):173–174; William H. Jordy, *Progressive and Academic Ideals at the Turn of the Century,* American Buildings and Their Architects Series, 4 vols. (New York, 1976), 3:326–327; and *Gore Hall: The Library of Harvard College 1838–1913* (Cambridge, Mass., 1917).

8. Van Brunt, "Library Buildings," 296.

9. Ibid.

10. Winsor, "Library Buildings," 1:465.

11. William F. Poole, "Library Buildings," *The Library Journal* 4 (1879):294.

12. Ibid.

13. Ibid., 293.

14. *The American Architect and Building News* 3 (1879):25.

15. Ibid. The librarians "answered" this editorial with one of their own, written by Charles Ammi Cutter, which appeared August 1879 in *The Nation* 29 (1879):125–126.

16. William F. Poole, "The Construction of Library Buildings," *The American Architect and Building News* 10 (1881):131. This paper was also published in *The Library Journal* 6 (1881):69–77 and reprinted as *U.S. Bureau of Education, Circular of Information,* no. 1 (1881). It was surprisingly well-received by the editors of *The American Architect and Building News,* which probably explains their willingness to republish it. For their reaction to this see *The American Architect and Building News* 9 (1881):85–86.

17. This was noted the following year in William F. Poole, "Progress of Library Architecture," *The Library Journal* 7 (1882):131.

18. Ibid., 130–134. For the Library of Congress see Helen-Anne Hilker, *Ten First Street, Southeast: Congress Builds a Library, 1886–1897* (Washington, D.C., 1980), 1–38.

19. *The Library Journal* 8 (1883):272.

20. Ibid., 270–272.

21. Ibid., 270.

22. Among them, for example, was Melville Dewey. See Ibid., 273–274.

23. John L. Smithmeyer, *Suggestions on Library Architecture* (Washington, D.C., 1883); and William F. Poole, *Remarks on Library Construction* (Chicago, 1884).

24. *The American Architect and Building News* 15 (1884):145.

25. "Small Library Buildings," *The Library Journal* 10 (1885): 250–256, 328–335. See also Breisch, "Small Public Libraries," 298–302.

26. "Small Library Buildings," 251, 256.

27. Ibid., 256.

28. Ibid., 252.

29. Ibid., 251, 256.

30. *The Library Journal* 12 (1887):387; and Hoyt Public Library of East Saginaw, Mich., Board of Trustees, *Invitation to Architects* (n.p., 1885). A copy of these specifications may be found in the Boston Public Library. See also Breisch, "Small Public Libraries," 289–291, 302–312; William J. Hennessey, "The Architectural Works of Henry Van Brunt" (Ph.D. diss., Columbia University, 1979), 154–163; and James Cooke Mills, *History of Saginaw and Saginaw County, Michigan,* 2 vols. (Saginaw, Mich., 1918), 1:304–307.

31. Mills, *History of Saginaw,* 1:305.

32. In addition to helping to introduce the freestanding metal stack shelving into the United States at Gore Hall, Harvard, in 1875, Van Brunt also had completed by 1883 a second major library designed along similar lines, at the University of Michigan, just south of Saginaw. In 1885, moreover, he still held the distinction of having been the only architect ever invited to speak before a national conference of the ALA. For Richardson's libraries see Breisch, "Small Public Libraries," 202–263, 280–291; James F. O'Gorman, *H. H. Richardson and His Office—Selected Drawings* (Boston, 1974), 55–74; and Jeffrey Karl Ochsner, *H. H. Richardson: Complete Works* (Cambridge, Mass., 1982), 174–179, 183–187, 226–231, 313–317. These included the Winn Memorial Library in Woburn

(1875–1879), the Ames Memorial Library in North Easton (1877–1883), the Crane Memorial Library at Quincy (1880–1882), and the Converse Memorial Library in Malden, Mass. (1884–1885).

33. *Harper's Weekly* 27 (1883):251.

34. That Richardson's own library designs were deeply influenced by his knowledge of Labrouste's library cannot be doubted. See Breisch, "Small Public Libraries," 217–239. For an analysis of the Bibliothèque Ste.-Geneviève see Neil Levine, "The Romantic Idea of Architectural Legibility: Henri Labrouste and the Neo-Grec," *The Architecture of the Ecole des Beaux-Arts,* ed. Arthur Drexler (New York, 1977), 325–416.

35. K. A. Linderfelt and Adolph Meinecke, "Notes on Library Buildings, Visited November 3–26, 1890," Appendix 1, *Reports of the Proposed Library and Museum Building for the City of Milwaukee* (Milwaukee, Wis., 1890), 44.

36. Letter from C. F. Adams, Jr., to Albert Crane after a visit to the library in May 1905. Quoted in I. Draper Hill, Jr., *The Crane Library* (Quincy, Mass., 1962), 25.

37. Ibid., 25–26.

38. H. H. Richardson, *The Hoyt Public Library: East Saginaw, Michigan* (Boston, 1888), 4–6; Hoyt Public Library, *Invitation to Architects.* A copy of Richardson's perspectus can be found in the Houghton Collection at Harvard University. This same collection has in its possession forty-three drawings that have been identified by O'Gorman as belonging to the Hoyt project. See O'Gorman, *Richardson,* 171–174.

39. Quoted in O'Gorman, *Richardson,* 171.

40. According to the architect, the arrangement of the book room had been "suggested by the twelfth-century library at Merton College, Oxford." See *Dedication Services of the Memorial Library and Grand Army Hall at Manchester-by-the-Sea, Massachusetts, October 13, 1887* (Boston, 1888), 4.

41. Although this building has been heavily remodeled since its completion, it has been possible to reconstruct a conjectural arrangement for Van Brunt's original plan. See Van Brunt and Howe, *Specifications for the Construction of the Hoyt Public Library in the City of East Saginaw, Michigan* (East Saginaw, 1886).

42. O'Gorman, *Richardson,* 171–174, appears to be the first author to mention it.

43. Prints of the exterior and plan were also published in *The Library Journal* 13 (1888):316–318. For a contemporary description of the Howard Library see "Howard Library: An Important Addition to the City's Architecture," *The Times-Democrat,* 13 January 1889.

44. *The Nation* 47 (1888):272.

45. *The American Architect and Building News* 24 (1888):165.

46. *The Library Journal* 13 (1888):276.

47. William I. Fletcher, "Architects and Librarians: An Irenicon," *The American Architect and Building News* 24 (1888):198.

48. Ibid.

49. Ibid.

50. Normand S. Patton, "Architects and Librarians," *The Library Journal* 14 (1889):160. For the Hackley Public Library see *The Hackley Public Library of Muskegon, Michigan, Dedication, October 15, 1890* (Chicago, 1891); and Kenneth A. Breisch, "The Hackley Public Library of Muskegon, Michigan: Its Evolution, Design and Place in Late Nineteenth-Century America," (master's thesis, University of Michigan, 1976).

51. Patton, "Architects and Librarians," 160.

52. Normand S. Patton, "Address," in *The Hackley Public Library of Muskegon, Michigan, Dedication, October 15, 1890* (Chicago, 1891).

53. *The Library Journal* 16 (1891):4.

54. Normand S. Patton, "Address," 42.

55. Ibid., 40. Upon entering the building, even without Richardson's ecclesiastical gallery, he also noted: "Your eye will first meet the hospitable fireplace and the tables of catalogues. [Then] you will instinctively turn towards the end of the room. There you will see row after row of shelves, each filled with volumes. . . . Can such a sight fail to whet your appetite for a taste of their treasures?"

56. Breisch, "Small Public Libraries," 312–318.

57. Letter from Robert W. Steele to W. F. Poole, 30 January 1888, in the "William F. Poole Papers," Newberry Library, Chicago. For the Dayton Public Library see *American Architect and Building News* 19 (1886):66. According to *The Dedication of the Dayton Public Library Building, January 24, 1888* (Dayton, Ohio, 1888), 10, "The interior arrangement [of this building] was adopted upon the recommendation of Mr. William F. Poole of the Chicago Public Library, who was consulted by our Library Committee upon the best method of library construction."

58. Poole also had been a strong advocate for a departmentalized plan for the Newberry Library in Chicago. This was composed of a series of subject rooms of the type he outlined first in 1879. Even though it was Poole's plan that was eventually constructed, it might be said that it was the architect, Henry Ives Cobb—advocating as he did a combination of this arrangement with a freestanding stack capable of storing some 600,000 books—who at the time was more progressive. By 1893, the year in which the Newberry was completed, Poole's system was already considered by most architects and even librarians to be something of an anomaly, even though—perhaps somewhat ironically—in recent years it has begun to return to favor in many of our largest American public and university libraries. See Houghton Wetherold, "The Architectural History of the Newberry Library," *The Newberry Library Bulletin* 6 (November 1962):3–23; and Jordy, *Progressive and Academic Ideals* 3:324–325.

CHAPTER 4

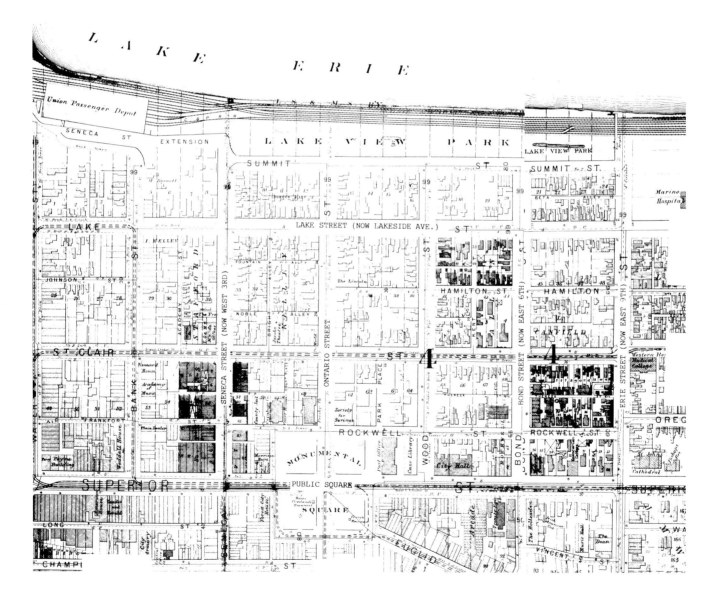

CLEVELAND'S STRUGGLE FOR SELF-IDENTITY

Aesthetics, Economics, and Politics

WALTER C. LEEDY, JR.

After the Civil War, sweeping technological changes challenged the basic structure of American society. A national railroad system, combined with telegraph and eventual telephone networks, revolutionized communications. Coupled with new methods of production, extraction of mineral resources, techniques of preserving food, and mechanized agriculture, basic industries began to specialize and multiply to create a national market. The concepts of the national corporation and national advertising were born. As a consequence, centers of production and distribution experienced rapid population growth. Practically overnight, villages metamorphosed into towns and cities. Though these transformations carried the promise of increased wealth for the nation, the physical and social structure of cities lagged behind economic and technical innovation.

Growing from a population of 57 in 1810 to 260,000 in 1890, Cleveland emerged from its pioneer, log-cabin days to become a major industrial center of 381,000 by 1900, which made it the seventh largest city in the United States. Attracted by the chance of industrial employment, immigrants flooded into the community (almost 125,000 were foreign-born in 1900), making the city a hodgepodge of ethnic enclaves. Twelve-hour work-

days left little time or energy for these new Clevelanders to contemplate what their city could look like. Political decisions were oftentimes left, out of loyalty and obligation, to ward bosses and parish priests, who assisted immigrants in securing employment and in becoming naturalized. One problem that Cleveland's leaders articulated was how might they educate the immigrant to live in a democratic society.

Since Cleveland was a research as well as a manufacturing center, it fostered an atmosphere of experimentation. It was the first city in the world to have its streets extensively lighted by electricity and the first place in the United States to make a commercial success of the Bessemer process; and it was home to several pioneer firms in the American mixed paint and varnish industry. Cleveland's business leaders, however, were financially conservative. Though there were no bank failures and comparatively few business failures during the recession from 1893 to 1896, the working class was extremely poor, and unemployment was high. Because the business community was enormously successful, Samuel Mather was able to present with confidence a lecture entitled "The Businessman—His Responsibilities as a Citizen" to the Cleveland Chamber of Commerce in 1895. He praised Joseph Chamberlain, who took time away from business to serve in public office, and appealed to his fellow Cleveland businessmen to follow Chamberlain's example of working for municipal excellence. Although common for the period, Mather's exhortation was seminal in Cleveland in uniting to philanthropic investment the necessity of service as an important contribution to civic life. In this spirit, and because of councilman Morris Black's vigorous opposition to corruption and fraud in city government, Harry A. Garfield and Frederic C. Howe, both members of the chamber of commerce, established the Municipal Association, an organization that equated reform with republicanism.[1] Leadership for innovation in Cleveland, therefore, was to come not from the oppressed or from disaffected reformers but from the establishment.

In the 1890s, cultivated Clevelanders dreamed that their city could rival Europe's finest achievements in civic architecture. Driven by competitive ambition, their quest to create an image for Cleveland ultimately resulted in a consensus amongst the city's political and economic leaders that this vision could become reality. To this end, but only after a complex series of events followed by a highly orchestrated effort, a plan was put forth in 1903. Laid out by a board of supervision chaired by architect Daniel Burnham of Chicago, a group of public buildings—a civic center—was envisioned to symbolize Cleveland. As one of the first large-scale planning efforts of the twentieth century, it served as an exemplar to other American cities. An understanding of how this plan was generated and accepted helps to clarify how planning goals were articulated and implemented in the period before planning became institutionalized within city government. Furthermore, as a case study, this paper investigates the impact of economic, political, and other forces that resulted in the eventual group plan, thereby giving special insight into the nascent years of city planning in America.

Cleveland was not entirely without an interesting architectural heritage. Two of her finest buildings were completed in 1890: the Cleveland Arcade, and Burnham and Root's Society for Savings Building. The Arcade, an interior, skylighted, commercial space that also functions as a passageway with office blocks at each end, is a typical nineteenth-century urban building type (fig. 4.1).[2] It was a response to traffic congestion present in the downtown area that forced pedestrians inside and led to a loss of the identity of the street as a locus for community activity. As innovative and as magnificent as its interior spatial conception and detailing are, the Cleveland Arcade looked backward to a relatively low and level concept for a city.

Fig. 4.1. John Eisenmann and George H. Smith, the Cleveland Arcade, Cleveland, interior before later changes, ca. 1890. (Cleveland Public Library)

By contrast, the Society for Savings Building looked forward to the future, being Cleveland's first skyscraper (fig. 4.2). It was not, however, the typical commercial office block of its day. Visually designed to communicate its purpose to the citizens of Cleveland and located at Cleveland's heart, Public Square, it proudly soared upward proclaiming itself to be a financial citadel. New materials and methods of construction were used in conjunction with Gothic architectural forms to create a truly ornamental structure.[3]

Myron T. Herrick, who was secretary and treasurer of the Society for Savings, helped promote the Arcade and later, in conjunction with entrepreneur James Parmelee, was part owner of the Cuyahoga Building (1892), designed by Daniel H. Burnham and Company.[4] Herrick, Parmelee, and Burnham were all Republicans. Political and personal allegiance was to become an important factor in later developments.[5] In retrospect, the construction of the Society for Savings Building and the Cuyahoga Building, in union with the Western Reserve Building (1891), accomplished one other important thing: it introduced Daniel Burnham to Cleveland's business elite. Thus in 1895 he participated in a closed competition to design a new building for the chamber of commerce.[6] In addition, Burnham was known in Cleveland for his leadership role in the World's Columbian Exposition of 1893, which for Cleveland area resident Charles E. Bolton created the impression that he "stepped upon a neighboring planet, where civilisation and art had been purified . . . and . . . [where] for a moment he was permitted to behold the glories of the New Jerusalem."[7]

Because enormous growth was taking place in Cleveland and new building technology made tall buildings viable, the physical environment of the city was undergoing radical change. Civic boosters boasted about the material wealth and progress the city was making but failed to acknowledge its ugliness. While celebrating Euclid Avenue, a famous street of fine homes, they tended to ignore actual conditions in the rest of the city.[8] The city did not have either a garbage collection or an adequate sewage system.

Cultivated Clevelanders began to notice their visual environment and put forth ideas to improve it. A letter to the editor in 1894, for example, suggested that Cleveland, like Paris, should regulate the height but not the style of buildings to make the streets more uniform in character. This, it was argued, would permit variety yet impart a feeling of harmony and dignity to the city.[9] Unlike those who believed tall buildings were totally unsuitable for human activities of any sort, the

Fig. 4.2. Burnham and Root, Society for Savings Building, Cleveland, under construction, ca. 1889. (Cleveland Public Library)

writer was only reacting to the jumbled mix of the new, taller buildings interspersed with older, lower ones. Another letter, published in 1895, called for the construction on Public Square of a new city hall of moderate height that would occupy considerable ground space in order to distinguish it from business buildings;[10] thus, one Clevelander articulated the crisis of identity inherent in the architecture of the period. The Group Plan of 1903 was to offer a solution to this predicament.

The city was in critical need of new and expanded facilities for a city hall. In fact, Cleveland city offices had been in rented space since 1875. When the city tried to erect a new headquarters on Public Square in 1895 — digging had actually started for the foundations — the plan had to be aborted. Herrick's Society for Savings had obtained an injunction: the city did not have the right to build there. The society did not want a building on its front lawn.[11]

The city was not the only institution that civic leaders felt needed new facilities. An editorial in *The Cleveland Plain Dealer* called for a new library building, citing the usefulness of the library as a public educator and also as a place of "mental recreation in this age of stress and anxiety."[12] A new federal building (post office) was also needed, as well as an art museum and an adequate music hall. There was no question that the city needed new facilities. On the other hand, the county courthouse, although twenty years old, was still creditable.[13]

The first concerted effort of Cleveland's architects to respond to such calls came in 1895 when the Cleveland Architectural Club, which recently had been founded, began to conduct educational exercises in the form of monthly juried competitions. Stimulated by real need, and by the court of honor of the World's Columbian Exposition, the assignment for their first competition in March 1895 was to provide a site plan for Cleveland's public buildings. This competition, however, was not realistic: expenses were not considered and, as a result, plans submitted would have destroyed blocks of the city with great impunity.

There were fifteen entries. The jury was composed of three architects, an artist, and Professor Charles F. Olney. Olney was a member of the leisure class, a Democrat, and a cultural leader who through ancestry and marriage had entrée into Cleveland society.[14] First mention went to a design by W. Dominick Benes that wiped Cleveland's old and venerable Public Square out of

existence, making it part of a grandiose scheme running to the lake (figs. 4.3, 4.4). Second mention went to Herbert Briggs, who proposed an axial mall from Public Square to the lakefront. Large in area, it was to run from Bond (now East Sixth) to Seneca Street (now West Third) (fig. 4.5). His objective, according to *The Cleveland Press,* was to reclaim the tenderloin district. He included a site for an exposition hall and recognized the importance of landscape by providing for fountains, statuary, asphalt pavings, parks, and little nooks. Third mention went to Frederick Baird, who proposed an artistic center in the vicinity of Euclid Avenue and Erie Street (now East Ninth) (fig. 4.6). Many thought this site was actually more desirable than those downtown on or near Public Square or the lakefront.[15]

These three designs posed arguments that were to emerge later on. First, what should be done with Public Square? Second, should downtown be decentralized to help alleviate traffic congestion? And third, should the group be apart from the business district on the lakefront? This was an area where land prices were low in the colorful but scandalous tenderloin district, a district whose reputation worried Cleveland businessmen. Known to be "full of low dives, . . . low saloons, . . . houses of prostitution, and one hundred and one objects that . . . [made it] Cleveland's bowery," the tenderloin district was tolerated by Republican mayor McKisson's administration. His police chief was against any campaign to clear out the district — the prostitutes would only be scattered throughout the city — and the Brewers Association and Saloonkeepers Association were potent forces in local politics. In the late 1890s, Cleveland's reform leaders, the clergy, and the clubs formed for the purpose were unsuccessful in their efforts to combat prostitution, gambling, and liquor abuses.[16] To them the tenderloin district epitomized corruption: it had to go. There was a split within Republican ranks because the Republican Municipal Association, which supported reform, did not support McKisson.

The 1895 designs were published in *The Cleveland Press,* which characterized them as "Napoleonic." For the time being, however, nothing concrete resulted from this competition. These architects' ideas were utopian rather than realistic. In spite of this, the Cleveland Architectural Club accomplished what it set out to do: the contest gave publicity to their newly founded organization, thereby helping to create a need for their services. As an early advocacy group, they established an asso-

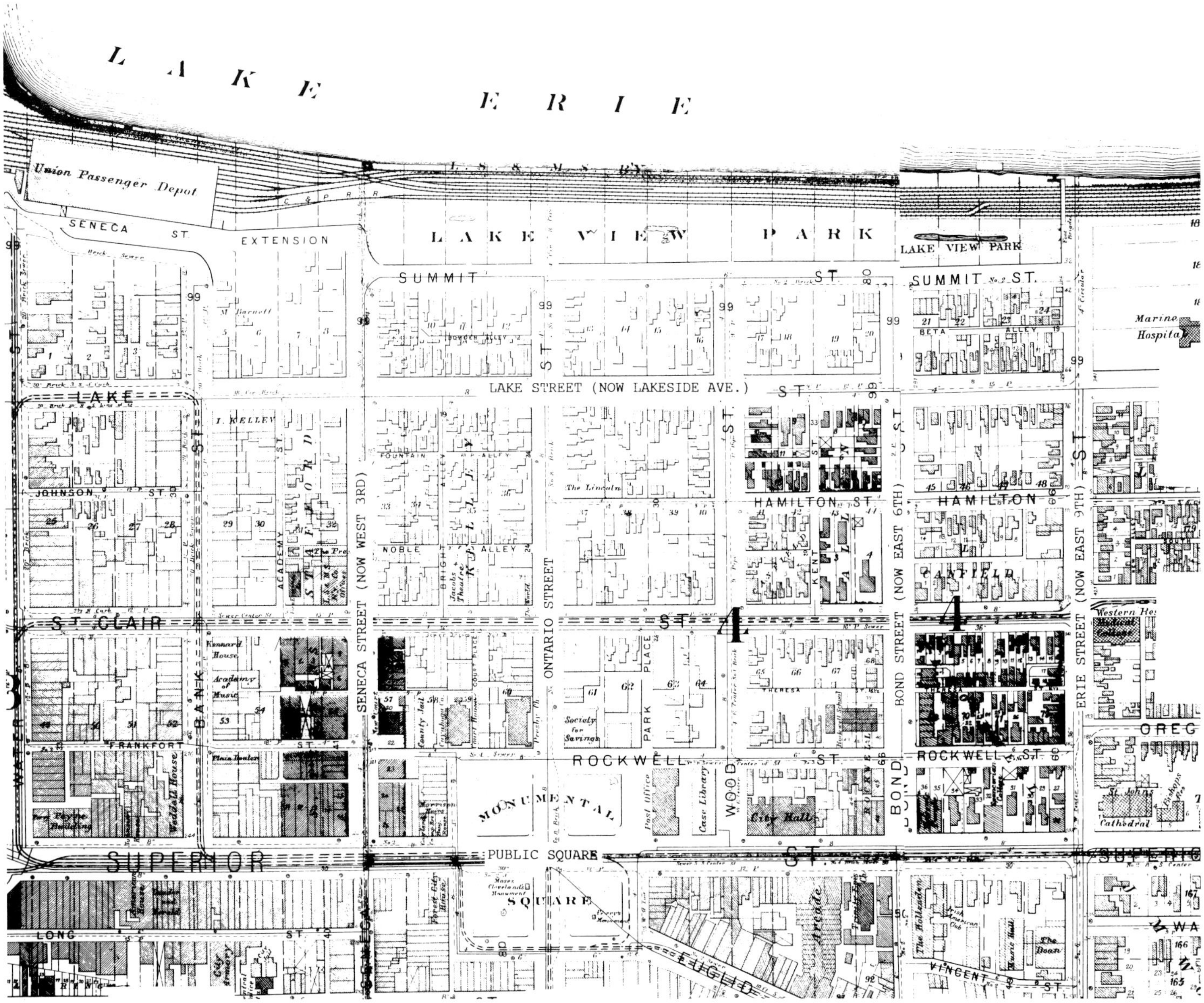

Fig. 4.3. Downtown Cleveland, Ohio, plan, 1892. (*Atlas of Cuyahoga County and the City of Cleveland,* Chicago: Geo. F. Cram, 1892)

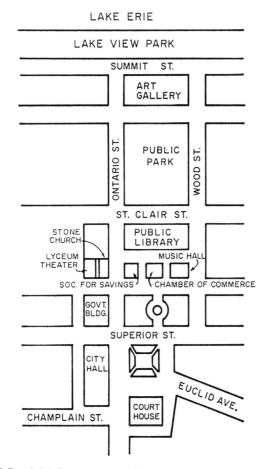

Fig. 4.4. W. Dominick Benes, proposed grouping scheme for Cleveland, plan, 1895. (Redrawn from *The Cleveland Press,* 2 Apr. 1895)

ciate membership that was open to the many who had an interest in architecture. The theme for their April competition was more mundane—boat- and bathhouses for Edgewater Park.

Immense political problems would have to be overcome to turn the early dream for a civic center into reality. Even at the local level, wholesale remodeling of urban districts required power, and, although power in a democracy is dispersed, this was especially so in Cleveland. The Ohio legislature made all major decisions, keeping local governments under its close control until Home Rule was established in 1912–1913. Fortunately for those who were promoting the group idea, the state legislature at that time was dominated by Republicans. But how could all the different commissions—city, county, federal, and pri-

vate—first be established, if this had not already been done, and then be brought together to correlate their plans, let alone be persuaded the group concept was a good idea? Why would the citizens of Cleveland appropriate resources for aesthetic benefits when the city was faced with immense social, educational, and economic problems due to large-scale immigration and industrialization?

With returning prosperity in the late 1890s, concern increased for the physical fabric of the city. Although the World's Columbian Exposition offered what was thought to be a utopian urban vision, there were no American exemplars of contemporary, large-scale planning that could serve as a starting point for new developments. Even historical American cities had little to offer the imagination. By the end of the nineteenth century, the Mall in Washington, D.C., had long disappeared; it had yet to be recreated. In Williamsburg, Va., only vestigial remains indicated that it had had an axial plan.

Because of advances in communication and transportation, American tourists, architects, and artists traveled more widely. As a result, European urban scenes became more familiar, and viewers were struck by what they thought to be disturbing contrasts between the artful civic scenes of Europe and the artless city scenes of America. Perhaps, therefore, out of necessity, thinkers came to focus on Europe rather than America for aesthetic precedent. They may also have looked to Europe out of a search for acceptance or out of a need for psychological release from the stress and anxiety caused by the visual jumble and fast-paced life of the American industrial city.

Stimulated by the civic architecture of great European cities like Vienna, Paris, Budapest, Dresden, and Munich, Frederic Howe was to recall in his *Confessions of a Reformer* the role that he and fellow Harvard graduate Morris Black played when Cleveland was on the verge of erecting new public buildings. They invited the editorial writers of each Cleveland paper to join the Beer and Skittles Club, a dining and drinking society they had started, and "unfolded to them a plan of developing a great civic center." With this in mind, they prepared illustrated stories of European groupings for the Sunday papers. Working behind the scenes—"nobody knew from what source the continued agitation was directed or that any particular group was keeping the subject alive"—they induced the local chapter of the American Institute of Architects (AIA) through the Cleveland

Fig. 4.5. Herbert Briggs, proposed grouping scheme for Cleveland, plan, 1895. (Redrawn from *The Cleveland Press,* 2 Apr. 1895)

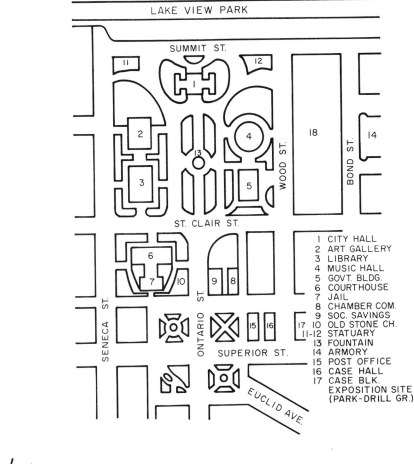

1 CITY HALL
2 ART GALLERY
3 LIBRARY
4 MUSIC HALL
5 GOVT. BLDG.
6 COURTHOUSE
7 JAIL
8 CHAMBER COM.
9 SOC. SAVINGS
10 OLD STONE CH.
11-12 STATUARY
13 FOUNTAIN
14 ARMORY
15 POST OFFICE
16 CASE HALL
17 CASE BLK.
EXPOSITION SITE
(PARK-DRILL GR.)

Fig. 4.6. Frederick Baird, proposed grouping scheme for Cleveland, plan, 1895. (Redrawn from *The Cleveland Press,* 2 Apr. 1895)

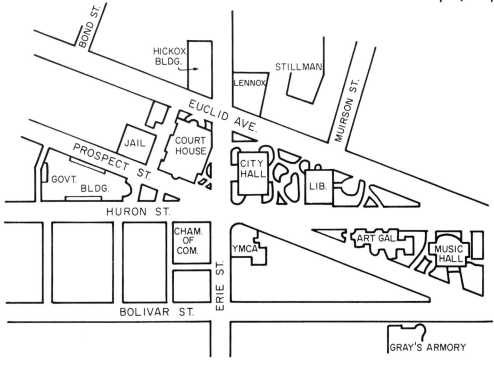

Architectural Club to hold a competition, and they asked Harry A. Garfield, then president of the chamber of commerce, to appoint a committee to further the idea.[17] Besides being founding members of the Municipal Association, Garfield and Howe worked together in the same law firm. Of equal importance, Cleveland architect Frank E. Cudell brought the idea to Elbert Baker, editor of *The Cleveland Plain Dealer,* whose paper was to take an advocacy position.[18] Thus, the idea for a group of public buildings began to gain momentum.

Even before Howe's campaign, the chamber of commerce had established committees to promote new public and cultural buildings for Cleveland. As early as 1896 they had a federal building committee. Chaired by the successful Republican banker Myron T. Herrick, they lobbied Congress for a new federal building. In December 1896 a special art museum committee was set up to work toward the unification of three separate bequests so that one art museum of world significance could be founded instead of three smaller ones.

In August 1897, the chamber of commerce received a communication from County Auditor Albert E. Akins suggesting the chamber consider the question of the erection of a new city hall and courthouse. His request was referred to the public buildings committee.[19] By September 1897, the committee had developed a policy: it would not arrogate to itself the decision on location of public buildings. The committee viewed its role as working for the best interests of the whole community by aiding the proper authorities in selecting sites and obtaining the necessary legislation and money that would make public improvements possible.[20]

Cleveland, like all other American cities, had neither an existing growth plan nor a mechanism to develop one, so recommendations had, by necessity, to originate externally. In the 1890s the city had built a major park system. Thus, unlike many other cities, it had at least some experience in developing and implementing a large-scale project. However, the Park Board was a single, specialized group. How could Cleveland's various commissions come together in a cooperative effort to develop a unified plan?

Continuing its work, the public buildings committee in March 1898 sent a delegation to inspect the county offices. During that meeting county officials argued they lacked not only space but adequate fire protection for legal records.[21] This ra-

tionale made sense to businessmen, for at a general chamber of commerce meeting on 15 March 1898, the public buildings committee recommended that new city and county facilities should be built. Also, they advocated that the facilities be in close proximity, centrally located to ensure accessibility from all parts of the region, and be situated in the vicinity of other public buildings. Furthermore, they recommended that the county should proceed to acquire sufficient land adjacent to their present location—they did not foresee a new site—and erect a building large enough to accommodate government for the distant future. The committee additionally suggested that a joint city/county building could be built to save money and in case the city itself should become a county. Clearly, functional considerations were paramount in their minds. The committee had yet to articulate a group concept based on ideological or artistic rationale.

On 29 March 1898, the chamber of commerce held a special meeting to consider the proposed state legislation initiated by Mayor McKisson for the erection of a city hall. Because the resulting bond issue would raise the city's debt limit beyond 5 percent to 7 percent, they came out against passage. Other reasons were also given that revolved around site selection, cost, and the method of appointing a commission to oversee implementation. More importantly, however, they cited the report of the Citizens Commission of 1896 and believed that similar conditions still existed: "We would be glad to see the city officers more comfortably housed, yet in our opinion . . . other improvements . . . urgent for the health and welfare of all citizens . . . [are needed. Therefore,] we think this matter should be postponed for the present."[22] Following through, the chamber sent a delegation to Columbus to oppose the authorization of bonds for a new city hall and, furthermore, for a new courthouse.[23]

In spite of opposition from the chamber of commerce and from other Republicans, but because Republican mayor McKisson and his allies aggressively lobbied for it, the Ohio legislature passed a statute that authorized the issuance of bonds and the establishment of a commission to select the site and construct a new city hall.[24] Mayor McKisson, as was required by the statute and with the approval of the Cleveland City Council, appointed a nonpartisan commission on 22 August 1898.[25] The commission held its first meeting on the following day.[26] In February of 1899, Mayor McKisson announced that the commissioners had been directed from the start to arrive at a plan that would "be in harmony with the other public buildings now being contemplated."[27] Whether he was retrospectively taking credit for the idea or in reality so directed the commission in August 1898, it is impossible now to determine. In either case the creation of this city hall commission constituted a significant step in the advancement of the group idea. This commission, whose membership was constant, was destined to play a vital political role; later, under Democratic mayor Johnson, they were to exercise considerable initiative in conferring with those representing the other buildings.[28]

In October 1898, the Cleveland chapter of the AIA sent a communication to the city hall commission requesting the commission "to provide a spacious site for the new City Hall, and to make efforts to harmonize that building, the Public Library, and the County Court House in a group."[29] This suggestion may have influenced the direction that the city hall commission was to take. By this time it was apparent that new buildings were going to be erected, and it was only a question of where and how. It was now clear that if the chamber of commerce did not reverse its earlier position against the building of a new city hall and courthouse, it would be left out of the decision-making process.

On 20 December 1898, Harry A. Garfield submitted to the board of directors of the chamber of commerce a resolution drafted by Professor Olney to appoint a special subcommittee of the public buildings committee to consider and report upon a plan for erecting the proposed new federal building, city hall, courthouse, public library, and educational headquarters under a harmonious architectural plan. As the resolution was a substantive one, action on it was deferred. Two days earlier Olney's plan for a grouping at Erie Street (now East Ninth) and Euclid Avenue had been discussed in the press.[30]

Three days after Olney's ideas appeared in print, on 21 December 1898, it was announced in *The Cleveland Press* that the Cleveland Architectural Club was conducting a competition as to the location of public buildings.[31] The club's objective was to get the best possible scheme, particularly from the architectural point of view. In contrast to the utopian 1895 competition, cost of the site was to be considered, but not to the detriment of the monumental or architectural effect. Obviously, with interest in the group idea growing, local architects recognized the opportunity to contribute their expertise and to secure some healthy commissions.

Pursuing efforts going back to 1896, the chamber of commerce recommended passage of a bill introduced in Congress by Senator Marcus Hanna for a new federal building to be located on Public Square at Superior Avenue. To this end the chamber sent a delegation to Washington in January 1899 to appear before the House Committee on Public Buildings. The bill was signed into law in March 1899 by President McKinley, who was doubtlessly influenced by his campaign manager, Senator Hanna. Thus, the site for the new federal building was determined. This site was accessible by streetcars from every quarter of the city. It was also close to the new chamber of commerce building, across the street from the relatively new Cuyahoga Building, which had replaced the "notorious old Hoffman block," and close by the Society for Savings Building. Although this site in part was already occupied by the present federal building, the chamber's objective in recommending this location should not be seen only as an attempt to save money, but can be interpreted as an effort to create a cluster of new buildings that would create a contemporary, modern image for the city. New York architect Arnold Brunner won the competition to design the structure.[32] The decision to construct a new federal building constituted a major breakthrough after years of talk and negotiation.

Meanwhile, after several meetings, the board of directors of the chamber of commerce finally presented on 17 January 1899 Professor Olney's resolution to appoint a committee to consider the grouping idea to the full chamber. It was passed with the amendment to "contribute to public utility and convenience" and with the understanding that the resolution did not contemplate any change in the site for the federal building.[33] A harmonious architectural plan was not enough for these men of business: it had to be practical. It took some time to find the right people to serve on the grouping plan committee, which was not appointed until 28 February 1899. If Frederic Howe's testimony is to be believed — and there is no reason it should not be — his influence with Harry A. Garfield was critical in getting this resolution initiated and passed. The road ahead was not easy; it would be almost a year before the grouping plan committee would make its report. Immediately following the creation of this committee, the library board sent a resolution favoring the grouping of public buildings to the chamber of commerce.[34] Professor Olney was a member of the library board and no doubt was extremely influential in bringing the board to this decision.

As a result of an informal meeting in January 1899 between Professor Olney, F. J. Pool, Howe, and F. H. Baer of the library board, it was suggested that the Cleveland Architectural Club hold a meeting and issue invitations to select individuals to promulgate the group building idea. The club did, but at this time it was very unclear exactly what buildings might constitute a grouping.[35]

The club's meeting was held on 24 January 1899.[36] In attendance were one hundred representative citizens—including the members of the city hall and courthouse commissions, the library board, school officials, and high-ranking clergymen anxious to view plans, drawn by the club's members and others, that showed proposed locations of public buildings. These drawings had been done in response to the competition announced the previous December.

The stated purpose for the meeting was to discuss the feasibility of the project and to stimulate the then small sentiment in its favor, rather than to adopt any specific design or location. Sketches for each proposed site, which had been developed for the competition, were carefully explained by architect Benjamin Hubbell. He, while commending and criticizing the various proposals, did not endorse any specific one but supported the idea in its abstract form. Knowing that politics and business would affect the decision, Hubbell expressed the hope that the buildings' location would be based on the true merits of a particular site. Addresses were then given by several of the city's leading citizens. One of them, Ambrose Swasey, spoke enthusiastically about Vienna's Ringstrasse, stating that "we have no Emperor Francis Joseph to group our buildings." Swasey understood what it would take to implement such a plan—a central authority. Charles E. Bolton spoke next. Earlier he had circulated a number of pamphlets advocating plans for public buildings he favored, but he concluded that the idea for grouping the buildings was superior. He went on to lecture the commissioners on how to do their job: "It will be a crime for us to neglect this opportunity, and the responsibility will rest upon the various commissions if they do not thoroughly investigate the group question and reject it only when it is proved impracticable." Bolton did not favor grouping the library and art museum with

the city hall, courthouse, and federal buildings. He stated that the former were buildings for a finer, higher purpose.

Harry A. Garfield, president of the chamber of commerce, was more guarded in his remarks. He believed the group idea warranted serious consideration, but he was not ready to decide on a site and asserted that the chamber of commerce would devote "no little attention" to a consideration of the idea and possible location of the buildings. Following the meeting the drawings were placed upon exhibition at the Case Library, where the public at large might view them. By doing this, the club hoped the idea would be looked upon as being meritorious, and therefore possibly would be adopted.[37] The next day librarian William H. Brett appealed to the public's imagination by recalling memories of the Columbian Exposition: "The grouping of the buildings, as compared to scattering them on sites selected independently, will do for them just what the grouping of the buildings at the world's fair did. If we will imagine the buildings at Chicago scattered through various streets and separated by business blocks, and compare this with the court of honor, we will have a suggestion of what may be gained. . . . The grouping . . . will place Cleveland on this continent where Vienna and Paris are in the old world."[38] Thus, the public campaign to educate and enlighten Clevelanders gained momentum.

The educational crusade did not stop here. Members of the architectural club presented the idea for a grouping before men's leagues and similar organizations. They utilized the competition drawings to illustrate their lectures.

The Cleveland Plain Dealer aggressively led the campaign, and in an editorial on 24 January 1899, it suggested that every street call meetings to debate the matter, after which a general mass meeting should be called where the educational value of stereopticon slides could be exploited. Pictures, along with words, were to be used to educate the masses. Earlier in the month the paper ran an editorial that spoke in favor of making public structures monuments of art, for a building testifies to the city's ignorance or knowledge, pride or penuriousness, dignity or disgrace. Public buildings, proclaimed the editor, form the nucleus from which growth can develop.[39]

In late January 1899, Daniel Burnham was in Cleveland to confer with New York architect George Post about the coordination of the design for the proposed new Williamson Building with Burnham's earlier Cuyahoga Building. This consultation may have been suggested by Myron T. Herrick, who was part owner of the Cuyahoga Building. At that time, Burnham's views on a proposed grouping were reported in the press: "From a business standpoint artistic and imposing buildings pay. . . . Such buildings make a city famous." Moreover, Burnham felt it should front on Ontario Street and open onto the lake with its "glorious skies and everchanging cloud effects."[40] There is no doubt, however, that Herrick was the first to suggest this location.[41]

On 16 February 1899, Charles W. Pratt, chief engineer for the park board, made public his plan for a grouping. He suggested a site in Lake View Park, which the board was presently developing.[42] At the end of 1899, Pratt's design was to play a critical role; it was to be espoused by the chamber of commerce.

In February 1899, the chamber received a letter from Rabbi Moses J. Gries in which he offered the use of the temple, where the chamber could sponsor a public meeting on the group concept. The chamber declined. Instead, they suggested that the Temple Society sponsor the event and issue a formal invitation to the chamber to attend.[43] In this way the chamber sought to involve the community in their endeavor. No doubt since Rabbi Gries showed interest and because he was an important community leader, he was appointed to the chamber's newly established grouping plan committee along with other very influential and supportive Clevelanders.[44]

At their first meeting on 4 March 1899, the grouping plan committee, chaired by William G. Mather, decided upon a plan of action. As soon as practicable, the committee would meet with the commissions having in their charge the erection of the city hall, county buildings, public library, and art museum.[45] Following *The Cleveland Plain Dealer*'s lead, the subject of having public meetings in which stereopticon lectures illustrating successful groupings in other cities was favorably discussed. In the week that followed, the committee informally examined various grouping designs by the members of the Cleveland Architectural Club.

In May of 1899, Myron Herrick campaigned further for the Ontario Street site. It was announced that a new union railroad station would be built where the present depot stands, thus assisting the development of Ontario Street. Furthermore, Herrick suggested that Lake View Park be extended to the station, thereby reclaiming more of the lakefront (fig. 4.3).[46]

Because of the announcement that a new station was to be constructed, and for other reasons, the grouping plan committee wrote in June to each railroad company requesting that a grouping plan be considered before definitive action was taken. Committee chairman Mather spoke with President William H. Newman of the Lake Shore and Michigan Southern Railway and obtained his cooperation. And another committee member received verbal assurance and cooperation from President William H. Canniff of the New York, Chicago, and St. Louis Railway and from General Superintendent Leonard Loree of the Pennsylvania Railway.

At the time of the convention of the Architectural League of America held in Cleveland in June 1899, the chamber of commerce sponsored a public lecture by New York sculptor Henry Kirke Bush-Brown on the grouping of public buildings. Cleveland's foremost citizens attended. Bush-Brown made it clear that he favored the Ontario Street site. *The Cleveland Plain Dealer* reported that Bush-Brown had conceived the idea of grouping New York's buildings and that Herrick was one of the chief movers to implement the idea in Cleveland.[47]

The grouping plan committee decided to change its approach at its meeting of 6 June 1899. It organized a joint consultative committee with two representatives from each board interested in the grouping idea. By expanding its membership, the committee became more representative and influential: elected and appointed public officials now became directly involved. The committee also decided to secure plans and suggestions from architectural experts in various cities.

With committee approval, Chairman Mather corresponded with John Carrère, member of the architectural firm of Carrère and Hastings of New York City and chairman of the board of architects of the Pan-American Exposition in Buffalo. He was invited to lecture on the advisability of grouping public buildings before the chamber of commerce on 18 October 1899. Carrère enthusiastically volunteered his services for the cause.[48] He was selected, no doubt, because he created "exhibition" architecture, which appealed to upper-class Republican taste.

Both Bush-Brown and Carrère forcibly advocated that vistas be provided and that streets must lead up to architectural monuments. Public sentiment began to grow in favor of the grouping idea. The chamber's modus operandi—the calling in of outside experts to testify to the efficacy of the idea—was astute:

it separated the argument from local politics and placed it on a higher, national level. At this time Carrère undoubtedly gained the chamber's innermost confidence.

Acting with great political acumen throughout 1899, the grouping plan committee avoided commitment to any specific location until the idea itself found acceptance in the community. Feeling a sense of urgency, however, at their meeting of 7 December 1899, they decided to report out. In fact they had no choice, since the public library was anxious to erect a building without delay. If a library were to be built without reference to the other needed buildings, the group idea would have run the risk of being seriously endangered. As a stopgap measure, the committee requested that the library board delay action until a final report was submitted to the full chamber for consideration. While the library board's action was the catalyst, the grouping plan committee also had a plan they could recommend, that

drawn up by engineer Pratt of the park board. The earlier decision to invite two representatives from each board was productive because Pratt's plan was presented by Park Board commissioner McBride. Feeling the pressure of time, a draft of the report was finished by 15 December for committee discussion, and the final version was submitted on 19 December 1899 to the full chamber of commerce for consideration.

Pratt's layout was discussed in great detail (fig. 4.7). The proposed site was bounded on the west by Seneca Street (now West Third), on the east by Erie Street (now East Ninth), on the south by Lake Street (now Lakeside Avenue), and on the north by Summit Street (now abandoned), or Lake View Park. Next to the site on the east were the Government Hospital Grounds and the Lakeside Hospital. The report ranked its virtues in this order: beautiful, popular, economical, and practicable. Beauty was an important criterion.

Fig. 4.7. Charles W. Pratt, proposed grouping scheme for Cleveland, plan, 1899/1900. (Courtesy of Extensions Division, Cleveland Museum of Art)

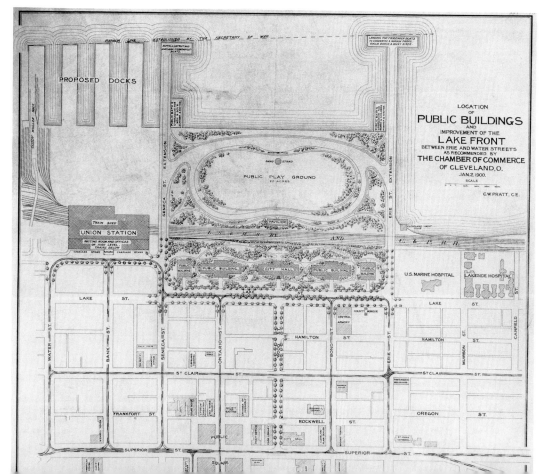

The site incorporated the lakefront, the advantages of which had been sadly and incomprehensibly neglected. Lake View Park, already existent, was to be expanded to fifty acres. Provided with wharves for passenger and excursion boats, a water basin and bathhouses, skating rinks, and other entertainments, this proposed lakefront development, like the midway at the World's Columbian Exposition, had great public appeal.[49] Cleveland's leaders thought of it, however, as essential to the group concept; it would form the necessary backdrop, or frame, essential to set off noble buildings. Only those approaching it by water, however, would have been impressed.

The railroad tracks, which cut the park off from the proposed site, were an obstacle that could be overcome through design. The railroads, it was thought, would cooperate with the city either by spanning the tracks with numerous bridges of attractive design or by completely covering them, as on Park Avenue in New York. In the latter solution, there would be no visual break from the buildings to the lake. It would also be of help if the railroads could use smokeless fuel: "The dense smoke which pours out of the stacks of the passing locomotives of the Lake Shore Railroad blackens the foliage and causes the falling of the same before it arrives at maturity. Very little can be done to improve these trees materially, except abating the smoke nuisance."[50] The question of suitability for a park on the lakefront was to be hotly debated in the years ahead.

The committee thought of Pratt's proposal as an integral part of Cleveland and not just as a discrete civic embellishment. On the west it could be connected by a high-level driveway or boulevard with Water Street, thence to the viaduct and the new boulevard to Edgewater Park, thereby making it an important link in Cleveland's magnificent scheme of parks and boulevards.

Broad streets were to connect it to the business district, and it was hoped that a new union railroad station would be built in the near future on an adjacent site. Traffic and access were also considered: there were to be streetcar loops up and down the streets between Seneca and Erie streets. Such arrangements, it was thought, would relieve the almost unbearable congestion present in and around Public Square and would connect all parts of the city with these buildings and the recreation grounds.

Other arguments for the site were that it would make an unsightly section beautiful and transform it into a notable monument of usefulness and of art. Most important of all, it would maintain the present business center.

One other virtue of the proposed lakefront site, perhaps the most important, was articulated in the report: "This will have been attained at small expense, for this land, though most centrally situated, is only valued on the tax duplicate at $415,000.00, although its area is 10.8 acres."

The goals for such a grouping were now well articulated. First, there was commercial value in the artistic phase of the problem, and second, there were economies to be realized in heating, etcetera. Third, there would be educational value in such a grouping. It would be uplifting and ennobling. The report declared that Cleveland must "group" to keep abreast of the onward march of improvement and civilization.

The report of 19 December 1899 also presented two ideas of importance that were related to implementation. First, it was not necessary to wait for all the various commissions to have their plans ready before beginning construction, and second, it was suggested that either an existing commission or one for which provision might be made during the current session of the Ohio State Legislature, be placed in charge of the work. It was recognized that one body must have the power to develop the proposal.[51]

On 2 January 1900, a special meeting of the chamber of commerce was called to act upon the report. The chairman of the grouping plan committee, W. G. Mather, supplemented the report with an outline of a plan for connecting the buildings on the lakefront site with Public Square, thus including the new federal building by making Wood Street into a boulevard. His suggestion was not part of the committee's report—but it was presented to the chamber in order that it might have consideration and publicity. In the future, Mather's idea would gain increasing support and can retrospectively be seen as the germinal point for a mall in this location.

While remarks in favor of Pratt's plan were delivered by several people, Professor Olney delivered the longest and most passionate plea for the passage of the committee's report: "We might here cite the preparations made at Athens, Rome, London, Paris, Vienna, Berlin, etc., etc., and also some of the cities of our own land,—preparations extending over a period of many years that the monumental buildings, when completed, might represent the highest intelligence of the period and command the admiration of the world." However, John Hutchins, a former judge and postmaster of Cleveland, gave insight into the real reason why the committee chose the lakefront site: "It is not unlikely that the committee individually and collectively may have preferred the Public Square, the Ontario Street site or the Euclid Avenue or Superior Street sites, but, evidently all of these sites appeared to them, upon investigation, out of the question on the score of price, and that for this reason largely they were finally remitted to the lake front site recommended in the report." Therefore, the location selected reflected Cleveland's financial conservatism,[52] and as the report indicated, the lakefront location did not disrupt the main business district, where many chamber of commerce members had vested interests.

More idealistic, or perhaps more self-serving, Myron T. Herrick was the only person who spoke in opposition to the adoption of the report; he favored the Ontario Street site. While he outlined what he felt were legal problems with securing the lakefront site and the difficulty of securing the enactment of a law authorizing a commission that would stand the test of the Supreme Court, he felt that the proposed lakefront site was too far from Public Square, the acknowledged center of business for the city. Presumably, he also desired the grouping to be close to his bank and other commercial investments. Despite Herrick's opposition, the report of the grouping plan committee was unanimously adopted.[53]

Immediately thereafter, the chamber of commerce set out to introduce the idea to state lawmakers. A "smoker" with refreshments was held on 13 January 1900 for the Cuyahoga County delegates to the Ohio legislature. The group plan was explained, and Andrew Squire of Squire, Sanders, and Dempsey, an international Cleveland law firm, spoke on the legal steps necessary for implementation.[54] Later in the year, the chamber asked Democrat Liberty E. Holden, president of the Cleveland Plain Dealer Publishing Company, to deliver an address on the architecture of public building that he had recently seen in Europe and on other features of municipal advancement.[55] The chamber was now in the process of strengthening nonpartisan consensus for the grouping idea.

The efforts and events of 1900 familiarized Cleveland's leaders with the subject, and they came to believe that this was a unique opportunity to erect a group of public buildings in a way that would make Cleveland favorably known throughout

the United States, if not the world. Optimism was high that Cleveland would shortly have larger, better, and more beautiful buildings in which to house and transact the varied municipal, governmental, educational, art, and civic functions. The dramatis personae—the architects; members of the chamber of commerce, city, county, and federal government and private boards; and cultivated citizens—were all identified. The plan was about to go forward when Democrat Tom L. Johnson became mayor of Cleveland in May 1901.

Johnson, a Progressive mayor, endorsed the idea of a grouping. This was somewhat surprising since the main proponents of the idea were Republican members of the chamber of commerce—men of privilege.

Across America, improvement efforts were becoming identified with Progressive reform. These efforts were supported by the nearby Chautauqua Institution, which published study guides.[56] Urban beautification expressed the social optimism of the Progressive Era. Beauty was to invoke, or at least express, a regenerated civic life.[57] In this particular instance, however, politics as well as idealism played a decisive role. The editor of *The Cleveland Plain Dealer,* who supported Johnson in his bid for mayor, urged him to embrace the group plan idea.[58] As public architecture was not on Johnson's reform agenda at first, it seems that a pragmatic reason—the harnessing of political support—influenced Johnson's decision to include it. In any event, business and Progressive government came to the same conclusion: a grouping of public buildings was in the city's best interest. Later, Johnson was to employ extraordinary political leverage to influence the final design. One other point is worth making. Johnson was a successful businessman but abandoned active business because, as he later declared, "the requirements of my work didn't square with my principles." While his enemies found his sincerity suspect, they always respected him. Johnson's personality was genial and jovial, his manner unaffected and easy unless aroused; he could be gruff though never abusive, and he treated opponents fairly. He also was a Francophile and learned; he continually read French and knew *Gibbon.*[59] He was a man with whom the chamber of commerce could deal.

In spite of support from the mayor, all was not going well. The newspapers printed interviews with county commissioners to the effect that they did not propose to participate in the group plan. In front of a joint meeting of the grouping plan committee and the municipal committee of the chamber of commerce on 6 January 1902, County Commissioner Case responded on behalf of the commissioners. He claimed that they never entertained the idea of forsaking the plan to group the buildings, that they would without question purchase the site for the new courthouse within the group plan district, and that they would consult with the committee after the bond issue was sold, before purchasing their site. The reason for the "negative" interviews in the newspapers, he stated, was to reduce land values within the territory affected by the plan! Obviously, political pressure was being used to good effect. The chamber of commerce was indeed powerful.

February 1902 was a critical time for decision making. On the fourteenth of the month, Charles Leach, a Republican and collector of customs of the port of Cleveland, presented a plan by Arnold Brunner to the grouping plan committee (fig. 4.8). This plan placed the federal building at the end of an imposing court of honor, or mall, which was over 350 feet wide and 1,000 feet long. Additional sites were proposed for the courthouse, city hall, music hall, art gallery, public library, and board of education. The newly erected chamber of commerce building was to be included in the grouping. At lake level, on axis with the court of honor, a union station was proposed. Leach, who was not necessarily supporting this scheme, stated that it was favored by Mayor Johnson, who had requested Brunner to make the drawing. Because of the lack of a quorum, no action was taken. The grouping plan committee understood the message: Mayor Johnson did not embrace Pratt's plan.

The initiative was now passed from the chamber of commerce to the mayor's office. Johnson was now fully committed to the concept of a group plan, probably for political as well as ideological reasons. Civic centers came to symbolize regenerated civic life, the ideal modern city. The achievement of such would doubtlessly add to a politician's reputation. An alliance was being forged between Democratic and Republican leaders to go forward with the group idea. Brunner's plan was immediately published in *Municipal Affairs* as a fait accompli.[60]

On 1 March 1902 the mayor and the various commissions consulted and sent the chamber a missive: they had "unanimously decided to adopt, as the scheme for grouping the proposed public buildings, the general plan providing for the widening of Wood Street into a Court of Honor, etc." Furthermore,

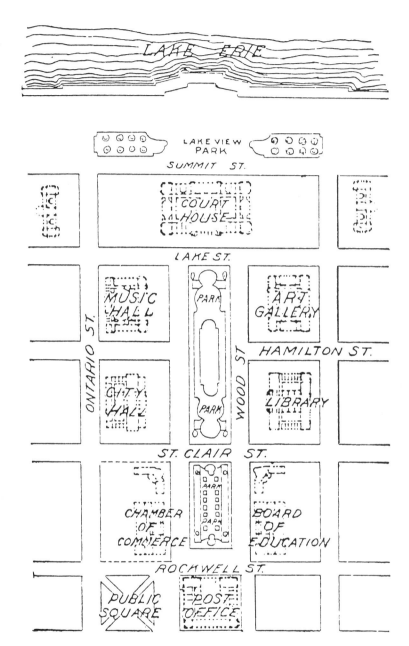

Fig. 4.8. Arnold W. Brunner, proposed grouping scheme for Cleveland, plan, 1902. (Drawing published by *Municipal Affairs*)

they authorized a bill for a bond issue of approximately $1.5 million, the proceeds of which "shall be exclusively used to acquire and improve the necessary land for the establishment of parks, boulevards, sites for public buildings and approaches thereto" in the city.[61] The city was willing to make a larger investment than what was previously thought to acquire a site close to Public Square. Cleveland and Cuyahoga County had a Democratic majority at the time. This no doubt helped the mayor build a consensus between the various local governmental commissions.

At its meeting of 3 March 1902, the grouping plan committee, being concerned over this proposed new location, suggested the establishment of an advisory committee of architects to take all the grouping plans that had been suggested and work out the one that might seem best to them. Mather and Andrews then conferred with Mayor Johnson and the members of the commissions relative to this subject, and by 12 March, Mayor Johnson approved the idea for a supervisory commission. Afterward, Andrew Squire drafted the bill. At another meeting the wording of the bill was unanimously endorsed by the members of the various building commissions, the mayor, members of city council, the Builders Exchange, and the American Institute of Architects. It was then introduced into the state legislature.[62]

At a luncheon meeting held at the aristocratic Union Club on 26 March 1902, the grouping plan committee—since they had virtually no choice—endorsed Mayor Johnson's proposed location. Their recommendation hinged, however, on the city's ability to acquire all of the land surrounding the proposed court of honor to prevent the construction of buildings not of a public character on the court. Also, if so much money were to be spent, the subject of the location of the group should be considered by an expert commission. Moreover, since they questioned whether the land could actually be acquired for $1.5 million, they advised that a precise cost estimate be made. To say the least, the committee was suspicious of this grand scheme.

At the meeting on 18 April 1902, the full chamber of commerce endorsed the idea of the expanded project, if the result was to be a grouping of buildings similar to that proposed in the so-called Brunner plan. Thus, although they abandoned their earlier support for Pratt's plan, they did not endorse any specific new location. That decision, they felt, should be made only after

an authoritative recommendation on the subject was obtained from experienced experts. Cleveland's business elite wanted to assure that public decision-making officials were well informed. In spite of the chamber's guarded endorsement, Mayor Johnson confidently reported to the city council on 21 April that the group plan had grown in public favor and that it would be carried out.[63]

In the face of Mayor Johnson's energetic leadership, the grouping plan committee tried to regain control. The committee invited John Carrère and Mr. Blake of the New York architectural firm Carrère and Hastings to Cleveland on 29 April 1902. In the morning the architects and the committee surveyed the site north of Rockwell Street and between Seneca and Erie streets. At a luncheon attended by select members of the chamber of commerce, W. D. Benes, now president of the Cleveland chapter of the AIA, and Mayor Johnson, Carrère submitted a hasty sketch illustrating his ideas. He suggested, as the mayor's office had earlier proposed, that Wood Street be retained as the axis of the scheme. Developing the idea further, he contemplated appropriating the blocks north of Lake Street from Seneca to Erie as sites for the courthouse and city hall and appropriating the half blocks east and west of Wood Street and north of Hamilton Street as sites for the music hall and library building. The courthouse, Carrère suggested, should be sited directly on axis with Ontario Street and the city hall about opposite the foot of Kent Street. Those present at this momentous luncheon decided that it was desirable for the county commissioners to take immediate steps to purchase the two blocks north of Lake Street from Seneca to Wood Street for the courthouse site.

To this end, county commissioners Case and Harms, along with City Hall Commission chairman Hill, were sent for and the general ideas developed earlier that day were explained to them by Carrère. The county commissioners expressed approval of the plan. The chamber of commerce adopted a resolution requesting the county to proceed with the purchase of land.[64] The site for the county courthouse was thus decided upon. A compromise was struck. The chamber of commerce secured what it wanted—influence over the design, since Carrère was their man—and the mayor gained support for an expanded scheme. However, there was still no authorized board to put the plan into action.

The bill to create a board of supervision passed the Ohio legislature on 6 May 1902.[65] At this time the Republican majority in the Ohio legislature was so vexed with Johnson that they decided that all local bills for Cleveland must first be approved by two Republican businessmen of the city—Myron T. Herrick and lawyer Homer H. Johnson.[66] Herrick's support of the plan was critical in securing this legislation.

The law authorized cities with populations over 380,000 to establish a board of supervision, which was to consist of three people, two of whom must be architects. They were to consider the location, size, height, style, and general appearance of public buildings. Objectives to be achieved were usefulness, safety, and beauty. The bill gave no authority to the supervisory board to purchase land or to expend the public money. The precedent for the formation of such a commission of experts was close at hand, since one year earlier the United States Senate had appointed the McMillan Commission to study Washington, D.C.[67] Burnham was the head of that commission. Carrère, too, may have originally suggested a board because he was a strong advocate of establishing one in New York.[68] Publicly the romantic spirit of professional cooperation and teamwork, which harked back for the early twentieth-century architect to the Renaissance, was stressed. But twentieth-century realities demanded that a board with authoritative control be formed; the project had no chance of succeeding without it. The idea to keep the board at three people was significant. Myron T. Herrick had earlier recognized the importance of this. In reference to a different situation, he wrote that a "decision usually made by a number of men together in conference . . . is usually more comprehensive than one evolved from the working of a single mind—though if the circle be broadened still further . . . the ends sought are often diverted, if not altogether rendered abortive."[69]

Next, Cleveland city councilman Frederic C. Howe prepared a resolution, which he submitted to the city council on 2 June 1902, to carry into effect the law authorizing the appointment by the governor of a board of supervision. The wording of the resolution was more conditional than state law required, and before submitting the resolution to the city council, Howe had secured its prior approval by the chamber of commerce.[70] Probably out of concern that non-Clevelanders would be appointed to the board, Howe's resolution was amended on 9 June 1902. Be-

fore the resolution passed, Chairman Mather of the grouping plan committee conferred with Mayor Johnson on the personnel for the board. With the chamber of commerce's approval, Mather suggested D. H. Burnham, J. M. Carrère, and A. W. Brunner be appointed.[71] On 14 June, James Parmelee wrote to Burnham, who replied the next day: "I will look over the copy of the Ohio Legislature['s bill authorizing a board of supervision] which you enclosed, and shall be willing to go on it if it is not too much of a political thing." Burnham may have been reacting to his experience on the McMillan Commission.[72] Howe's resolution passed city council on 16 June 1902 by a vote of sixteen for, four against.[73] At the same meeting, the city council adopted a resolution introduced by Howe to request the governor to appoint at least one member from the city of Cleveland.[74]

There had been opposition from the Master Plumbers Association to appointing any non-Clevelanders to the board, and the Cleveland Builders Exchange lobbied for at least one Clevelander.[75] In a letter to the city council, architect Frank Cudell most eloquently argued that since "the grouping commission originated among a few members of the Chamber of Commerce . . . [it was an] instrument to control the whole building enterprise REGARDLESS of our legal home authorities. . . . Three men from distant states would be more likely to take directions from the Chamber than a commission of two home men and one stranger." Cudell felt one should not "sacrifice self-government." He was also against appointing Burnham to the board.[76]

No one in the inner circle was surprised, however, when on 20 June 1902 Governor Nash appointed Daniel Burnham, Arnold Brunner, and John Carrère. After all, the board, according to Howe's resolution, was "to consist of three persons . . . experienced in the matter of the arrangement and construction of public buildings and familiar with the best architectural work, both in America and abroad."[77] Brunner unquestionably was chosen because he developed a proposal that the mayor had favored earlier. Also, he was the architect of the federal building then in the design stages, which everyone hoped would be included in the group. After his appointment on 1 July 1902, Burnham wrote a letter of thanks to Frederic Howe. This board was to set only the location, height, and style for all the buildings; individual architects would actually design the buildings.

At Burnham's initiative, work commenced promptly.[78] The

board met on 15 July and elected Burnham as chairman and Brunner as secretary. Clevelander Edward Roberts handled the board's correspondence, arranged meetings, and coordinated its efforts with city hall, seeing to it that the board received what it needed. As one of its first acts, the board immediately met with committees from the public library, chamber of commerce, the county, city architects, and the board of education to assess their needs. A special office was set up in New York, where the drawings were done.[79] Burnham definitely took the lead in defining the issues. On 18 July 1902 he wrote to Carrère, "Railway arrangements will modify any design we make and should be considered at once." Three days later he sent another letter to Carrère in which he began to set priorities: "The town needs the *best* railway station."

By the end of July, less than two months after their appointment, the board made a tentative decision to locate a mall along Wood Street: We "practically adapted an arrangement for a court of honor at the head of which will stand the U.S. government building now being designed. . . . It is evidently impracticable to turn the building around so as to use the principle [*sic*] facade at the head of the avenue. Brunner made a new design for the northern facade at the head of the avenue, . . . which is very satisfactory to us."[80] Brunner's design, which was based on late eighteenth-century French prototypes, therefore determined the general design characteristics for the other buildings. Burnham would have to convince the federal government to accept Brunner's modified design and later would have to fight for granite instead of a local stone that darkened quickly[81] so that the court of honor would not turn into "a court of horror."[82] The decision not to have the entrance for the federal building on the mall was to have far-reaching consequences: this building came to serve more as a stage set than as an active participant. The decision to have a mall leading to the federal building had one other important consequence: the relatively new chamber of commerce building would be included in the grouping.

Business was already reacting to the proposed new mall. Perhaps stimulated by the decision to have the federal building at the head of a court of honor, James Parmelee wrote to Burnham about expanding his nearby Cuyahoga Building. Burnham replied, "It will be possible to put two more stories of a very light construction on the present Cuyahoga Building."[83] Land prices in the area were rising significantly.

In August, the railway issue became paramount in Burnham's mind: "Nothing can be done until the railway matter is settled. It seriously modifies the whole thing and it becomes the principle [*sic*] matter."[84] On 17 August, the board met with the mayor and city council relative to the civic center.[85] Throughout August, the effect the depot would have upon the general layout was considered. On 29 August 1902, Burnham wrote to John Carrère, "In the great[est] possible secrecy I am sending you today the layout for the Railway Station. This is not even to be seen by Mr. Brunner." Actually, Burnham had an agreement with the Lake Shore and Michigan Southern Railway to design a new station for Cleveland,[86] and at this time he was working with the Big Four and the Pennsylvania to persuade them to join with the Lake Shore to build a union station. His designer, Pierce Anderson, was in charge of plans.[87] Burnham was anxious for all the railroads to cooperate and wrote to Carrère on 4 September, "I feel railway people will probably unite on the scheme. . . . We must keep it to ourselves at present." As architect for the railroads, Burnham was very concerned that the Cleveland general plan they were developing not transgress railroad requirements. He was later to argue that the future of the city depended on the railroad.

One can only speculate as to why Burnham did not want Brunner to see the proposed layout for the railway station. Since everyone knew that Burnham's architectural firm was designing the station, this does not suggest competition amongst board members for commissions. If a later newspaper account is accurate, it may reflect an internal conflict; Burnham may have proposed to build a skyscraper depot.[88] Although providing an economic rationale for the railroads to build a monumental station, this would have meant the inclusion of a commercial structure in the development. Brunner may have been opposed to this change in concept.

On 26 August 1902, Chairman Hill, on behalf of the city hall commission, reported to the grouping plan committee of the chamber of commerce on progress being made in purchasing land between Wood and Erie streets and Lake and Summit streets for the city hall.[89] Thus, before the board of supervision could make its report, three sites—for the federal building, county courthouse, and city hall—were determined. Any decision to change them might endanger the whole undertaking.

While Carrère was working out ideas and sketches on the

block plan, Burnham began to conceptualize the central idea for the grouping. After meeting in September with James McCrea, vice president of the Pennsylvania Railroad, Burnham wrote to him on 18 November 1902:

> The railway station, as it becomes the vestibule of the city is of the very first importance. It cannot be let out of the plan we are to make. In my judgement there is no other proper place for it except the one the railways have chosen. From the point of view of the people themselves, the placing of this vestibule to their city is of just as much importance as is the placing of a government, city or county building. This scheme . . . is not one for parks but for buildings. If a park seems . . . [the] proper thing it will of course be suggested. . . . We are going on as we have been for the last two years since the agreement was made with yourself, Mr. Ingalls and Mr. Newman to develop the best plan for a station for Cleveland.

It began to look doubtful that Burnham could get all the railways to agree among themselves. If they should agree, they would still have to make an agreement with the city for the site. The work of the board of supervision had been at a standstill since the end of August pending a decision regarding the inclusion of a union station. To force the railroads into a decision, in December 1902, Burnham wrote to the city to get an answer from Mayor Johnson.[90] There is no question that Burnham had a keen interest in the commercial aspects of the project.

The technical problems involving the station were becoming a real challenge to Burnham. On 12 December 1902, he wrote to Carrère, "I do not see my way clear to making even a tentative report; . . . it may be possible that the park idea may have to be partially given up." This was important for Carrère to know as he was working on the general layout. At this time, Burnham was elected as an associate member of the chamber of commerce.[91]

In January 1903, the city council adopted a resolution to include in the grouping a future park on made land north of Lake View Park.[92] By this action, the council tried to influence the outcome; the board became well aware of how deeply entrenched the park idea had become and the political obstacles they would have to face if they did not recommend a park. By the middle of February work was well along and a preliminary scheme was in hand. The city wanted Burnham to make a preliminary report, but he was not interested in making a public

presentation at that time:

> I do not think a public meeting had better be held. I think we should . . . go over the general scheme . . . and when we are thoroughly ready, then a public meeting might be called to which these things might be submitted, although I am not a believer in town meetings. They do not seem to have any permanent effect at all. I believe the best way to go at it would be after making a statement, with a plan, to place the whole matter in the hands of the Mayor and ask him to consult with the proper officials and proper citizens and then to advise me.[93]

Problems involving the railways had yet to be resolved, and it is clear from the correspondence that Burnham wanted to take this matter up with city officials while he was in Cleveland instead of presenting a tentative report.

All was not going as planned. In February 1903, Lehman and Schmitt, who had the commission to design the county courthouse, submitted their preliminary plans for informal discussion. In spite of the fact that they had met earlier with the board of supervision,[94] they persisted in presenting a design that was totally unacceptable. Given the state of planning for the entire scheme, it was too early to decide upon the size of the building. At this time, Burnham said that within six months at the outside the board would have its proposal ready for submission to the public. Also, it was thought that within two months the railroads would be ready to begin negotiations with the city relative to the construction of a new union depot. Furthermore, he stated, it would take at least six months to make the working drawings after the preliminary plans were approved and, in his judgment, the construction of the station would take at least two years.[95] Burnham was overly optimistic: negotiations with the city would drag on until 1915, when an agreement was finally reached to build on the lakefront site. World War I intervened, circumstances changed, and the lakefront site was finally abandoned in 1919.

By 25 February 1903, Burnham felt confident that he knew all that he was likely to know about the elements or units of the plan, and he suggested he go to New York to spend a day at Carrère's office and give exclusive time to the project. In March he continued to push Carrère toward making an early report: "Are you ready yet to take up with me the final layout for Cleveland? I do not see why we should not make a report very soon if you and Mr. Brunner can agree. I still think we should present two schemes, one like the last you and I talked about in New York, which I believe to be the best, and the other showing the City and County buildings out on the Lake Shore."[96] Carrère was obviously working on the general layout, and Burnham wanted him to get on with it.

On 16 May 1903, Burnham sent Carrère and Brunner a rough draft of the report concerning the grand axis and lake-park and the railway station. He suggested that there be a connection from the court of honor to the parks east and west of the city. To this end, he requested Carrère to prepare a small map of the city showing the route of the park boulevards. Undoubtedly, Burnham was building on an idea, already expressed in an editorial in *The Cleveland Plain Dealer* and by the park engineer, that equated the boulevards to both the importance of the beautiful as a feature of city life and as an advertisement for the city.[97] The inclusion of the boulevard system had great ideological value. The proposed civic center was to be seen symbolically and physically tied to and at the heart of the city.

The board of supervision made its report on 1 August 1903.[98] Burnham was its principal author. Printed in New York at the Cheltenham Press, it is impressive in format, 22.5 by 15.5 inches. Large-scale and beautifully rendered illustrations, two of which are magnificent bird's-eye views, present the proposed improvement. The title page was devoid of doodads and flourish and has little actually to read. With no reason to linger, the reader quickly turns to the substance of *The Group Plan.* Printed in Cheltenham type font, which was designed by architect Bertram Goodhue and based on his theories of readability, it stood out with great distinction from the nondescript and graceless types then in common use.[99] Elegantly and convincingly written, *The Group Plan* is a magnificent display of visual and rhetorical power.[100]

From the beginning, the report appealed to Cleveland's vanity and to the gravity of the project: "The opportunity of grouping . . . with proper setting . . . has never before come to any city, and your Commissioners have felt the great responsibility of the task, which . . . has splendid opportunities." It was "very inspiring that public opinion should have risen to a full realization of this great opportunity."

After this preamble, a historical account of the planning process—from the conception of the idea—was given. The aim of this was to demonstrate how exhaustive was their present report; every previous suggestion, no matter when it was made or where it came from, was considered. The report acknowledges that there was a predilection to locate the grouping between Public Square and the lake and that the decision had already been made to purchase the sites for the county courthouse and city hall, but the "Commission has nevertheless seriously considered every other possible solution of the problem." In reality, this statement was probably an exaggeration.

The board members knew there was opposition to them because they were not Clevelanders, and they already were aware that Cudell had different ideas;[101] it is for these reasons the report probably states that after "numerous studies, and . . . much time in consultation and in consideration of local conditions . . . [and] with the conditions definitely imposed, . . . the most advantageous grouping . . . can be obtained in the territory already considered by the Chamber of Commerce." Burnham knew to whom he had to appeal: the chamber of commerce's relatively new building was to be at the southeastern corner of the proposed mall, thus conjoined symbolically and physically with Cleveland's civic architecture. Because the report gave no facts on which its conclusions were based, it reinforced the authority both of the board and the chamber of commerce and made criticism of *The Group Plan* difficult.

In the proposed plan a major axis runs down the center of the composition, perpendicular to the lake (figs. 4.9, 4.10). A secondary axis runs along Lakeside Avenue, thus forming a Roman cross (fig. 4.11). Furthermore, two tertiary axes are formed by Ontario and East Sixth streets (fig. 4.12). All of these axes would constitute important urban vistas.

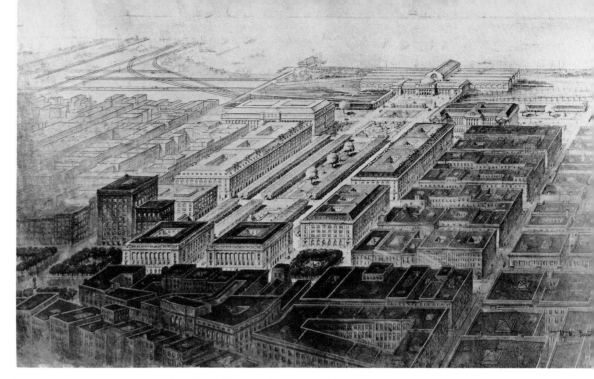

Fig. 4.9. Daniel H. Burnham et al., *The Group Plan* of 1903, plan. (Courtesy of Extensions Division, Cleveland Museum of Art)

Fig. 4.10. Daniel H. Burnham et al., *The Group Plan* of 1903, bird's-eye view looking north. (Courtesy of Extensions Division, Cleveland Museum of Art)

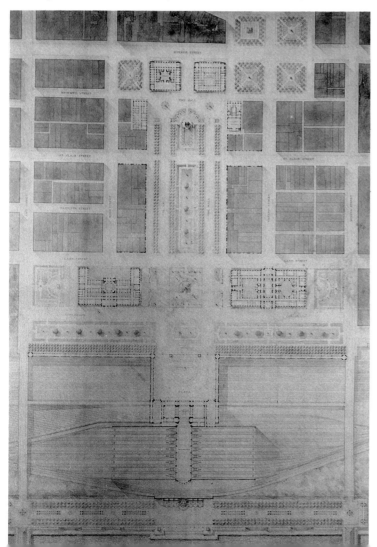

Fig. 4.11. Lakeside Avenue, Cleveland, showing the county courthouse and city hall, ca. 1920. (Cleveland Public Library)

Fig. 4.12. East Sixth Street, Cleveland, looking north, photographed 1987. (Walter C. Leedy, Jr.)

More importantly, they were planned to form monumental spaces, which would act as outdoor rooms. The federal building, whose site and design were already established, was associated with a library at the south end of a commodious mall. Their symmetrical placement is reflected by the axial placement of the railroad station at the mall's north end on the lakefront. The county building and city hall were to be placed on the lakefront with their axes on Ontario and East Sixth streets respectively, creating a bilaterally symmetrical composition around the north-south axis of the mall. Also, by fostering closure they create a definable street environment. Space, therefore, was as important as the buildings which surround it. Furthermore, by serving as conspicuous organizational devices, these buildings establish a clear, permanent, and lasting framework, thus ensuring the future development of the whole area. In addition, each building establishes a monumental presence in its immediate area rather than being mere classical embellishment. Burnham once remarked, "Beauty of the whole is superior to that of each of the several parts of the composition exploited separately."[102] By developing a symmetrical plan, the board of supervision may have been following Henry Van

Brunt's conviction that symmetry is the visual expression of unity.[103]

The determination of the exact location of the main axis of the composition within the city's street layout was of critical importance. That decision determined the amount of land necessary, which impacted on its ultimate cost. More important for aesthetic and symbolic reasons, the placement of the main axis determined the width of the court of honor or mall. All of these factors, the report indicated, were taken into consideration. Not surprising to those in the know, the main axis was located down the center of Wood Street. Again, the report gave no specifics. How large was the mall to be? What would it cost? One factor that made the report seem credible was its continual reiteration that everything had been carefully studied and the best solution was being proposed.

The report captured the reader, and mustered support for the plan, by the slow unfolding of the proposed layout before the reader's eyes. Each part was carefully introduced, so it could be thought about, digested, and *felt*. A narrative was thus created that took the reader emotionally, as well as intellectually, into the decision-making process. The persuasive arguments for the plan were reinforced by presenting a picture of fair, impartial consideration of all problems by distinguished experts. For example, before the report introduced the railway station, it stated that the north area "required much study." While "the Commission would have preferred to carry out the popular idea of a park and playground, . . . the conditions . . . are not ideal." Appeal was also made to the community's self-interest. The reasons for including the station were given, followed by the statement, "The railroad ought to be willing to make serious concessions to the city in exchange for these privileges. An arrangement can undoubtedly be made on this basis that will be to the greatest advantage of both parties, which means the greatest advantage to the City of Cleveland." Thus, Burnham implied that Cleveland would be getting something that it badly needed for little outlay. Then, and only then, did he give the reasons why a large park would be unattractive in this location. After reading this, could anyone doubt the authority of the commission?

Burnham appealed repeatedly to civic pride: "In bringing the visitor to Cleveland through a magnificent entrance into the most attractive section of the City, his first impression, which is usually the most lasting, would be a favorable one." Implicit in this statement is that the benefit will be permanent, not transitory, no matter what the rest of the city looked like. Then, he cited analogous situations in other great cities to support his point. Though he questioned whether the city and the railroads could reach an agreement, with great adroitness he presented an alternative scheme that replaced the railroad station with a beautiful park, only to argue against it. He understated the scheme he supported by stating in a tone of measured objectivity, it "meets the practical and artistic conditions in a satisfactory and reasonable manner."

The practicality of the scheme was continually stressed and reiterated. The landscaping was simple, mostly trees, and simply massed. There would be little individual detail, yielding a satisfactory and beautiful result. The court of honor or mall was to occupy "the minimum amount of land adequate for a scheme of this importance, and it does not seriously interfere with any improved property of great value." As an example, Burnham mentioned the power plants, but he could also have been appealing to the Society for Savings and to the chamber of commerce, whose buildings were to be saved. Implicit in this testi-

mony is the conclusion that something of little value will be traded for something of great substance.

Before the totality of the scheme was presented, the report introduced ideas for its implementation. Of greatest concern to Burnham was how to control the design of buildings to be constructed on the east and west sides of the mall, for at that time there was only the assurance that four buildings—federal building, library, courthouse, and city hall—would be built. He first proposed city ordinances in conjunction with public spirit to control the design, stating that selfish interests could destroy much of the mall's visual effect. Then he presented the ideal solution: the city should acquire all the land facing on the mall and dispose of it under well-defined restrictions. Knowing that this may be impossible to achieve, he stated that "while it would be unfortunate not to secure or control the grounds on each side of the Mall, it would not, however, be fatal to our scheme, which is complete and consistent in itself." He explained that the trees would hide any incongruous buildings. Each segment of the argument was built upon point, counterpoint, coda, and conclusion. By taking this approach, the reader was won over, even before the entire extent of the proposal was presented.

Burnham then described the mall with its monumental railroad station opening out onto an imposing court of honor or mall surrounded by formal clipped trees. He introduced the human element by including what many planners today fail to—seats and drinking fountains. Giant fountains were placed at each end of the mall. The report related how the design for the fountain at the southern end had to be restudied. At first a simple one was proposed, but that was not sufficient to make it as important as the facades of the library and the federal building. He created a plan for a ceremonial city, a dream city, which would make Cleveland famous. This illusion was constantly reinforced by incessantly repeating the phrase "Court of Honor," which invoked the mental image of the World's Columbian Exposition. Recognizing the need for appeal to practical civic leaders, he described how streetcars and pedestrians would approach the station. He admitted that there would virtually be no view of the lake from the mall, and what one might see would be unattractive (railroad yards, smoke, cinders). To appease those who wanted a plan that had lake views, he said, "The view of the lake from the northerly end of the waiting room of the railroad station and from the Park on the lake front, will be wholly unobstructed by any objectionable foreground, and the view from the buildings over the trees will be even finer." At lake level a park was planned on the other side of the railroad tracks. Although the city had been filling in the lake to make land in that area since 1894, the park's inclusion and development as recreation grounds was an earlier idea he adopted and developed to appeal to popular demand.

Burnham then summarized his argument thus far: "It is our belief that a maximum of effect can be produced at a minimum of expense, that the scheme can be carried out in its entirety within a reasonably short time, and . . . that it is of such a character as to become more beautiful." Thus the report introduced the hope or fantasy that the proposed plan could become a reality sooner than anyone previously had thought possible.

Flattering the desire of a provincial city to achieve stature, he compared this solution to specific European exemplars from which the Cleveland design was derived, pictures of which were published in the report. Not only was vanity appealed to, but readers might respond to the pictures as visitors to the World's Columbian Exposition had done — with *astonishment*. Burnham's stated reason for using pictures of already built sites was given later that year in a letter to Willis Polk of San Francisco: "The human brain is not comprehensive enough to evoke . . . [a design] without seeing the important things men have already done for similar locations."[104] This was followed by a discussion as to why the buildings must be of one style, and why that style must be derived from the motifs of the classic architecture of Rome. "It needs no argument; . . . [it was] the lesson taught by the Court of Honor of the World's Columbian Exposition of 1893." He then again summarized the whole argument in favor of the scheme he favored, adding more detail, but stressing practicality. He ended on what must have been a reassuring note to members of Cleveland's ruling elite: "Our report . . . must . . . be considered as a first or preliminary report. . . . After it has received due consideration by you, it may have to be modified. . . . We therefore lay the matter before you with . . . suggestions and recommendations for your consideration and decision, and await your further instructions." Burnham, master politician and rhetorician, realized he could not appear to be heavy-handed.

Burnham conceived the railroad station to be the gateway to Cleveland and the mall to be its vestibule. At a time when most people came to Cleveland by train, this grouping of public buildings, rather than any individual building, was to symbolize Cleveland. Clearly defined by a distinct architectural edge, softened by rows of trees, fountains, statuary, and terraces, the design fused urban qualities with those of a large city park. When exiting the station, tourists and businessmen alike could immediately gawk at Cleveland's achievements upon arrival in the city. When the report was published, the monumental size of the mall was immediately recognized and criticized.[105]

Beautification was not only to stimulate a regenerated civic life.[106] For Burnham beauty was an important ingredient of economic well-being. An attractive city should promote tourism, enlarge trade, and revitalize the local economy. The court of honor was to serve as a national advertisement for the city of Cleveland. It was also to stimulate private investment.[107] For Cleveland's cultivated citizens, beauty had one more important function: a beautiful environment was thought to be morally uplifting and ennobling. Beauty had educational value for Cleveland's immigrants and would help in the quest for social and moral cohesiveness. This cohesiveness was based, of course, on values established by Cleveland's ruling elite.

The same style for all the buildings, academic classicism, and a common cornice height unified the composition and distinguished these buildings, marking their public purpose.[108] Style served, therefore, as a form of communication at a time of large-scale European immigration.

Furthermore, academic classicism gave a sense of continuity with the past by fostering a romantic attachment to Greece and Rome and by evoking late eighteenth- and early nineteenth-century American architecture. It could form the basis of a civilizing influence that could alleviate the effects of what was seen as the overly materialistic values of post–Civil War society, as exemplified in Samuel Mather's speech of 1895. The employment of academic classicism can moreover be understood as an exercise in vanity on the part of the ruling elite, who were European descended and male-dominated.[109] The architecture of the mall was to emphasize the greatness of Cleveland by visually linking it to European cities.

The idea of the mall appealed to the masses, for it answered the need for relief from the drab, disorderly, and blighted conditions of the city. It became a rallying point for civic pride. Thus, a pre-modern architectural style was employed as a symbol of modernity.

The Group Plan can be read like a multilayered visual text. First, the district was to be an image in the city. Uniformity of style and academic classicism were to give the area an identifying character. Public buildings would be easily recognizable. Second, this civic center was to be the image for the city of Cleveland. After arrival in the railway station, the traveler emerged into the mall, the vestibule of the city. Not one building but several were to characterize Cleveland. Third, on a universal level, it expressed a utopian image of the city, for it was to express two important aspects of the human condition—peacefulness and repose—which Burnham thought to be the true basis of contentment.[110] Thus Burnham recognized the multivocal potential for urban design and was able to articulate it.

By uniting economic and ideological benefits, *The Group Plan* directed attention away from more threatening reform agendas, such as inadequate housing and population congestion.[111] It convinced the proponents of the idea that they were correct all along.

The Group Plan was quickly accepted. On 17 August 1903, the city council received the report. Members of the chamber of commerce, along with other civic leaders, met the following day in the city council chambers and in a general way approved the plan submitted.[112] *The Cleveland Plain Dealer* endorsed the plan on 19 August, while *The Cleveland Leader* held off until 17 September. Criticism began to mount when architect Frank Cudell published a circular letter on 1 September 1903 in which he was highly critical of the report and suggested alternative solutions.[113] This action may have prompted the chamber of commerce to invite the board of supervision to present their plans. Burnham did not accept, but Carrère and Brunner made a presentation on 15 September 1903. Invited to this presentation were members of the Cleveland Builders Exchange, the Cleveland chapter of the American Institute of Architects, the Cleveland Architectural Club, and the Associated Technical Clubs. Carrère showed stereopticon slides illustrating the proposed plan and of public buildings in European cities, while Brunner addressed the chamber on the general outline of the plan and described the proposed federal building.[114]

In December 1903, Mayor Johnson let it quietly be known to the chamber of commerce that he opposed putting the city hall on the lakefront site. Perhaps in response to Cudell's criticism of its being too far away, he suggested the city hall stay where it was then located, on Superior Street. However, he did not intend to publicly oppose the lakefront site unless the chamber of commerce concurred with his opinion.[115]

Over the next year the grouping plan committee of the chamber of commerce did an extensive evaluation, publishing its findings in September 1904. The report concentrated on the financial aspects of the project. It included estimates, for example, of how much the land would cost and how it would be paid for. In addition, there was an estimate of the cost of the structures and the landscaping, fountains, statuary, etcetera, for the mall. To carry out the board of supervision's recommendation to control the land around the mall, the committee had the state legislature pass an act that empowered cities to acquire land contiguous to public buildings and parks and to resell it with restrictions. Total first cost was estimated to be $12,953,325. Since the city needed the buildings anyway, the committee argued, and profit was to be made from the resale of land, the net cost would be lower, only $3,374,780. The city was urged to acquire the land as fast as possible as there was wide variance between these new cost estimates and estimates made just two years ago—the difference: $753,000.[116] The chamber of commerce, therefore, not only played a role in developing the plan, but its help was essential during implementation.

Preliminary plans for the courthouse were approved in November 1904 and working drawings in May 1906. City hall preliminary drawings were approved in March 1906. In April 1907, the city council passed a resolution approving the site for the public library. In 1910, the federal building was the first building to be completed, followed by the county courthouse in 1912, the city hall in 1915, and the public library in 1925.

Other buildings along the east side of the mall included a public auditorium (1922) with adjoining music hall (1929), and the headquarters for the board of education (1930). On the west side a county office building was constructed in 1956 (fig. 4.13).[117]

By accepting Wood Street as the axis for the mall, the board of supervision followed the latest planning theories relative to the location of civic centers. Located between radial lines of development, the mall did not interfere with the major traffic arteries. The mall did not intrude on the business center but was placed in juxtaposition to it. Removed from the direct flow of business, the mall was to gain in repose and strengthen the public sense of dignity and responsibility of citizenship. The real reason, however, for siting the mall in this location, as Carrère was later to report, was the result of the consideration of vested interests. The board of supervision could not disturb the business center without creating opposition that they felt might not be possible to overcome.[118] The plan, therefore, was practical and politically expedient rather than idealistic. It can also be seen as reflecting a value system that placed great importance on the commercial aspect of the modern city. As a result of this momentous decision to site the mall in this location, the mall was, and is still, both of Cleveland and apart from it.

Because the railway station was never built, because the major buildings on the mall have their main entrances on the side streets, because of the overwhelming, monumental scale of the mall itself, and because of its location, the mall only obliquely affects the lives of Clevelanders. Thus, in the last analysis a plan that promised so much was to result in the creation of a static model for the city, devoid of human reference. But this undertaking, because of the persuasiveness of the original report, the brilliant placing of four buildings, and the energy and struggle for its realization, resulted in concomitant commitment.

By 1930, $38 million had been spent on the civic center, and yet it was far from completed.[119] As Charlotte Rumbold, a member of the Cleveland City Plan Commission, wrote at that time, the civic center "has been of incalculable value in welding into a unity of feeling the whole citizenship about a hope of achieving a beautiful thing. . . . Pride in their city . . . is one of the intangibles that in the long run outweigh many concrete, visible achievements."[120]

Attempts have been made in recent years to enliven the mall with festivals and other civic events, such as the National Rib Cook-Off, which attracted 150,000 people during an August weekend in 1987 and caused some officials to complain that festivals disrupt downtown traffic and present an undue burden for the city.[121] Thus, the mall today takes on a role never envisioned by its creators, that of emulating the entertainment function of the midway of the World's Columbian Exposition.

The Group Plan was to symbolize Cleveland. But, as it turned out, that honor went to the Terminal Tower (fig. 4.14). Part of a high density, multifunction development located at a major transportation node, Public Square, and with good distance views, Terminal Tower became Cleveland's most important cognitive marker. Opened in 1928, it was an immediate commercial and symbolic success.[122] By that time the skyscraper was the undeniable symbol of the modern metropolis, and in civic centers across the country tall buildings came to symbolize civic pride.

Fig. 4.13. The Mall, Cleveland, aerial view looking south, photographed 1977. (Walter C. Leedy, Jr.)

The greatest success of the board of supervision is not, therefore, in the actual execution of the plan and its intended results but is in the lessons it taught about how successful urban imagery could function, and in how the board was able to forge all of the constraints of this particular situation into a conceptual whole and effectively communicate it. As a consequence, the Group Plan was destined to influence the development of other cities across America.

"Sorely throb my feet, a-tramping city pavements (Ah, the springy sod upon an upland moor!)"

Fig. 4.14. Graham, Anderson, Probst, and White, Terminal Tower, Cleveland. (Van Sweringen Co., sales brochure, ca. 1928)

Notes

I became interested in Daniel Burnham in 1984 when I attended a National Endowment for the Humanities Summer Institute, "Urban Architecture: A New Perspective," held at DePaul University and directed by Professor Sally Chappell.

I am indebted to Ms. Karen Martines of the Public Administration Library of the Cleveland Public Library and to Mr. Martin Hauserman, archivist for the city of Cleveland. For a critical reading of this essay in draft form and for helpful suggestions, I am grateful to Professors John Cary and Edric Weld of Cleveland State University.

The letters and scrapbooks of Daniel H. Burnham cited below are preserved at the Art Institute of Chicago. The minutes of the Cleveland Chamber of Commerce and its committees cited below are preserved in the Western Reserve Historical Society, Cleveland, Ohio, MS. 3471. Cleveland city archives are located in the Cleveland City Hall.

1. See Thomas F. Campbell, *Freedom's Forum* (Cleveland: The City Club, 1963), 19ff, and idem, "Background For Progressivism: Machine Politics in the Administration of Robert E. McKisson, Mayor of Cleveland, 1895–1899" (master's thesis, Western Reserve University, 1960), 40, 89.

2. Mary-Peale Schofield, "The Cleveland Arcade," *Journal of the Society of Architectural Historians* 25, no.4(1966):281–292.

3. See Eric Johannesen, *Cleveland Architecture, 1876–1976* (Cleveland: Western Reserve Historical Society, 1979), 39ff. The Society for Savings realized the commercial implications of being visible; later they sold an adjoining small parcel of property to the chamber of commerce for their new building with the stipulation that the chamber build no higher than six stories: 13 March 1902, minutes of the directory, Cleveland Chamber of Commerce, in which this prior agreement is recalled.

4. According to Samuel P. Orth, *A History of Cleveland, Ohio,* 3 vols. (Chicago-Cleveland: S. J. Clarke, 1910), 3: 316–317, Herrick was involved with many of the details of construction and arrangement of the Society for Savings Building. Herrick was to go on to the presidency of the Society for Savings in 1894. A leading Republican, he later became governor of Ohio and ambassador to France.

5. Herrick and Burnham apparently knew each other quite well. They exchanged Christmas cards (preserved in Burnham's scrapbooks), and Burnham wrote to Herrick on 18 July 1902 asking him to help his nephew find a job.

6. Three hundred dollars was paid to D. H. Burnham and Company, 15 May 1896, executive committee minutes, Cleveland Chamber of Commerce.

7. Charles E. Bolton, *A Model Village of Homes and Other Papers* (Boston: L. C. Page, 1901), 196. Bolton was the mayor of the village of East Cleveland, 1899–1901. He was opposed to the annexation of the village to the city of Cleveland, which would mean "saloons, crime, [and] increased taxation." His ideal village was patterned on the English Lake Country, which he had visited and given illustrated lectures on to the citizens of East Cleveland. His *A Model Village of Homes,* which describes East Cleveland, was originally published in *The American Monthly Review* (1899). See Ellen Loughry Price, *A History of East Cleveland* (1970), 81.

8. One such description published in *The Cleveland Press,* 19 May 1897, describes a section of downtown with an odor so vile that it gagged one when entering. Alleys and side streets, which never appeared on city maps, were full of mud, filth, and dirt; decaying fruit and vegetables were strewn over the pavements, etcetera. See Campbell, "Progressivism," 3.

9. *The Cleveland Plain Dealer,* 4 November 1894, letter to the editor from R. C. P. This most likely was Richard C. Parsons. As a lawyer and public official, he was instrumental in expanding and securing Cleveland's harbor.

10. Letter to the editor from John E. Ensign, *The Cleveland Leader,* 17 March 1895. Ensign was a member of the chamber of commerce.

11. See *The Cleveland Plain Dealer,* 4 June, 3, 24 July 1895. The proposed city hall was to span two quadrants of Public Square. Ontario Street was to be bridged. For a complete description of the plans see *The Cleveland Plain Dealer,* 14 July 1895. The courts continually found that Public Square was owned by the people and not by the city.

12. Ibid., 9 December 1894.

13. Elroy McKendree Avery, *A History of Cleveland and Its Environs* (Chicago and New York: Lewis Publishing, 1918), 1:466.

14. The architects were W. S. Dutton, C. W. Hopkinson, and F. A. Coburn. The artist was Otto S. Ruetenik. In 1893, the Olney Art Gallery was completed and was opened by private invitation to Cleveland art circles. It was designed by Coburn and Barnum. Olney was a forceful advocate for the arts in Cleveland. See *In Loving Memory of Charles Fayette Olney, 1831–1903* (Cleveland, 1903), 5–12; and Carl Wittke, *The First Fifty Years: The Cleveland Museum of Art, 1916–1966* (Cleveland: John Huntington Art and Polytechnic Trust and the Cleveland Museum of Art, 1966), 18, 21. According to *The Cleveland Leader,* 25 February 1900, Olney's love of beauty was based on higher grounds than mere pleasure.

15. *The Cleveland Press,* 2 April 1895. For additional information, see Herbert B. Briggs, "Cleveland Architectural Club," *The American Architect and Building News,* 6 April 1895, 7.

16. *The Cleveland Press,* 20 August 1894 and 29 November 1895. See Campbell, "Progressivism," 25–31.

17. Frederic C. Howe, *The Confessions of a Reformer* (New York: Charles Scribners, 1925), 80–81.

18. Archer H. Shaw, *The Plain Dealer: One Hundred Years in Cleveland* (New York: Alfred A. Knopf, 1942), 278.

19. 17 August 1898, minutes of directory meeting, Cleveland Chamber of Commerce.

20. 21 September 1897, public buildings committee report, Cleveland Chamber of Commerce.

21. 15 March 1898, minutes of public buildings committee, Cleveland Chamber of Commerce.

22. 29 March 1898, minutes of special meeting, Cleveland Chamber of Commerce.

23. 11 April 1898, minutes of directory meeting, Cleveland Chamber of Commerce.

24. 1898 Ohio Laws, 132L, passed 19 April 1898, "AN ACT to authorize cities of the second grade of the first class to secure the necessary land, and to borrow money therefor, and for the purpose of building and erecting thereon a city hall, and the furnishing of the same."

25. Robert E. McKisson, *An Address by Robert E. McKisson to the People of Cleveland: Reviewing What Has Been Done by the Present City Administration* (Cleveland: Brooks, 1899), 12, 15, 29–31. The commission was established on 22 August 1898. See Cleveland City Council, *Proceedings, 1898–1899,* 31: 188, File No. 22039. Members appointed to the board of the city hall commission were Thomas W. Hill, Stephen C. Gladwin, Matthew F. Bramley, Nathan I.

Dryfoos, and Frederick W. Gehring.

26. William Ganson Rose, *Cleveland: The Making of a City* (Cleveland and New York: World Publishing, 1950), 591.

27. McKisson, *An Address by Robert E. McKisson,* 29–31.

28. See below and Charles Mulford Robinson, "New Dreams for Cities," *Architectural Record* 17 (1905):413.

29. Quoted in Edwin C. Baxter, "The Grouping of Public Buildings in Cleveland," *American Monthly Review of Reviews* 31, no. 5 (May 1905):562.

30. Olney would have the city hall, courthouse, public library, Case Library, and art museum facing each other on a court of honor with appropriate fountains and monuments in the center: *The Cleveland Leader,* 18 December 1898, 9. Later in 1899, Professor H. W. Hulbert of the Old Stone Church suggested a court of honor further out on Euclid Avenue; he recognized that the center of population and commercial industry was shifting to the east: *The Cleveland Press,* 4 February 1899.

31. Herbert B. Briggs, "The Municipal Building Problem in the City of Cleveland," *Architectural Annual* (1900), 43.

32. See Herbert Croly, "The United States Post Office, Custom House, and Court House, Cleveland, Ohio," *The Architectural Record* 29, no. 3(March 1911): 193–213.

33. Minutes of the chamber of commerce. This was reported in *The Cleveland Press,* 18 January 1899.

34. 23 January 1899, minutes of the directory meeting, Cleveland Chamber of Commerce.

35. *The Cleveland Press,* 20 January 1899. The paper went on to say, "The group building advocates say they do not consider the fixed location of the postoffice as a black eye to their project. They say other buildings might be grouped exclusive of the postoffice, and, perhaps, of the court house, too."

36. This meeting was publicly announced in *The Cleveland Leader,*15 January 1899, 12. At that time the agenda was listed as (1) to organize, (2) to consider the question of grouping, and (3) to discuss the location. The article went on to state that similar projects had been started in New York and San Francisco. Members of Cleveland City Council were formally invited: Cleveland City Council File No. 23397.

37. *The Cleveland Plain Dealer,* 25 January 1899. According to the paper, Wilson M. Day was one member of the committee that passed upon the sketches submitted to the club. Day was president of the chamber of commerce, 1895–1896.

38. *The Cleveland Press,* 25 January 1899, 3.

39. Ibid., 15 January 1899. These ideas came from Phebe [Phoebe] Hearst of San Francisco, who was a recent member of the Architectural Review of Boston. See also editorials on 21, 30, 31 January 1899.

40. *The Cleveland Press,* 1 February 1899.

41. "The Ontario St. plan was originated by . . . Herrick," *The Cleveland Press,* 23 May 1899.

42. *The Cleveland Press,* 16 February 1899. Charles Wheeler Pratt (b. 1865) attended MIT. He worked in the office of E. W. Bowdich, of Boston, 1881–1891. He was employed by the Cleveland Park Board as chief engineer from 1894 until 1900, when he entered private practice. He designed Ambler Heights and Euclid Heights allotments, amongst other things. See Samuel P. Orth, *A History* 2: 43–44. Pratt's plan bears remarkable similarity to Wight's later plan for the development of Chicago's lakefront.

43. 17 February 1899, minutes of the directory meeting, Cleveland Chamber of Commerce.

44. Other members were William G. Mather, president of Cleveland Cliffs Iron Company, attorney Horace E. Andrews, banker George A. Garretson, and manufacturer George W. Kinney. The committee was appointed at the regular meeting of the chamber of commerce on 28 February 1899.

45. Earlier in the year a call for a joint meeting was issued by Harry Dixon, secretary of the library board. This meeting was proposed by members of the Cleveland Architectural Club, according to Judge Hutchins, president of the library board. See *The Cleveland Plain Dealer,* 24 January 1899, 15.

46. *The Cleveland Press,* 23 May 1899.

47. *The Cleveland Plain Dealer,* 2 June 1899; 3 June 1899, 3, plus an editorial, 4.

48. 24, 31 August 1899, minutes of the grouping plan committee, Cleveland Chamber of Commerce.

49. The Cleveland Industrial Exposition and Carnival was held there, 7–19 August 1899. There was a midway, an anchored balloon, and two bandstands. A theater was at the foot of Ontario Street and a fishery exhibit opposite Bond Street. The site plan was published in *The Cleveland Press,* 19 May 1899. Thus, the general public became aware of the recreational potential that the lakefront location offered.

50. Michael Horvath, "Report of the Forester," in *Seventh Annual Report of the Board of Park Commissioners of the City of Cleveland, 1899* (Cleveland: Cleveland Printing and Publishing, 1900), 91.

51. This report was printed in Cleveland Architectural Club, *Catalogue of Its Third Exhibition* (1900), 21–26.

52. Per capita expenditure for all purposes in 1900 was $16.68. In New York it was $30.35, and in Boston $45.37. See Frederic C. Howe, "Cleveland – A City 'Finding Itself'," *World's Work* 6 (October 1903): 3997.

53. 2 January 1900, minutes of special meeting to act upon the report of special committee on grouping plan for public buildings, Cleveland Chamber of Commerce.

54. Undated memorandum, minutes of the grouping plan committee, 1899–1900, Cleveland Chamber of Commerce.

55. 20 June 1900, minutes of the directory meeting, Cleveland Chamber of Commerce.

56. For a summary of efforts up to 1907 see Clinton R. Woodruff, "The National Impulse for Civic Improvement," *The Chautauquan: Organ of the Chautauqua Literary and Scientific Circle* 47, no. 1(June 1907): 24–31.

57. See Thomas S. Hines, "The Paradox of 'Progressive' Architecture: Urban Planning and Public Building in Tom Johnson's Cleveland," *American Quarterly* 25(1973): 426–448.

58. Shaw, *The Plain Dealer,* 278, 284.

59. Hoyt Landon Warner, *Progressivism in Ohio, 1897-1917* (Columbus, Ohio: Ohio State University Press, 1964), 54–78.

60. John de Witt Warner, "Civic Centers," *Municipal Affairs* 6, no. 1(March 1902):19. The fact that Johnson requested Brunner to design a plan was recalled c.1921 by Peter Witt. See Western Reserve Historical Society MS. 3281: "The Union Depot on the Public Square and Other Grafts."

61. An important conference was held on 9 October 1901 in the city hall council chamber, which eventually led to the decision of 1 March 1902. See 9 October 1901, 26 March 1902, minutes of the grouping plan committee, Cleveland Chamber of Commerce.

62. 3, 12 March 1902, minutes of the grouping plan committee; 19 March 1902, minutes of the regular meeting, Cleveland Chamber of Commerce.

63. Cleveland City Council, *Proceedings, 1902-1903,* 35: 2, Mayor's Mes-

sage, File No. 37284.

64. 29 April 1902, minutes of the grouping plan committee, Cleveland Chamber of Commerce.

65. 1902 Ohio Laws, 258L, passed 6 May 1902, "AN ACT to create a board of supervision in the erection simultaneously of public municipal and county buildings (Cuyahoga County)."

66. Clarence H. Cramer, *Newton D. Baker* (Cleveland and New York: World Publishing, 1961), 37–38.

67. See Jon A. Peterson, "The Nation's First Comprehensive City Plan, A Political Analysis of the McMillan Plan for Washington, D.C., 1900–1902," *Journal of the American Planning Association* 51 (Spring 1985): 134–150.

68. See Harvey A. Kantor, "The City Beautiful in New York," *New York Historical Quarterly* 57 (April 1973): 149–171.

69. 21 September 1897, minutes of the Cleveland Chamber of Commerce.

70. 19 May 1902, minutes of the grouping plan committee, Cleveland Chamber of Commerce. See also *The Cleveland Press,* 2, 5 June 1902.

71. 19 May 1902, minutes of the grouping plan committee, Cleveland Chamber of Commerce.

72. See Peterson, "The Nation's First."

73. Cleveland City Council, *Proceedings, 1902–1903,* 35: 72, 79–80, 99–100, File No. 37970. For the complete file see Cleveland city archives. Adoption was recommended by the board of control, who suggested that it be amended in the area of their compensation and that the composition of the board consist of three "persons" instead of three "experts." It was so amended in spite of a recommendation not to do so from corporation counsel.

74. Cleveland City Council, *Proceedings, 1902–1903,* 35: 100, File No. 38223.

75. Cleveland City Council, *Proceedings, 1902–1903,* 35: 95, File Nos. 38191-1/2 and 38192, 11 and 17 June 1902.

76. 16 June 1902, letter, partly damaged, preserved in Cleveland city archives, city hall, City Council File No. 38197, noted in Cleveland City Council, *Proceedings, 1902–1903,* 35: 96. Cudell wrote an earlier letter relative to the appointment of the architects to city council. Unfortunately, that letter, City Council File No. 37985, is now lost or misplaced.

77. Cleveland City Council, *Proceedings, 1902–1903,* 35: 99.

78. Letter, Burnham to Carrère, 24 June 1902, to arrange a meeting in Cleveland with Brunner; letters, Burnham to Harvey Goulder, president of chamber of commerce, and to Carrère, 30 June 1902, in regard to meeting arrangements; letter, Burnham to Carrère, 2 July 1902, to prepare a list of all possible buildings entering into the arrangement; letter, Burnham to Hollendon House Hotel, Cleveland, 11 July 1902, for hotel reservations.

79. Charles Moore, *Daniel H. Burnham, Architect, Planner of Cities* (Boston and New York: Houghton Mifflin, 1921), 1: 183, 202; letter, 15 July 1902, Burnham to B. Davey; Arnold Brunner, "Cleveland's Group Plan," *Proceedings of the Eighth National Conference on City Planning, Cleveland* (New York, 1916), 15.

80. Letter, 30 July 1902, Burnham to James Taylor, supervising architect of the U.S. Treasury.

81. 11 September 1902, letter, Burnham to Taylor, U.S. Treasury: "The highest beauty rests on order and system. . . . All future government buildings [should be] . . . uniform in style [to achieve a] dignified effect. . . . We wrote the clause regarding style in government buildings which was used in the code for the agricultural building competition. . . . A good design does not mean expensive materials." Letter, Burnham to Marcus Hanna, 2 July 1903: "Stone shown to

us . . . [is] a dark color unsuitable for monumental City Architecture of any sort. If used by the government I fear that the effect will be exceedingly disappointing. . . . The general effect . . . will be depressing, and all delicacy of details depending on the play of light and shadow will be lost."

82. *The Cleveland Plain Dealer,* 20 December 1902. The decision to use granite met with vehement protests from owners of local sandstone quarries, who sent a committee to Washington to influence the action of the architect, Senator Hanna, and Representative Burton on this issue. Labor also demanded sandstone. After a bitter and protracted fight both in Cleveland and Washington, granite won. See Shaw, *The Plain Dealer,* 316.

83. Letter, Burnham to Parmelee, 11 August 1902.

84. Letter, Burnham to Roberts, 16 August 1902; see also letter, Burnham to Thomas Rodd, chief engineer, Pennsylvania Railroad Company, 26 August 1902, in which Burnham states that the work of the commission has come to a standstill pending a decision on a union station.

85. Moore, *Daniel Burnham,* 1: 185.

86. Letter, Burnham to N. B. Ream (New York City), 8 October 1901: "We have in hand the Cleveland station of the Lake Shore and Michigan Southern Railway."

87. "Mr. Anderson, designer, in charge of Cleveland work," in a letter, Burnham to G. W. Kittridge, 22 November 1902.

88. "There is a hint in official quarters that the general plan of the railroad architect is to build a skyscraper depot," *The Cleveland Press,* 18 February 1903.

89. 26 August 1902, minutes of the grouping committee, Cleveland Chamber of Commerce. On 16 February 1903, the city hall commission reported on the completion of the purchase of the entire block. First options to purchase were recorded in a communication to Mayor Johnson on 9 December 1901. See Cleveland City Council, *Proceedings, 1902–1903,* 35: 498.

90. Letter, Burnham to Roberts, December 1902. *The Cleveland Plain Dealer,* 2 January 1903, advocated putting the railroad station in the group plan. The board of supervision carried out all the negotiations with the railroads.

91. Letter, Burnham to F. A. Scott, secretary, Cleveland Chamber of Commerce, 31 December 1902.

92. Cleveland City Council, *Proceedings, 1902–1903,* 35: 444, File No. 40572; letter, Burnham to Roberts, 26 January 1903: "This amounts to almost an order as I understand it."

93. Letters, Burnham to Roberts, 10, 14 February 1903. And again on 16 February 1903: "I believe it would be much better not to have a general meeting; . . . [it] is an extremely bad thing in its effect unless we are prepared on every point to conduct it properly. I should much prefer to wait until we have gone over our affairs together carefully in order that we may know just where we stand."

94. *The Cleveland Plain Dealer,* 16 January 1903; see also letter, Burnham to Roberts, 3 December 1902: "The Board of Supervision has not approved the plans of the Courthouse."

95. 21 February 1903, minutes of committees of grouping plan and new union depot, Cleveland Chamber of Commerce.

96. Letter, Burnham to Carrère, 27 March 1903.

97. For insight into boulevard and park system, see the editorial in *The Cleveland Plain Dealer,* 18 January 1903. Park engineer Williams completed plans to connect all Cleveland parks by boulevards, including the new mall. For a complete description and map, see *The Cleveland Plain Dealer,* 22 January 1903.

98. Cleveland, Ohio, Board of Supervision for Public Buildings and Grounds, *The Group Plan of the Public Buildings of the City of Cleveland, Report Made to the Honorable Tom L. Johnson, Mayor, and to the Honorable Board of Service by Daniel H. Burnham, John M. Carrère, Arnold W. Brunner, Board of Supervision* (New York: Cheltenham Press, 1903). The text and illustrations were reprinted in *Architects and Builders Journal* (Baltimore), (November 1903): 17–29. The plans were exhibited at the American Institute of Architects convention held in Cleveland (October 1903).

99. Frank Denman, *The Shaping of Our Alphabet* (New York: Alfred A. Knopf, 1955), 14–18, and Geoffrey Ashall Glaister, *Glaister's Glossary of the Book,* 2 ed. (Berkeley: University of California Press, 1979), 199.

100. Dr. Edward Wolner is presently working on Burnham's methods of presentation for the Chicago Plan of 1909. He gave a paper on the subject at the 1987 annual meeting of the Society of Architectural Historians, to which I am indebted.

101. Letter, Burnham to Roberts, 3 December 1902.

102. Daniel H. Burnham, "White City and Capital City," *Century Magazine* 63 (February 1902): 619.

103. Henry Van Brunt, *Architecture and Society: Selected Essays of Henry Van Brunt,* ed. William A. Coles (Cambridge: Belknap Press, 1969), 245.

104. Letter, Burnham to Willis Polk, 12 November 1903.

105. See F. C. Cudell, *The Grouping of Cleveland's Public Buildings,* circular letter, 1 September 1903. Copy in the Western Reserve Historical Society.

106. See William H. Wilson, "The Ideology, Aesthetics and Politics of the City Beautiful Movement," International Conference on the History of Urban and Regional Planning, in Anthony Sutcliffe, ed., *The Rise of Modern Urban Planning, 1800-1914* (New York: St. Martin's Press, 1977), 165–198.

107. Daniel H. Burnham, "Extract from a paper on the Commercial Value of Beauty," United States Senate Committee on the District of Columbia, *Park Improvement Papers,* no. 11 (January 1902).

108. Academic classicism was viewed as having lofty purpose, as witnessed by this letter from Stanford White to Burnham, 23 September 1903, preserved in Burnham's scrapbooks: "I think the cheap carpenter's Gothic patchwork of Cram, Goodhue, and Fergusson is a public calamity, and the fact that the great Military Academy at West Point is to be completed in this style seems to me to be a body blow to all those who are striving to raise architecture out of the heterogenous muck into which it has fallen."

109. See James E. Vance, Jr., "The Classical Revival and Urban-Rural Conflict in Nineteenth-Century North America," *The Canadian Review of American Studies* 4, no. 2 (Fall 1973): 149–168; Brooklyn Museum, *The American Renaissance* (New York: Pantheon Books, 1979); Richard W. Longstreth, "Academic Eclecticism in American Architecture," *Winterthur Portfolio* 17 (1982): 55–82; and Richard Guy Wilson, "Architecture and the Reinterpretation of the Past in the American Renaissance," *Winterthur Portfolio* 18 (1983): 69–87.

110. *The Group Plan,* n.p.

111. This was recognized shortly thereafter. See George B. Ford, "Digging Deeper into City Planning," *The American City* 6 (March 1912): 557–562.

112. 18 August 1903, minutes of the grouping plan committee, Cleveland Chamber of Commerce.

113. Cudell, *The Grouping.* His opposition was unrelenting. In a circular letter to the people of Cleveland, "Group Plan, Initiative and Referendum," October 1908, he asked: "Shall our seat of government have the location of a seashore hotel, or that of a city hall?" and he felt "structures of high character . . . should face the community and be near the principal thoroughfares." Later in 1912 he published another pamphlet, "The Group Plan Question: A Nine Years Study and a Warning."

114. 11 September 1903, minutes of the directory meeting, Cleveland Chamber of Commerce; 15 September 1903, minutes of the chamber of commerce.

115. 5 December 1903, memorandum, minutes of the grouping plan committee, Cleveland Chamber of Commerce.

116. *Report of the Grouping Plan Committee of the Chamber of Commerce approved by the Chamber, September 27, 1904* (Cleveland: City of Cleveland, Board of City Hall Commissioners, 1904).

117. For a more complete, later history of the mall, see Eric Johannesen, "Making and Sustaining a Legacy, Cleveland's Group Plan," *Inland Architect* 31, no. 6(1987): 30–35.

118. John M. Carrère, no title, remarks before the Thirty-seventh Annual Convention of the American Institute of Architects, October 1903, *Proceedings of the American Institute of Architects* (Washington, D.C., 1904), 112.

119. An early critic of the plan said that "it is extremely doubtful whether the public at large has any very clear conception of just what the group plan implies." And, "there may be strenuous objection to bonding the city and boosting the tax levy to meet the increased expense," printed in "Group Plan of Cleveland, Ohio," *Architects and Builders Journal* (November 1903): 30. There were comparatively few problems in funding the mall. The main problem was with the railroads and the building of a union station. However, as the public library building had to be the same size as the federal building, this resulted in a greater expenditure than what was anticipated.

120. Charlotte Rumbold, "What a Civic Center Means to the Citizens Who Create It," in *Planning Problems of Town, City and Region, Papers and Discussions at the Twenty-Second National Conference on City Planning* (Philadelphia: Wm. F. Fell, 1930), 196.

121. *The Plain Dealer,* 10 December 1987.

122. Designed by Graham, Anderson, Probst, and White, which was a successor firm of Burnham's. See Walter C. Leedy, Jr., "Cleveland's Terminal Tower – The Van Sweringens' Afterthought," *The Gamut* no. 8 (Winter 1983): 3–26.

CHAPTER 5

FRANK LLOYD WRIGHT AND VICTOR HUGO

SIDNEY K. ROBINSON

When Frank Lloyd Wright sat down to design, he did not look at the blank paper only to conjure up images of buildings. He brought to his architectural task experiences of ideals as well as forms. We would expect him to visualize with the help of things he had seen, but it is surprising when he makes use of a storybook in his work. Throughout his life Wright acknowledged the important things about architecture he had learned from, of all people, the great Romantic writer Victor Hugo. In *Notre Dame de Paris* Wright did not pick out decorative motifs or compositional principles. Instead he found a statement of architecture's place in a cultural context that guided his life's work.

To begin this review of how much Victor Hugo there is in Frank Lloyd Wright, notice the similarities in two bird's-eye descriptions of great metropolises. The first is Chicago seen from the highest office building in the world in 1892:

> Go at nightfall, when all is simplified and made suggestive, to the top of our newest skyscraper, the Masonic Temple. . . . Beneath you is the monster stretching out into the far distance. High overhead hangs a stagnant pall, its fetid breath reddened with light from myriad eyes, endlessly, everywhere blinking. Thousands of acres of cellular tissue outspread, enmeshed by an intricate network of veins, and arteries radiating into the gloom. . . . The

> labored breathing, murmur, clangor, and the roar—how the voice of this monstrous force rises to proclaim the marvel of its structure! . . . Then the darkened pall is gradually lifted and moonlight outlines the shadowy, sullen masses of structure. . . . Remain, to reflect that the texture of the city, this great machine, is the warp upon which will be woven the weft and patterns of the democracy we pray for. Realize that it has been deposited here particle by particle, in blind obedience to law.[1]

So wrote the thirty-four-year-old architect nearly twenty years after he had read Victor Hugo's description of medieval Paris seen from the heights of Notre Dame. Hugo blends the sights of angular roofs closely packed, clinging together between streets rushing down to the river's edge with the sounds of bells making a "symphony with the mighty uproar of a tempest."[2] Seeing the great buildings as "the residuum left by the successive evaporations of human society . . . [as] each wave of time leaves its coating of alluvium,"[3] Hugo asks us to

> look through that amazing forest of spires, towers and steeples; . . . project sharply against an azure horizon the Gothic profile of old Paris; let its outline float in a wintry mist clinging round its numerous chimneys; plunge it in deepest night, and watch the fantastic play of light and shadow in the sombre labyrinth of edifices; cast into it a ray of moonlight, showing it vague and uncertain, with its towers rearing their massive heads above the mists.[4]

One great Romantic echoes another. But it was not only in vivid description of a great city that Wright learned from Hugo's *Notre Dame de Paris* published in 1831. Later in the novel, Hugo inserted a chapter on architecture, which first appeared in the 1832 edition, that Wright, at age ninety, called "the most illuminating essay on architecture yet written."[5] Wright reported that he first read Hugo's *Notre Dame* in Madison before he went to Chicago in 1887.[6] He would mention Hugo from time to time over the next seventy years. Any source encountered in youth that is drawn upon throughout a man's life surely invites close scrutiny. Wright first makes use of Hugo's architectural essay in the 1901 Hull House talk from which the description of Chicago was taken. With some regularity, he returns to it either directly or indirectly whenever he is considering the broad history and significance of architecture, particularly in the 1920s and 1930s when he was much concerned with his impact on the culture of the United States. These instances occur in the professional journals; in his *Autobiography;* in his Princeton lectures, most explicitly in the third lecture, "The Passing of the Cornice"; in *Genius and the Mobocracy;* in *A Testament;* and in interviews.

When Wright first read Hugo, the great French author was enshrined as *the* Romantic writer of Europe, the fervent defender of Napoleon, the enemy of classicism and the creator of *Les Miserables.* His preface to *Cromwell* written when he was twenty-five and the *Hernani* controversy of 1830 had heralded him as an unquenchable literary and political force whose profligate energy carried him beyond his intellectual and formal limitations. Upon Hugo's death in 1885, when Wright was eighteen, American literary and cultural reviews variously assessed his stature. His own excesses were reflected in the adulation accorded him by his bourgeois public. For the *Dial,* published in Chicago, this reverence amounted to "hugolatry."[7] Melville Anderson softened his earlier criticism when his report on Hugo's funeral celebrated his humanitarian radicalism that had helped to make the "19th, the century of the *people.*"[8] At Hugo's death, the Boston-based *Literary World* wondered if Hugo was passé in a time that had displaced romance with analysis.[9] It too had anticipated Hugo's death three years earlier with a long review of his life and work entitled "The Grandfather of Humanity" in which it referred to *Notre Dame* as an "exceedingly powerful romance of Paris."[10] In 1887 *The Chautauquan* ran a twenty-five-page tribute to Hugo, and in 1902 various articles at the centennial of Hugo's birth reconsidered his contribution to the age.[11]

Hugo's effect on the American architectural world rested primarily on his early championship of the Gothic and his lifelong activity on behalf of historical preservation. In 1890 a review of Charles Herbert Moore's book on Gothic architecture began by referring to Hugo's comments on this high point of the art of architecture.[12] Four years later a passage from *Notre Dame* was quoted in support of American preservation efforts.[13] Beyond these scattered references, there was little concern for Hugo in the architectural press, although later, Irving Gill began his 1916 article "The Home of the Future" with a summary of Hugo's insight on the effect printing had on architecture. With nearly direct quotation, Gill went on to restate how architecture is the residue of successive evaporations of human society.[14]

When Wright went to Chicago and joined in the affairs of his uncle's Unitarian congregation, he also joined one of the study groups in reading *Les Miserables* that sent him back, he said, to reread *Notre Dame.*[15] Wright's apprenticeship with Louis Sullivan apparently did not reinforce his earlier contact with the French author; there is little Hugo in Sullivan. But Wright seems to have associated the two in his own mind when he wrote about Sullivan after his death. In June of 1924, Wright's tribute to his "Beloved Master" dwelled on the circumstances surrounding the neglect of Sullivan that forced him to reach the American public through books rather than buildings.[16] The displacement of one form of expression by the other was one of Hugo's most incisive critiques of the modern world. Wright could not ignore the shift but saw it as a challenge to utilize the means of the interloper to reestablish the ancient place of architecture. For Wright the printing press was the prototype of the machine. In the 1924 tribute he wrote that Sullivan was "forced to relinquish his chosen work in architecture, the great art of civilization, . . . and was compelled to win recognition in a medium that is the all-devouring monster of the age."[17] In 1949 when Wright fulfilled his promise to publish a book on Sullivan, he restated Hugo's assessment of the decline of architecture since the invention of printing in the fifteenth century: "The spirit of Architecture was dead. Human thought had found the printed book. The other arts had fled. Printing was the Machine."[18] The Renaissance had originated in the age of printing and lived on because of it. More than once Wright repeated

Hugo's acid phrase that the Renaissance was "the setting sun all Europe mistook for dawn," which first appeared in the famous chapter in *Notre Dame,* "Ceci Tuera Cela."[19] Wright often used two other castigations that Hugo hurled at the Renaissance. According to Hugo the fifteenth-century architect's response to the draining away of social and religious significance from the edifice was to substitute aesthetic image for religious content: "The Cathedral . . . escapes the priest and falls under the dominion of the artist."[20] He cited as an example of the instability resulting from this substitution Michelangelo's piling of the Pantheon on top of the Parthenon in St. Peter's in Rome.[21] Wright enjoyed repeating this disrespectful judgment of an icon of the Renaissance.[22] Hugo went on to characterize neoclassical architecture in terms that Wright would recall when he heaped scorn on the bare-bones International style. For Hugo the buildings of the sixteenth, seventeenth, and eighteenth centuries were nothing more than the bony framework of geometrical outline seen through the skin of an emaciated body. The edifice was reduced to a bare polyhedron.[23]

Wright's identification of the printing press with the machine intensified his ambiguous response to each. He elided the two when he paraphrased Hugo in an interview in the 1950s by saying that the machine destroyed the cathedral. The machine and the printing press could be used positively, but by merely trying to reproduce forms that predated their invention, their effect was to make "available to the poor and needy a cheap or debased form of what was once rare and precious."[24] The multiplicity of their products created a vicarious relation between individuals and words or material objects. "Society becomes consciously literate as the printed book absorbs ever more of the cultural energies of mankind. . . . Life itself became and continues to grow more and more vicarious."[25]

In the Princeton lectures, Wright, who was, in the late twenties, more deeply engaged in writing than in designing, acknowledged that he was "more accustomed to saying things with a hod of mortar and some bricks, or with a concrete mixer and a gang of workmen, than by speaking or writing. I like to write, but always dissatisfied, I, too, find myself often staring at the result with a kind of nausea . . . or is it nostalgia?"[26] Wright's use of the word *nostalgia* is striking. The nostalgia he feels is likely for the original condition of architecture as "the living . . . upstanding expression of reality"[27] that appears to him to be

lost in the words. The condition of nostalgia is the universal longing for original meaning to be right in front of us, not veiled by layers of representation, displacement, and writing. Wright goes on to castigate Vitruvius, Palladio, Vignola, and Vasari for taking up the new printing machine and reproducing architecture, for extending those aspects of buildings that can be captured, albeit very thinly and abstractly, on a page and unnaturally prolonging them beyond their original condition. Their literary efforts simply produced "the propaganda of the dead."[28] The representation that is writing, opposed to the "presence" of a material object, drains meaning from architecture. The impact of the picture on architecture is integrated into the discussion by noting that the "machine by way of the camera today takes the pictorial upon itself as a form of literature."[29]

The repetitiveness of the machine and the dispersal of word and object both fragmented the organic harmony and interdependence of society. Rather than different parts taking their places within an identifiable whole, much as the parts of a building contribute to a unified composition, the machine created a levelled, featureless surface. For both Hugo and Wright, the workings of the community are comparable to the necessary forces of nature that direct the sea, beavers, and bees. In following the law of nature, society resembles a tree whose trunk is the unchanging, underlying order that supports the variable foliage of fancy and symbol. Democracy and the machine replace this grand order with a shapeless swarm of alternatives. Dispersed compositions were shapeless by comparison with premachine compositions that were characterized by their concentration and hierarchy. Wright, however, was able to look beyond the immediate lack of composition to another arrangement that took advantage of the "perfect distribution, like ubiquitous publicity, [that] is a common capacity of the machine."[30] His championing of decentralization for the city was a clear expression of his belief in the ultimate significance of displacement at one scale in order to permit replacement at the individual scale.

Wright and Hugo struggled to combine the freedom of the individual, personified by the poet-architect, with the unity of the people. Hugo ridiculed the conventional, bourgeois world of the 1830s for mistaking regularity for beauty. And yet his popularity rested on his similarity with the average middle-class citizen. For Wright the oppressive doctrine of the common man enforced by a lock-step American democracy stifled individual liberty. The love and fear of the community, the love and fear of the machine, suffused both of these powerful artists.

Hugo's insights in the progress of architecture are not entirely represented by a few observations and memorable phrases. He outlined a far-reaching evolution of architecture beginning with primitive monuments uttering the first letters and syllables of what would become the language of architecture. The evolution of architecture proceeded in three cycles, each one working its way from theocracy to democracy. The cycles had begun in Hindostan, Egypt, and the Romanesque with the expression of authority, unity, and tradition. The cycles culminated in Phoenicia, Greece, and the Gothic with the expression of liberty, imagination, and progress. This evolution was shattered when printing killed architecture. No longer was the most noble record of society to be found in buildings, as Wright paraphrased Hugo in 1901.[31] The printing press presented the democratic phase of society with a tool that placed poetic expression in the hands of each individual. Personal access became possible whenever and wherever it was desired because the book was not unique in space and time, but multiple and portable. Paper received words "as infallibly as the gray matter of the human brain receives the impressions of the senses."[32] It was easier for an individual to express himself in print than in stone. Wright "saw the lifeblood of beloved architecture slowly ebbing, inevitably to be taken entirely away from the building by the book, the book being a more liberal form of expression for human thought. This mechanical invention was to become the channel for thought—because it was more facile and more direct. In the place of the art of architecture was to come literature made ubiquitous."[33] To dramatize the increase in volatility and ubiquity, Hugo had compared architecture to a mountain and printing to a flock of birds.[34] Although he did not specify the kind of birds, one does not imagine eagles or hummingbirds but the great middle class of the bird world. The apparent permanence of stone was replaced by the intangible persistence of the printed word. Wright echoed this in 1937 when he wrote, "the book is to become a means of recording life perhaps more enduring than the great edifice ever was."[35] And yet in the sixth Princeton lecture, he had lamented that a thousand years after the end of American civilization, antiquarians would find in the junk heap of our cities no record "of the cherished PICTURE we are making."[36] If architecture were the writ-

ing of past ages, at least its materiality persisted, its presence was preserved in some apparently direct form. Mobile, immaterial words apparently left no lasting trace. Their persistence was based on reproduction, not on resistance.

The famous chapter in *Notre Dame* helped to focus Wright's ambivalence regarding the machine in the service of architecture. He wanted to believe Hugo's conviction that buildings were the authentic record of humanity. Yet he could not simply ignore the effects of printing. The resolution lay in welcoming the machine to architecture. Machines would reinstate architecture as the rightful expression of democracy. If a machine could make literature the most effective voice of liberty, imagination, and progress, it could do the same for architecture. Hugo provided an analogy between printing and architecture that profoundly affected Wright's view of the role of architecture in the twentieth century. Printing transcended the edifice by replacing the mountain with a flock of birds. Wright would find a way for his architecture to do the same.

In the books explaining Broadacre City, beginning with the 1932 *The Disappearing City,* Wright divided primitive humanity into two opposing camps: the cave dweller and the nomad, paralleling Hugo's opposition between the mountain and the flock of birds. His estimation of these two representatives of mankind displays an ambivalence similar to his response to the architect/poet and the machine/printing press. The cave dweller, "ancient conservative," sought safety in the weight of masonry defenses called cities. The nomad "cultivated mobility for safety" through the use of the adaptable and elusive folding tent. Matter versus space. Wright's desire to have both is embodied in the cantilever: solid core of mass reaching out to the freedom of space. "In the affair of culture, 'shadow-of-the-wall' has so far seemed dominant, although the open sky of the adventurer appeals more and more today to the human spirit."[37] The progression is a corollary to the cycle from theocracy to democracy. It also can be seen as paralleling the two phases of Wright's own career, divided by the period of writing in the late 1920s; the cavelike masses of the Prairie house evolved into the light, folded roofs and walls of the Usonian house.

Before the invention of printing "whoever was born a poet became an architect" according to Hugo and Wright.[38] After the printing press, the individual poet could sing of himself as the representative of his people without having to assemble them in front of the cathedral. Printing had put the words of the poet in the hands of each individual. Architecture in the twentieth century would give each individual his own building. The machines of transportation, communication, and construction would make this dispersal possible. Wright dreamed of filling the land with representatives of an American architecture. Each individual would replace the vicarious experience fostered by the reading of books with the direct experience of personal buildings. Architecture would no longer be the mountain, the great, immobile edifice; it would become the ubiquitous, private house.

Hugo's flock of birds came to roost in Broadacre City.

Notes

This essay is an edited version of a paper delivered to the annual meeting of the Society of Architectural Historians in Madison, Wisconsin, in 1980.

The illustration on page 106 is *Notre Dame de Paris,* Facade Principals fig. 29, from J. Guadet, *Elements et Theorie de l'Architecture,* 1909.

1. Frank Lloyd Wright, *The Future of Architecture* (New York: New American Library, Mentor Book, 1953), 90–92.
2. Victor Hugo, *Notre Dame de Paris,* trans. Jessie Haynes (New York: Heritage Press, 1955), bk. 3, pt. 2, 85.
3. Ibid., pt. 1, 70.
4. Ibid., pt. 2, 84.
5. Frank Lloyd Wright, *A Testament* (New York: Horizon Press, 1957), 17. The chapter inserted by Hugo is "Ceci Tuera Cela," bk. 5, pt. 2.
6. Ibid., 17, and Frank Lloyd Wright, *An Autobiography* (New York: Duell, Sloan and Pearce, 1943), 78.
7. *Dial,* June 1882, 32.
8. Ibid., June 1885, 33–35.
9. *Literary World,* 30 May 1885, 188.
10. Ibid., June 1885, 181–184.
11. *Chautauquan,* May 1897, 115–145.
12. *American Architect and Building News,* 3 May 1890, 72.
13. Ibid., 1 September 1894, 84.
14. Irving J. Gill, "The Home of the Future: The New Architecture of the West," *The Craftsman,* May 1916, 140.
15. Wright, *An Autobiography,* 78.
16. Frank Lloyd Wright, "Louis Henry Sullivan: Beloved Master," *The Western Architect,* June 1924, 64–66.

17. Ibid., 65.
18. Frank Lloyd Wright, *Genius and the Mobocracy* (New York: Duell, Sloan and Pearce, 1949), xii.
19. Hugo, *Notre Dame de Paris,* bk. 5, pt. 2, 116. Wright, *Future of Architecture,* 125.
20. Hugo, *Notre Dame de Paris,* bk. 5, pt. 2, 111.
21. Ibid., 117.
22. Wright, *Future of Architecture,* 163.
23. Hugo, *Notre Dame de Paris,* bk. 5, pt. 2, 117.
24. Frank Lloyd Wright, "In the Cause of Architecture," *Architectural Record,* June 1927, 478.
25. Wright, *Future of Architecture,* 66.
26. Ibid., 80.
27. Ibid., 139.
28. Ibid., 221.
29. Ibid., 116.
30. Ibid., 192.
31. Ibid., 84.
32. Ibid., 91.
33. Ibid., 125.
34. Hugo, *Notre Dame de Paris,* bk. 5, pt. 2, 116.
35. Wright, *Future of Architecture,* 67.
36. Ibid., 197.
37. Frank Lloyd Wright, *The Living City* (New York: Horizon Press, 1958), 22.
38. Wright, *Future of Architecture,* 135; Hugo, *Notre Dame de Paris* bk. 5, pt. 2, 112.

CHAPTER 6

THE WRIGHT SPACE

The Parti of the Prairie House

GRANT HILDEBRAND

> Figural architecture, hence, does not consist of casual inventions, but of typical elements which may be repeated, combined and varied. We have already suggested that the typical elements are not just a matter of convention, but represent basic ways of being between earth and sky. They are given with the world, like spoken language, and the task of the architect consists in making them appear at the right moment and in the right place.
>
> Christian Norberg-Schulz
> *The Concept of Dwelling*

From 1900 to 1909 Frank Lloyd Wright developed a particular relationship of typical elements—fireplaces, walls, ceilings, glazing, and terraces—that comprised the major spaces of his houses. He used this particular relationship, which we could call a parti, for the rest of his life for reasons that to him must have been intuitive but that now can be more consciously described and understood.

In about 1900 Wright designed four houses of extraordinary interest. Three of them, the Warren Hickox and Harley Bradley houses in Kankakee, Ill., and the first *Ladies Home Journal* house (figs. 6.1, 6.2, 6.3), all have their fireplaces at the center of the plan, as by no means did a majority of Wright's prior houses. The fireplace in turn determines the interior edge of the living room. On each flank of the fireplace the living room opens to contiguous spaces. Opposite the fireplace is a wall of windows and glazed french doors; beyond this is a generous terrace. Thus, these three houses repeat a particular relationship of particular architectural elements.

The fourth of the interesting designs of 1900, that is the second *Ladies Home Journal* house, the "Small House with Lots of Room in It" varies the theme. There are two fireplaces, one for living, one for dining (fig. 6.4). As in the other three houses

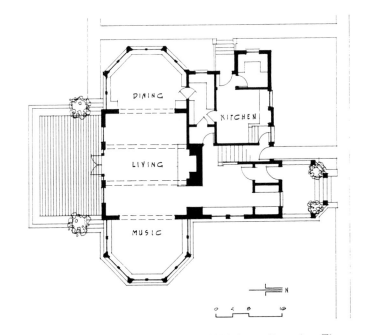

Fig. 6.1. Warren Hickox house, Kankakee, 1900, lower floor plan. The fireplace is the black **U**-shaped element located at the approximate center of the plan, as it will be in most of Wright's houses hereafter. (Grant Hildebrand)

113

they are at the center of the plan and at the inner edges of the rooms they serve. But each now is shown with an adjacent seat and screen on the flank that creates a kind of half-inglenook. The sectional perspective of this house also shows a lowered ceiling over the living room fireplace and its half-inglenook. The organization is asymmetrical. The passage to dining slides away from the living room fireplace zone. Terraces open from both living and dining rooms.

Fig. 6.2. Harley Bradley house, Kankakee, 1900, lower floor plan. (Grant Hildebrand)

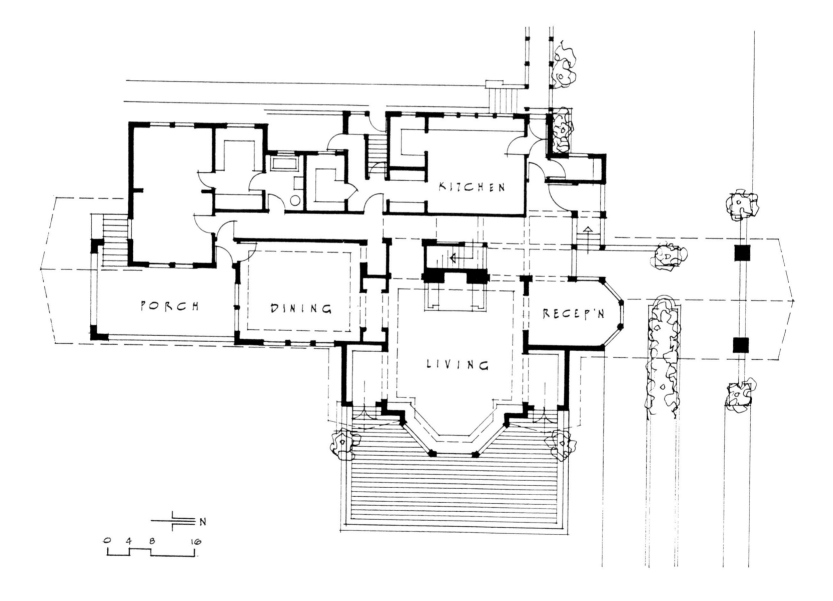

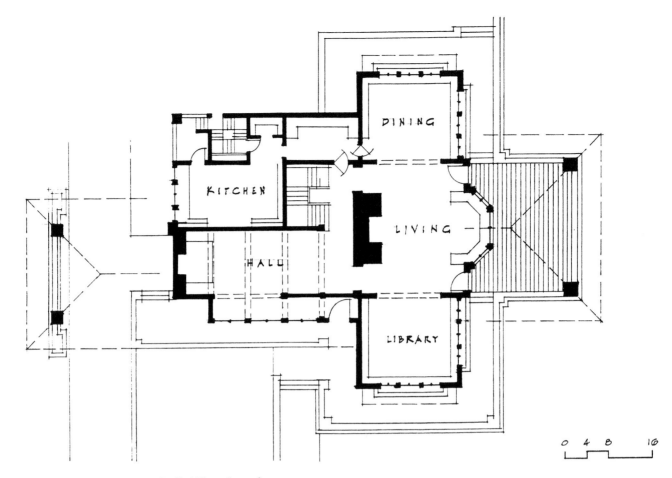

Fig. 6.3. Project: "A Home in a Prairie Town," for *Ladies' Home Journal*, February 1901. (Grant Hildebrand)

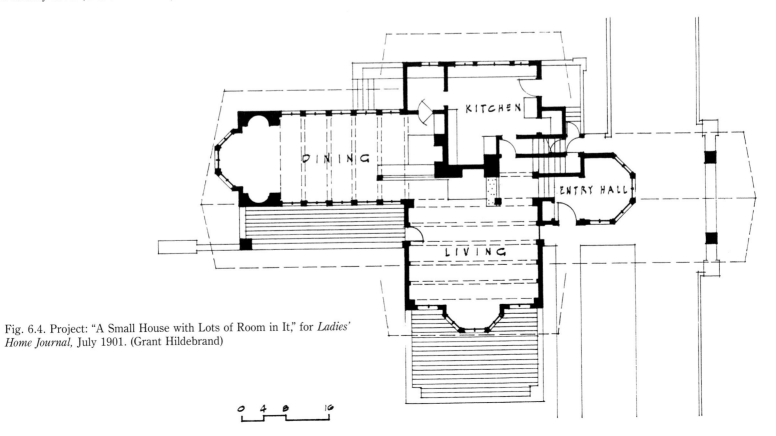

Fig. 6.4. Project: "A Small House with Lots of Room in It," for *Ladies' Home Journal*, July 1901. (Grant Hildebrand)

The organization put forward in this project was built, almost verbatim, in the house for Ward Willits in 1901 in Highland Park, Ill. (fig. 6.5). The differences are only in nuance. The polygonal projection of the living room is gone; vast rows of french doors are used from both the living and dining rooms to their terraces; ceilings are lowered over both fireplaces; and the terrace/porch off dining involves a more fluid and dramatic geometry. On the upper floor the master bedroom repeats the organization yet again (fig. 6.6).

Fig. 6.5. Ward Willits house, Highland Park, 1901, lower floor plan; compare with figure 6.4. (Grant Hildebrand)

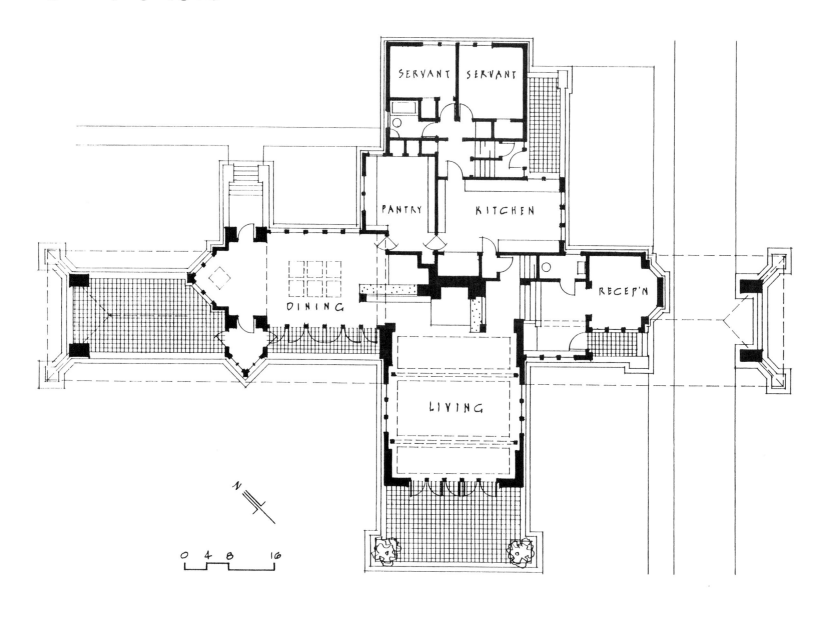

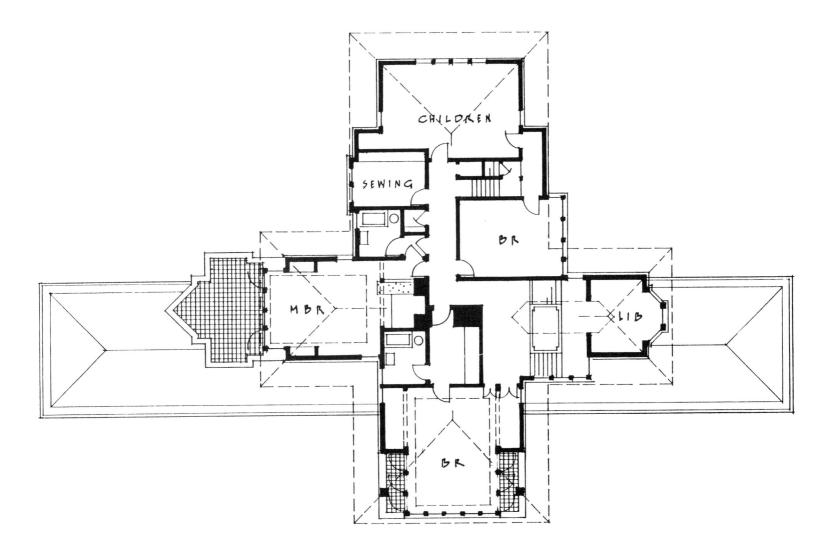

Fig. 6.6. Willits house, upper floor plan; master bedroom at left.
(Grant Hildebrand)

As in almost all other multistory houses, including all earlier ones in Wright's career, at the Willits house the major spaces are on the lower floor. This of course means that ceilings are more or less flat because of the floor above. There is some manipulation for change of height, but in the end there is necessarily a restricted ability to juxtapose and dramatize low and high spaces. There is evidence from all of Wright's subsequent career, and from his immediately subsequent major house, that he wanted to be free of this limitation. In fact in the first *Ladies Home Journal* house he had tried to solve the problem by opening the lower floor living room right up to the roof, but he himself noted that this was at the expense of two omitted bedrooms.

This constraint was broken in the design of the house for Arthur Heurtley in Oak Park, done perhaps just a very few months after the Willits house. In it Wright grasped the nettle of two-story house composition. For the first time in his work, and contrary to overwhelming precedent in the Western world, he thrust the major spaces up to the second floor, and so put them directly under the roof (fig. 6.7). Having put them there at

Heurtley, he kept them there for nearly every major work public and private for the remainder of his life. From here on it is almost true that if the major space is not contiguous to the roof the building is not by Wright. The advantage is apparent at the first usage in the Heurtley house. The living and dining rooms can and do borrow their ceiling configuration from the roof form. Thus the ceilings of these spaces can be significantly higher at the center, thereby contrasting and dramatizing the lowness of the edges (fig. 6.8). This attribute is conjoined at Heurtley with a revisiting of the essential plan relationships of Willits. Thus at Heurtley we have arrived at the parti: major spaces directly under the roof, their ceilings echoing the roof planes; fireplace deep in the heart of the building, its withdrawal emphasized by a low ceiling edge and enfolding accouterments; flanking and opposite walls open to the adjacent space and to glass and glazed doors; and a contiguous elevated terrace beyond. These characteristics are contained within a shell, the outer reflection of the parti, whose features are a deep overhanging roof, a central chimney, horizontal groupings of window bands, and conspicuous balconies (fig. 6.9).

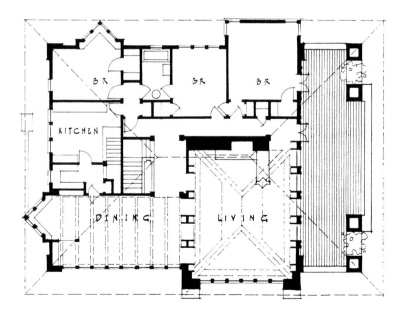

Fig. 6.7. Arthur Heurtley house, Oak Park, 1902, plans: (*left*), lower floor; (*right*), upper floor, with dining and living spaces to the front and terrace to the far right. (Grant Hildebrand)

Fig. 6.8. Heurtley house, living room with fireplace. The dining room and stairhead are to the left; the terrace opens to the right.
(By permission of Domino's Pizza Collection, Ann Arbor, Mich.)

Fig. 6.9. Heurtley house, exterior from sidewalk. The broad sweep of windows above the entrance arch is that of the dining room; the living room is to the right; at the extreme right, under the broad roof, is the terrace. (By permission of Special Collections Division, University of Washington Libraries, UW Neg. 9066)

This parti can be found in almost all of Wright's subsequent domestic work. In work by architects other than Wright, however, including even his own Prairie School colleagues, the parti in all its characteristics is so rare as to be nonexistent. Thus it constitutes a formal and spatial theme particular to Wright. As such it has historic and stylistic interest, but because it anticipates recent work in basic human choices of setting, it has broader significance as well.

The role of the fireplace, a key element in the parti, as symbol in a primordial sense is obvious, of course, and accounts for its continued popularity in houses generally, not only by Wright but by almost everyone else and even where its practical use is unlikely. But the hold it had on Wright's concept of dwelling was also obviously strong; it is a universal element in his domestic work. However, as these early examples show, he does not simply include it, he also composes all the other features leading outward from it in a particular and repetitive way that can now be seen to have fundamental meaning.

Christian Norberg-Schulz comments on this phenomenon: "Traditionally the human dwelling had been a refuge for the individual and the family. Wright wanted rootedness *and* freedom, and thus he destroyed the traditional 'box' and created a new interaction between inside and outside."[1] "Thus he opened up his plans to make them interact with the environment, at the same time as he created an inner world of protection and comfort."[2] These observations, though, do not take us much further than Wright's own statements of his intentions. More help is to be had from the recent work of Jay Appleton, working in the cognate field of meaning in landscape.

In 1975 Appleton outlined in *The Experience of Landscape* what has since become known as prospect-refuge theory.[3] Appleton argued that in landscapes chosen for human pleasure, as evidenced by designed landscapes, landscape paintings, and landscape-describing literature, certain characteristics occur across all cultures and across time, characteristics that he calls prospect and refuge. By prospect he means the unimpeded opportunity to see, thus the broad vista across land or water or both. Refuge is the opportunity to hide while at the same time being able to view the access to prospect, thus the sheltering grove, the cave, or the hill-pocketed ravine. Appleton further argues that while these characteristics pervasively occur in landscapes chosen, designed, or recorded for pleasure, they

were, deep in time, characteristics that served species-survival purposes. The prospect was the hunting or fishing space; the refuge was protection from our natural enemies. These characteristics are complementary; their juxtaposition yields an experience that can be summarized by the phrase "to see without being seen." Appleton points out, however, that as with other survival behaviors the choice is made, necessarily, not because of an awareness of any survival value but because the behavior provides pleasure or relief of discomfort. Thus Appleton is led to the conclusion that the choice of these fundamental and pervasive conditions of setting is not a result of culture, nor of aesthetics in any narrow sense, but is a part of our species-wide, pleasure-choosing genetic makeup.

Appleton's theory is related to habitat theory and as such should be considered in relation to architecture generally and houses particularly, though Appleton does so only briefly and with reference to their role as objects in the landscape. But a survey of well-known examples of house architecture from any period does not particularly show the prospect and refuge characteristics described by Appleton. Yet when one turns to Wright, the architectural manifestation is clear and consistent, and especially in that large part of his career that begins with the Heurtley house.

Houses, even the rudest huts or tents, offer the function of refuge and, given any opening at all, the function of prospect as well. But if Appleton is right, our predilections are based not only nor even primarily on the functional provision of these characteristics but on indications of the potential for doing so. Thus we may say that our pleasure, or a fundamental part of our pleasure in houses may be found not only in the refuge and prospect they offer us but in the signals they give of their ability to do so. Appleton notes particular external features of architecture that signal its refuge potential: "windows, alcoves, recesses, balconies, heavy overhanging eaves—all these suggest a facility of penetration into the refuge. Even if actual access is not practicable the suggestion of accessibility can stimulate the idea of refuge."[4] An emphasis on these features is a hallmark of Wright's work. At the Heurtley house they are already modeled with unique insistence (fig.6.9). And Heurtley conveys other refuge signals, especially the cave-mouth entry, itself given refuge by the masonry promontory that is the porch. Clearly, however, several of these features can also signal prospect. The horizontally grouped stretches of windows, the balconies, even the entry promontory, all convey the potential for panoramic view from within. And again such features emphatically handled are hallmarks of Wright's work.

As these exterior features signal prospect and refuge, interior features can signal these characteristics too. If we enter the interior of the Heurtley house, then, through the cave-mouth, we ascend through several right-angle turns and at the head of the stair find ourselves on axis with the fireplace at the heart of the structure. The fireplace focuses an interior refuge zone, – low, intimate, screened, and dark. It would be easy to call it a cave, but the word has to be used with care, as it can also denote a cold, damp, dark cavern. The presence of a fire, or the apparent potential for a fire, is therefore of essential importance in making the interior refuge suggest reassurance and comfort. This fire element, not a part of Appleton's theory, thus is necessary when one extends that theory to architecture. At Heurtley, Wright emphasizes the potential for this reassuring fire by the monumental treatment given to the fireplace. Thus the cave-refuge is inferred as habitable through strong signals of warmth and light. Above the fireplace, the ceiling ascends; to the north are openings to dining. These living and dining spaces, thus linked by vista, with higher ceilings and glass on three sides, are the interior architectural equivalent of prospect. Opposite the vista to dining, the living room opens by glazed french doors to the large terrace, the exterior architectural equivalent of prospect, which commands from its elevated surface the landscape prospect beyond. The occupant, having entered the interior of the larger refuge that is the house itself, therefore has, from within, an orchestrated sequence of spatial options from interior refuge to interior prospect to exterior prospect.

Heurtley is an example of Wright's well-known interest in the open plan. There is no solid wall between living and dining, nor between the living space and the entry condition leading to it. Transitions between spaces are articulated by freestanding architectural elements that clarify spatial transitions but offer no impediment to free passage from one space to another. The terrace is visible through the french doors, and the landscape beyond through ubiquitous glazing. Appleton's comments on choice between prospect and refuge are germane: "If the eye makes a spontaneous assessment of the environment as a strategic theater for survival, this must include some assessment of the opportunity for movement between the various key positions in the prospect-refuge complex."[5] Was the open plan created out of an intuitive sense of this need? Thus Heurtley marks in Wright's career the first appearance of a parti that will hereafter be pervasive in his work; and that can be seen to consist of a cohesive sequence of humanistically meaningful conditions.

In the design of the Edwin Cheney house of 1904, also in Oak Park, he repeats the parti with several important refinements. Entry to Cheney reinforces the idea of refuge in a way analogous to but different from Heurtley. One makes a right-angle turn off the sidewalk (fig. 6.10), then up six steps, a walk of twelve feet or so, up two more steps, and under the eave, another right-angle turn and then another, and the front door is reached, on axis with the fireplace cave; the whole process has entailed perhaps seventy-five to eighty feet of walking, eleven risers, and 360 degrees of turning. Having traversed this long sequence one arrives at the very heart and core of the house. Thus the refuge is a secret place, approached by an intricate process of revelation.

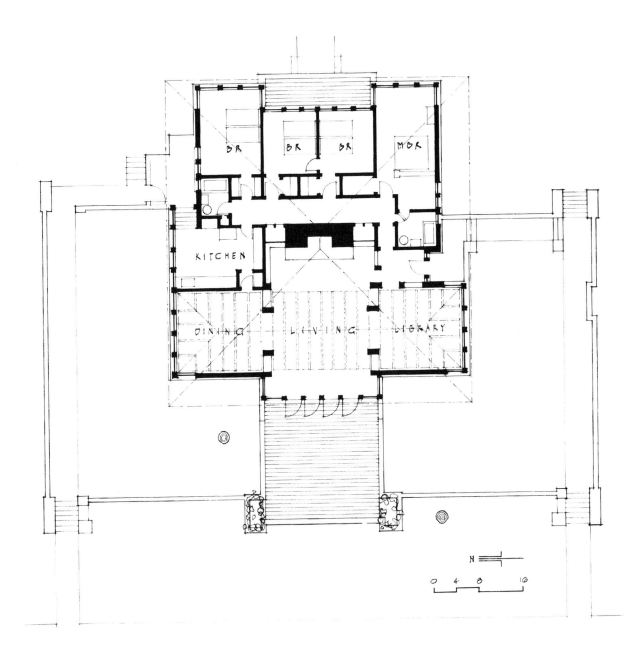

Fig. 6.10. Edwin Cheney house, Oak Park, 1904, upper (main) floor plan.
(Grant Hildebrand)

Fig. 6.11. Cheney house, living room toward fireplace. (Christian Staub, with permission)

Fig. 6.12. Cheney house, interior prospect: the vista across the three living spaces. (Christian Staub, with permission)

The Cheney house is in plan closer to Hickox than to Heurtley. But the plan and, equally importantly, the section, are modified to develop the parti. The fireplace in the living room is withdrawn behind the edges of the adjacent dining room and library. It lies under a low flat ceiling (fig. 6.11). To right and left the immediate fireplace zone does not open to contiguous spaces but is contained by solid book-lined walls creating a refuge, and a particularly powerful one, at the very core of the house. One moves forward from this refuge into the living room proper, whose ceiling planes again echo those of the roof above. But these planes continue uninterrupted to right and left into dining room and library, uniting the three spaces and extending the eye into them, establishing a prospect condition between them (fig. 6.12). At the edges of this ceiling, and especially in the zone of the french doors leading out from the living room, the height returns to that of the fireplace refuge and like the fireplace refuge includes an area of flat ceiling (fig. 6.13). Thus within the house itself there is a microcosm of the refuge-prospect sequence, more fully developed than that of Heurtley, while in a larger sense the interior, with its low edges all around, is itself again a refuge.

Fig. 6.13. Cheney house, living room toward french doors to terrace. (John Savo, with permission)

At this larger level of consideration, the french doors opposite the fire open out to the exterior prospect condition, the terrace as an architectural meadow (fig. 6.14). Here too there is a development beyond that of the Heurtley terrace. At Heurtley the terrace is entirely covered by the great roof whose eaves project well beyond; at Cheney the roof, a concise square, overhangs the french doors only slightly. As one moves out onto the terrace, therefore, the prospect is expanded not only laterally but vertically. It also offers a contrast in light quality not available at Heurtley. For as one moves from the Cheney living room out onto the terrace one moves from dark to light. Darkness, as Appleton notes, is associated with not being seen and therefore with refuge—do we need any further explanation for the often-noted darkness of Wright's interiors?—while light is associated with seeing and therefore with prospect. Thus this manipulation of the terrace condition not only releases sky views but intensifies the contrast between refuge and prospect. Here too Wright seems to have had an intuitive sensitivity to the value of this condition; hereafter his terraces are typically partly roofed, partly open.

Fig. 6.14. Cheney house, diagrammatic drawing. (William Hook)

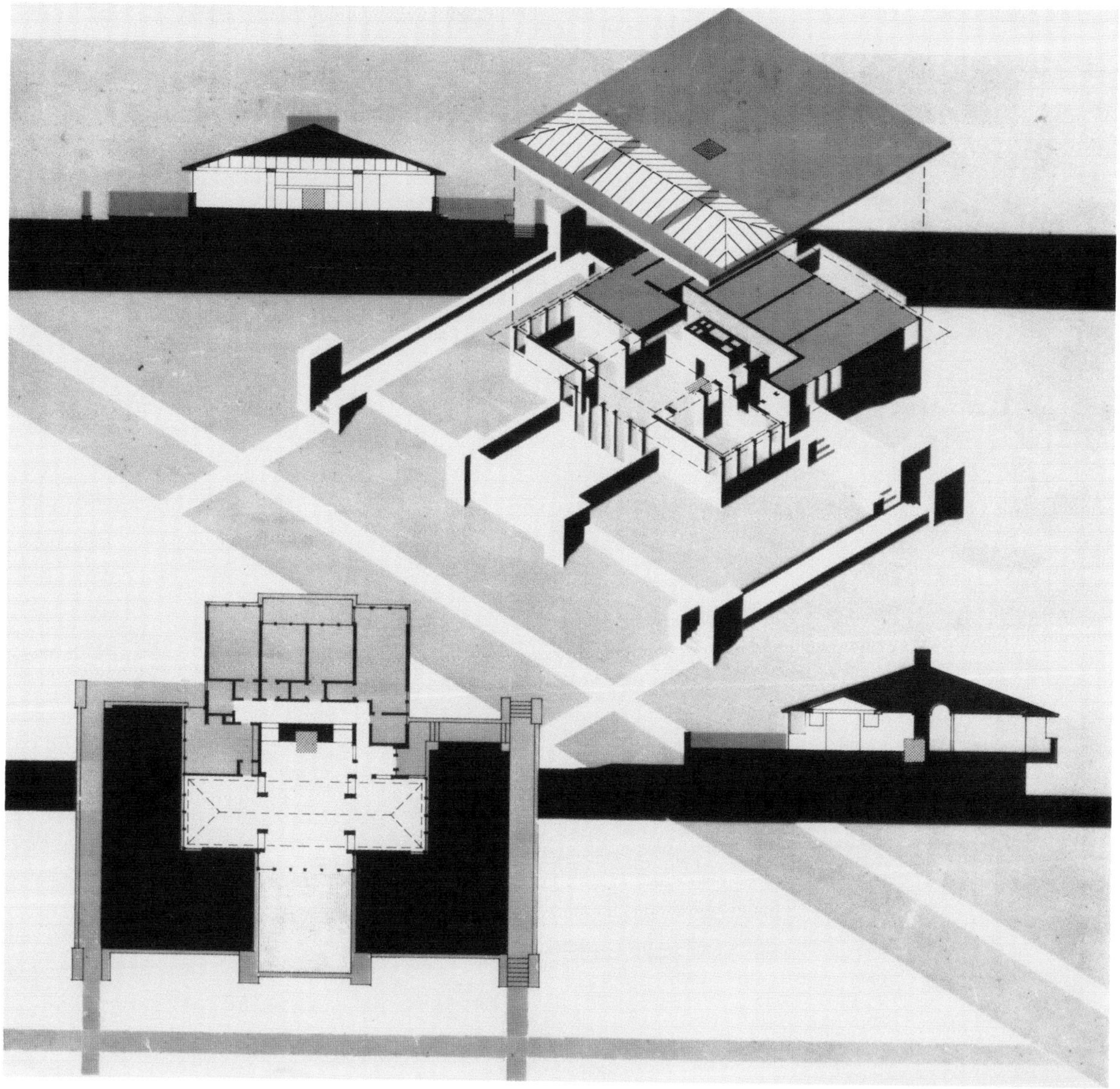

Having pushed the major spaces up under the roof at Heurtley, at Cheney, Wright brings these major spaces nearer the earth. The main floor is only about five feet above grade. Since Cheney lies much closer to the sidewalk than either Willits or Heurtley, and since, like them, its street-facing wall is largely glass, necessary for the conditions of the parti, Wright here had to solve a problem of privacy. By bringing the terrace wall out toward the sidewalk, and by locating the coping of its solid brick parapet over seven feet above sidewalk level, Wright controlled the sight line from the near sidewalk so that it intercepts the lower edge of leaded glass in the french doors to the terrace (fig. 6.15).[6] This brick parapet wall originally extended across the entire lot, ensuring privacy to the whole house and from diagonal as well as frontal views. This was essential, of course, to the development of refuge within a small, low house near a city street. Yet standing anywhere in the living room one sees the trees and houses on the opposite side of the street, so that privacy is controlled while prospect is retained; one can see without being seen.

The house for the Avery Coonleys in Riverside was done perhaps three years later than Cheney. It is much larger, and its plan is far more extensive (fig. 6.16). As at Heurtley and Cheney, Wright has raised the main floor. As at Cheney one moves through a series of ascending right-angle turns, but at the head of the stair is vista to right and left. One negotiates three more turns and arrives in the great living room. The fireplace, as demanded by the parti, is at the room's inner edge, pocketed by the high railings that edge the stairs to either side (fig. 6.17). The pocket thus created is lined with books below and an arboreal mural above on either side of the brick fireplace itself. From this the grand ceiling rises, now completely congruent with the roof planes above. Walter Creese has recently remarked that "the ceiling panels may represent the spreading clouds of the prairie sky, or the branches of Olmsted's trees."[7] Perhaps they are both. The space, considered as a hierarchical enlargement of the fireplace cave-refuge, thus becomes a gentler grove-refuge, in which the lighted edge-panels and the skylights of the adjacent hall ceilings suggest the light of the sky sifted through the branches of the grove. Within this interpretation the appropriateness of the arboreal mural flanking the fireplace is obvious.

Fig. 6.15. Cheney house, section showing sight lines toward and from the living room. (Grant Hildebrand and William Hook)

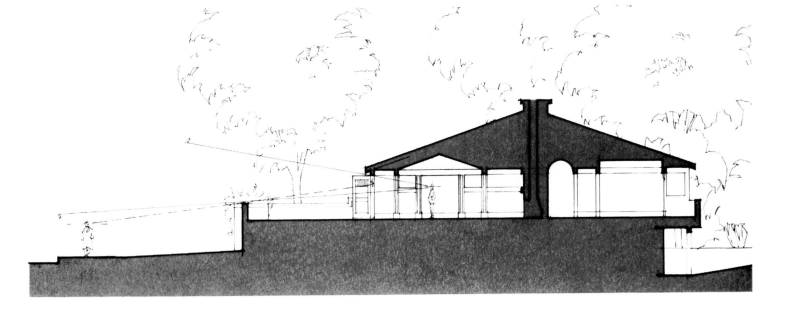

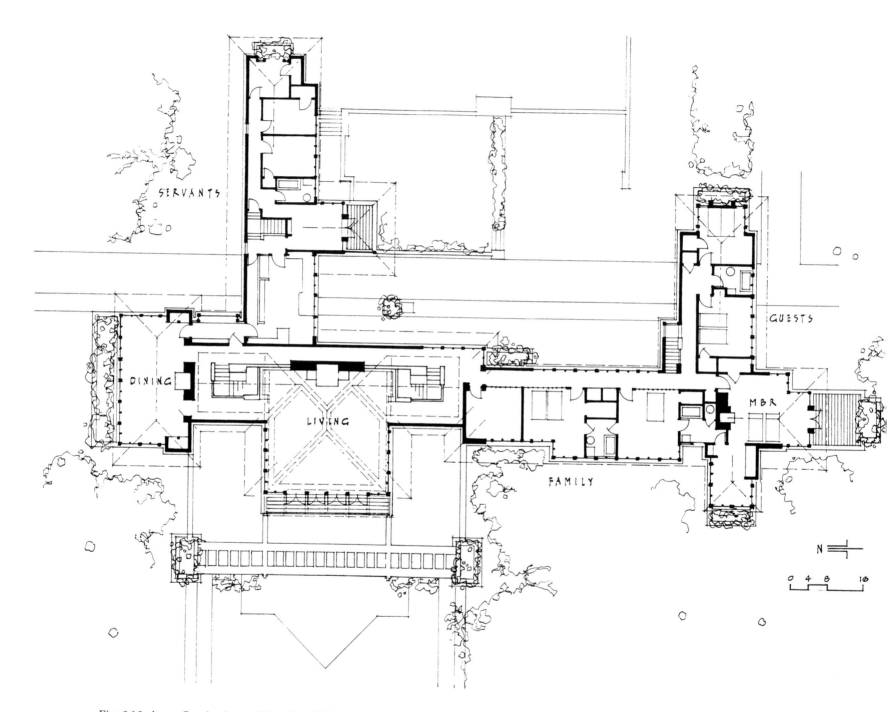

Fig. 6.16. Avery Coonley house, Riverside, 1906–1907, upper (main) floor plan. Entry is from extreme left on the floor below; one then ascends the stair to left of the living room. (Grant Hildebrand)

Fig. 6.17. Coonley house, living room toward fireplace. (By permission of Domino's Pizza Collection, Ann Arbor, Mich.)

Fig. 6.18. Coonley house, living room toward garden. (From Walter L. Creese, *The Crowning of the American Landscape: Eight Great Spaces and Their Buildings.* Copyright © 1985 by Princeton University Press. Reprinted by permission of Princeton University Press.)

Fig. 6.19. Coonley house, the view from the living room toward the garden. (From Walter L. Creese, *The Crowning of the American Landscape: Eight Great Spaces and Their Buildings.* Copyright © 1985 by Princeton University Press. Reprinted by permission of Princeton University Press.)

Fig. 6.20. Frederick Robie house, Chicago, 1909, exterior from southwest. (By permission of Domino's Pizza Collection, Ann Arbor, Mich.)

Like the preceding examples, the plan of Coonley is open; the eye can be carried out from the living room to the skylit hallways and stairwells, though actual movement is held away from the fireplace pocket. These low hallways lead to dining and bedroom pavilions, expansive and bright; movement is analogous to that of a woodland path leading from glade to glade.

Opposite the fire, at the edge of the ceiling/grove, three walls of glass open to the prospect of the house's own extensive grounds and Olmsted's Riverside beyond (fig. 6.18). Yet there were originally only modest planting boxes beyond these windows and no terraces. It has always seemed to me that, as in the photos of the original scheme, these are much missed. Wright may have felt this too, because eventually he added the pergola to suggest horizontal extension of the floor plane toward the horizon, and later still removed the planting boxes and replaced the windows with floor-to-eave french doors leading to a real terrace (fig. 6.19). This of course means that although originally the Coonley design lacked an element of the parti, ultimately it did not; in fact in the final version the parti is realized completely and with unprecedented richness.

The master bedroom pavilion at the terminus of the long bedroom wing, is, like that at Willits, a miniature version of the parti (fig. 6.16). This master bedroom was the one space of the original scheme to have had a terrace, called in early drawings a porch, which like Cheney was open to the prospect enrichment of the sky.

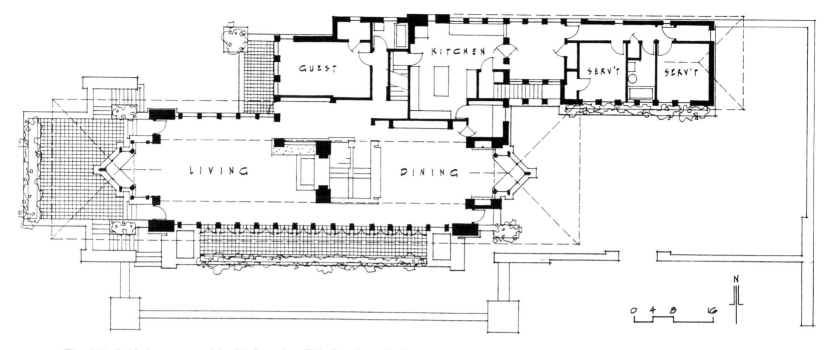

Fig. 6.21. Robie house, second (main) floor plan. This floor is reached from the lower entry floor by the stair adjacent to the fireplace. The stair at upper center leads to third-floor bedrooms. (Grant Hildebrand)

Wright's other great terminal masterpiece of the early period, the Frederick Robie house of 1908–1910, in Chicago, handles the parti differently. The exterior presents extraordinarily strong refuge-signals; deep overhanging eaves, balconies, window groupings, recesses, alcoves (fig. 6.20). It is common knowledge that for this house Wright chose to make living and dining a single architectural unit; on the exterior as seen from the south no division whatever is apparent. Thus the sweep of balconies and glass is more extensive than at Heurtley or Cheney, and more forcefully modelled too. The anchoring chimney signals the potential for fire. And, as at Heurtley, the window groupings and balconies suggest the potential of panoramic prospect as well, a suggestion reinforced by the vigorous outward-thrusting eave line just above the windows. As at Cheney the approach is circuitous, around to what inevitably reads as the back of the house, then up the usual twisting ascent flanking the fireplace mass. One arrives, again, at the very heart of the structure (fig. 6.21).

The fireplace is freestanding. There is not here, as there is at Cheney or Coonley, any spatial pocket defined by flanking full or partial walls (fig. 6.22). Wright used such freestanding fire-places rather often in his early period; other examples are the Gridley, Evans, Hardy, Martin, and Tomek houses, the latter a prototype of Robie. The effect in all such cases is to weaken the refuge characteristic, as it is more difficult to group sitting provisions around the fire. But at Robie the urge toward spatial unification, presumably, also led Wright to continue the living room ceiling and wall conditions through to the dining room without interruption, even parting the fireplace mass itself to allow the ceiling plane to be seen as continuous. This meant, of course, that the usual lower ceiling edge over fireplace could not happen here. And therefore the fireplace is doubly limited in its ability to suggest a refuge. Perhaps as compensation Wright provided the flanking screen/seat fixture of the Heurtley plan projecting from the north pier of the fireplace. This is now gone, but even in place it cannot have been fully effective, as it would have faced, and been rather close to, the continuous glazed french doors to the south. In the dining room the extraordinarily powerful enclosing character of the dining furniture is partial compensation, and perhaps intuitively was intended to be so, a room within a room, refuge within openness for the family at mealtime (fig. 6.23).

132

Fig. 6.22. Robie house, living room toward fireplace; an old photograph showing the half-inglenook seat. Stair and dining are beyond the fireplace. (By permission of the College of Architecture and Urban Planning, University of Michigan)

Fig. 6.23. Robie house, the dining room looking toward the stair. (By permission of Domino's Pizza Collection, Ann Arbor, Mich.)

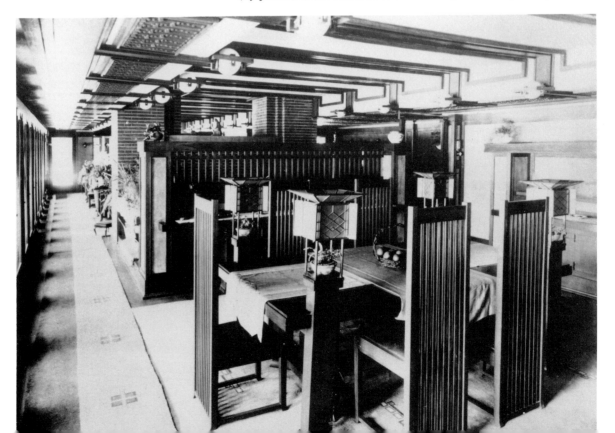

The containing ceiling rises, as usual, at the center, with low edges. The french doors to the south, and the prowlike projection to the west, lead to the ubiquitous terraces. Both of these are again only partly roofed, and one of the more unforgettable experiences at the Robie House is to go out to either of these and feel the power of release from the pressure of the low soffits to the expanse of the sky and trees. This experience must have been even more powerful in 1910, when the planter boxes, now empty and forlorn, would have softened a view that in those early days extended all the way to the old Exposition Midway two blocks to the south.

Like Cheney, the Robie house is close to a city street. Thus privacy, provided at Coonley by the sheer size of the site, had here to be dealt with again by manipulation of the architectural material. Robie himself put it tersely: "I wanted to be able to look out and down the street to my neighbors without having them invade my privacy."[8] Wright, working again through careful attention to section, managed this issue with precision and elegance (fig. 6.24). The parapet wall of the south terrace, solid as at Cheney but unlike Coonley, is disposed to intercept exactly a sight line from the center of the near sidewalk; a view from that position sees only the wood trim of the tops of the french doors and no glass at all of the main floor spaces. This can hardly be accidental, as the planter forward of the upstairs bedroom does exactly the same thing, to the inch.

Fig. 6.24. Robie house, section showing sight lines toward and from the living room. (Grant Hildebrand and William Hook)

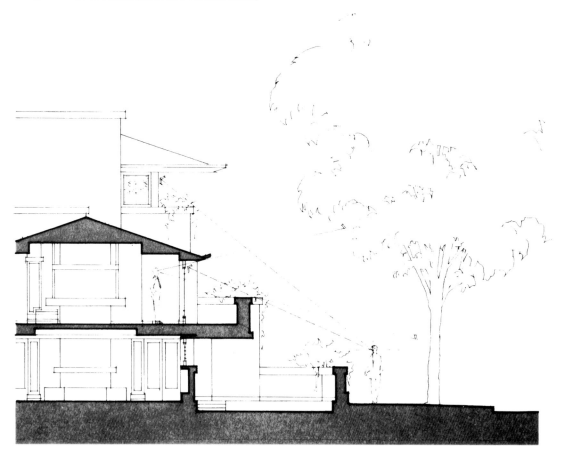

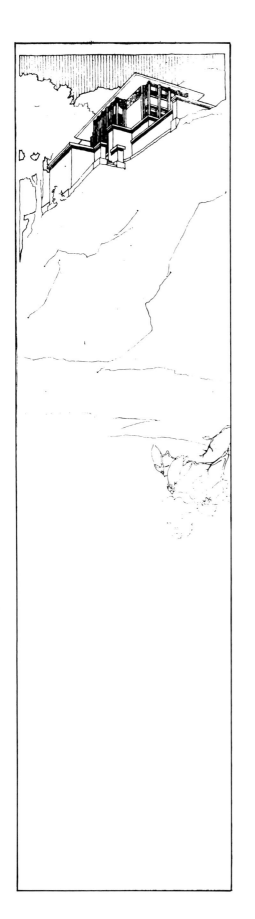

The Robie house, then, at least originally, was an exquisite platform for prospect and, taken as a whole, was meticulously managed to provide refuge from a busy public thoroughfare. The smaller refuge within the house however, the zone around the fireplace, is atypically weak in the context of Wright's work generally. Gaston Bachelard, writing before Appleton's work, describes the mood of refuge in his book *The Poetics of Space.* He first quotes Henri Bachelin, describing his childhood house:

> At these moments, I felt strongly—and I swear to this—that we were cut off from the little town, from the rest of France, and from the entire world. I delighted in imagining . . . that we were living in the heart of the wood, in the well-heated hut of charcoal burners; I even hoped to hear wolves sharpening their claws on the heavy granite slab that formed our doorstep. But our house replaced the hut for me, it sheltered me from hunger and cold; and if I shivered, it was merely from well-being.

Bachelard himself continues:

> Thus, the author attracts us to the center of the house as though to a center of magnetic force, into a major zone of protection. He has only to give a few touches to the spectacle of the family sitting-room, only to listen to the stove roaring in the evening stillness, while an icy wind blows against the house, to know that at the house's center, in the circle of light shed by the lamp, he is living in the round house, the primitive hut, of prehistoric man.[9]

Fig. 6.25. Thomas Hardy house, Racine, 1905, perspective from the lake. (From *Ausgeführte Bauten und Entwürfe von Frank Lloyd Wright,* Wasmuth, Berlin, 1910. Courtesy of Special Collections Division, University of Washington Libraries, UW 9064-A)

It is just this sensation that is so easy to project into the Cheney and Coonley houses, and so difficult to feel at the Robie house. The fireplace zone is too open, an island rather than a cave. Nor is there the fluid ambience of Coonley. It is a cliche that the Robie house is a free and open spatial exercise, and from one point of view there is truth in this. But it is a stiff freedom, more rigorous and more relentless than at Coonley.[10] It is impossible to experience here the Coonley sensation of movement along woodland paths between sun-dappled glades. Were these the reasons why, in spite of the unmatched drama of the Robie exterior, Wright claimed the Coonley house as his own favorite of those early years, the "most successful of my houses from my standpoint"?[11] In any event we have to agree with him not only from his standpoint but from ours; the Coonley house is the perfection of Wright's early prospect-refuge parti.

There is a cognate series of houses of this period, all on hillside sites, that have a story of their own in modifying the parti. The first of these is the Thomas Hardy house of Racine in 1905. This house is the subject of one of the most famous of Wright's drawings, the orientalized view from the lake that so dramatizes the precipitous character of the site (fig. 6.25). Such a site raises a real problem for the parti: the terrace cannot extend from the living room opposite the fireplace without cutting off the view downward, in this case to the lake. The Hardy house is a wonderfully vertical composition of spaces, unusual in Wright's domestic work and especially so at this early date. He modifies the parti in a way that is exactly appropriate. The terrace is displaced downward in the spatial stacking, opening opposite the fireplace of the lower dining room rather than that of the living room (figs. 6.26, 6.27). Thus the parti is more or less maintained. The living room lacks the horizontal extension of its floor plane, but since the terrace is seen from any point near the windows there is partial compensation, and the prospect to lake is ensured.

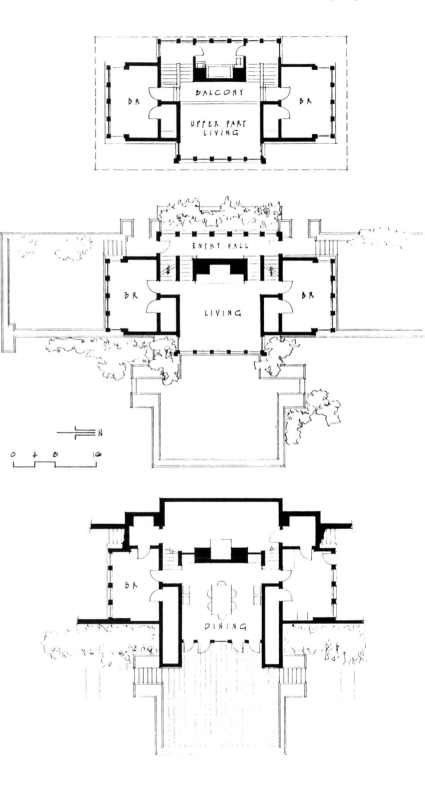

Fig. 6.26. Hardy house, plans. (Grant Hildebrand)

The W. A. Glasner house of about the same year, in Glencoe, also had to deal with the problem of a hillside view toward which the living room faces. But unlike Hardy, Glasner is of one level of axially disposed major spaces. Therefore the terrace cannot reasonably be moved downward. The Glasner terrace is displaced to one side as an entry porch, though it is unsatisfactory: awkward, almost grotesque as entry, and so small that it has no hope of counting as prospect (fig. 6.28). Its only redeeming feature is that it avoids blocking the living room view (fig. 6.29). Was the intended but unexecuted "tea house" Wright's attempt to provide a second prospect-claiming feature to counter the inadequacies of this porch?

Fig. 6.27. Hardy house, perspective. (From *Ausgeführte Bauten und Entwürfe von Frank Lloyd Wright,* Wasmuth, Berlin, 1910. Courtesy of Special Collections Division, University of Washington Libraries)

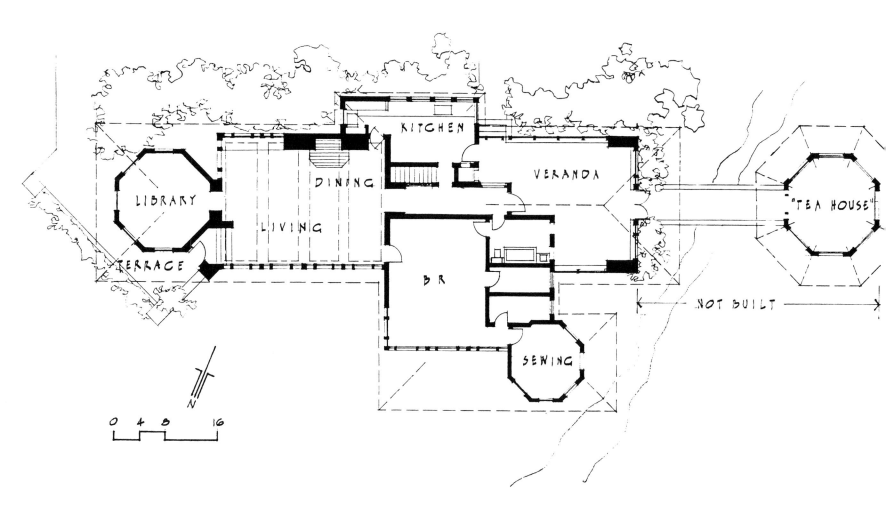

Fig. 6.28. W. A. Glasner house, Glencoe, 1905, main floor plan.
(Grant Hildebrand)

Fig. 6.29. Glasner house, perspective. (From *Ausgeführte Bauten und Entwürfe von Frank Lloyd Wright,* Wasmuth, Berlin, 1910. Courtesy of special Collections Division, University of Washington Libraries, UW 9061–A)

Unsatisfactory though the Glasner terrace is, it is a cousin to the laterally located terrace of the Heurtley house, and it leads on to a number of houses that use this lateral disposition advantageously. The well-known Isabel Roberts house of 1908, in River Forest (fig. 6.30), and its larger progeny the Frank Baker house in Wilmette, of 1909, both use the lateral terrace to keep distance from the street; unlike Cheney or Robie both have a floor level near grade so that privacy could not be had by parapet manipulations.

And a laterally disposed terrace was proposed for the great McCormick project of about 1907. The site was similar to Hardy, a magnificent lakeside bluff. Blockage of views from main spaces would have been unthinkable. The enormous terrace therefore was to be placed between living and dining pavilions and accessible from the flank of each through a connecting loggia (fig. 6.31). This family of terrace conditions can be compared with the terraces of the Cheney-Coonley-Robie family as evidence in each case of Wright's sensitivity to site-specific management of prospect.

Fig. 6.30. Isabel Roberts house, River Forest, 1908, main floor plan. (Grant Hildebrand)

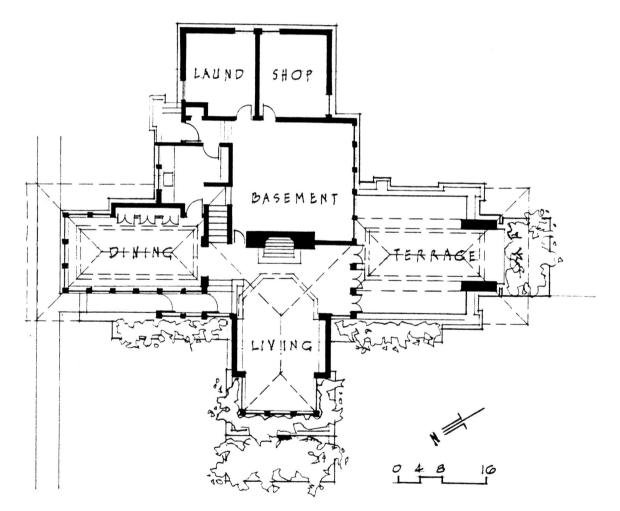

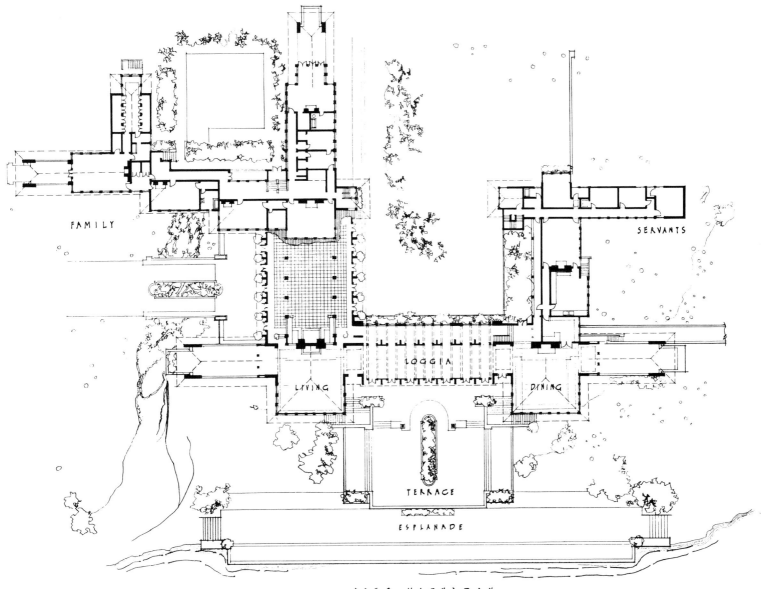

FAMILY

SERVANTS

LOGGIA

LIVING

DINING

TERRACE

ESPLANADE

LAKE MICHIGAN

Fig. 6.31. Project: Harold McCormick house, Lake Forest, 1907, plan.
(Grant Hildebrand)

Thus in the years from 1900 to 1909 Wright worked through a typical relationship of domestic architectural elements that I have called a parti. This consists, in each case, of both exterior and interior repetitive features. On the exterior are deep overhanging eaves, broad window bands, balconies or terraces, and refuge-signaling entry conditions. On the interior major spaces are directly under the roof, their ceilings lifted into the roof's volume; a fireplace is at the heart of the building and at an inner edge of the space served, with low ceiling or ceiling edge above[12] and flanking elements suggesting containment. Other flanking walls are open to contiguous interior spaces, to glazing, and to french doors that lead to a contiguous elevated terrace or balcony. This parti can now be seen to correspond to current thought about fundamental human spatial preferences as most clearly described by Appleton. Nine houses manifesting this parti, and five more that show its development, have been cited here. These include all of those that would commonly be considered to be Wright's major houses of that period with just three exceptions: the Susan Lawrence Dana house of 1903, in Springfield, the Darwin Martin house of 1906, in Buffalo; and the Mrs. Thomas Gale house of 1904–1909, in Oak Park. These fall out of the pattern for work after 1902 only in that the living room lies under a second story; otherwise the parti occurs in these houses as well. Is it necessary to point out that it is rare in other major houses of our time? Wright's own Prairie School colleagues use the parti rarely and, it would seem, by accident. None of MacIntosh's work qualifies. Aalto's Villa Mairea comes close, but nothing by Mies or Corbu does so, nor does Rietveld's Schroder house, nor – to jump ahead in time – does any work of which I am aware by Richard Meier, Michael Graves, or Peter Eisenman.

With Wright however the parti established by 1909 per-

vades his work for the remainder of his life. It informs all the major domestic rooms at Taliesin; it is the fundamental idea of Falling Water; it is found in the California work of the twenties; it is the starting point for the spatial disposition of the Usonians. Even at the Price Tower, where one would think the whole idea would be out of court, the parti appears in compressed form. And one key element of it, the major space contiguous to the roof and borrowing its character, happens in Wright's nondomestic work too: at Unity Temple, where as a religious building the condition is traditional, but also at the Larkin Building, Johnson's Wax, the Morris Gift shop, and the Guggenheim, where it is not.

Was Wright consciously aware of the value of this parti? There is no clear indication in his writings that he had at all begun the intellectual analysis carried forward at a much later date by Appleton, Norberg-Schulz, Bachelard, and others. There are hints of awareness, but no more. He speaks of the pleasure it gave him to see "the fire burning deep in the solid masonry of the house itself."[13] Obviously he took Robie's demand for privacy seriously. Of Taliesin he mentions the chimneys marking the gathering places within while the walls opened everywhere to views,[14] and at one point he refers to the site of Taliesin as refuge.[15] In connection with the early Prairie houses he notes the enlargement of prospect to be had from a slightly elevated viewpoint.[16] But these are provocative hints of intuitive awareness only. To read in them a veiled but conscious theory would be quite wrong. Nevertheless, his intuitive choice of prospect-refuge spatial manipulation was in practice accurate, convinced, and pervasive. He seems to have been extraordinarily sensitive to the value of these elements that might be repeated, combined, and varied, to "represent basic ways of being between earth and sky."

Notes

This essay is adapted from Grant Hildebrand, *The Wright Space: Pattern and Meaning in Frank Lloyd Wright's Houses* (University of Washington Press, forthcoming).

1. Christian Norberg-Schulz, *Genius Loci* (New York: Rizzoli, 1980), 192–194.

2. Christian Norberg-Schulz, *The Concept of Dwelling* (New York: Rizzoli, 1985), 99.

3. Jay Appleton, *The Experience of Landscape* (London and New York: Wiley, 1975).

4. Ibid., 105.

5. Ibid., 118–119.

6. Wright was for himself, of course, the measure of all things. Accordingly I have drawn all figures in these diagrams at 5 feet 8½ inches.

7. Walter Creese, *The Crowning of the American Landscape* (Princeton, N.J.: Princeton University Press, 1985), 237.

8. "Mr. Robie Knew What He Wanted," *Architectural Forum* 109 (October 1958):126.

9. Gaston Bachelard, *The Poetics of Space,* trans. Maria Jolas (Boston: Beacon Press, 1964), 30–31.

10. Few discussions of the Robie house consider its interior as a setting for human living. It is to William Jordy's credit that he does so in his *American Buildings and their Architects,* vol. 4 (New York and Oxford: Oxford University Press, 1974), 214. He hints briefly at the difficulty described here: "Of all his [Wright's] interiors, that of the Robie House is one of the more difficult for many to appreciate. A little cramped, and among the most insistently modeled, it is difficult to imagine it congenially furnished."

11. Frank Lloyd Wright, *An Autobiography* (New York: Horizon, 1932, 1943, 1977), 185. Wright continues "descriptions of ideals and the nature of my creative effort in house-building already given apply particularly to this characteristic dwelling."

12. As already noted the Robie house lacks this feature.

13. Wright, *Autobiography,* 165.

14. Ibid., 195–198.

15. Ibid., 191.

16. Frank Lloyd Wright, *The Natural House* (New York: Horizon Press, 1954), 15.

CHAPTER 7

MR. WRIGHT AND MRS. COONLEY

An Interview with Elizabeth Coonley Faulkner

THEODORE TURAK

The interaction between patron and architect exists as one of the most important determinants of architectural form. As in all ages, this factor operated in Chicago and its environs between 1871 and the First World War, the era of the so-called Chicago and Prairie schools of architecture. Chicago patrons had an element of uniqueness, however. They were uncompromisingly middle class, the bourgeoisie. They represented the culmination of several hundred years of social evolution and, on the Illinois steppe, they reigned supreme. Unlike the aristocracy they commanded no palaces and they were only marginally concerned with church-building. Their interests centered around their businesses and their homes. Not surprisingly, therefore, the business building (the skyscraper) and the detached, private, relatively modest home reached a point of technical and aesthetic development never before attained in the history of architecture. The domestic work of Frank Lloyd Wright and other Prairie School architects represented the ultimate expression of middle-class aspirations.

To be sure most Chicago clients preferred traditional homes designed by such talented architects as Howard Van Doren Shaw. A substantial minority, however, welcomed experiment and sought out Prairie School architects. According to Professor Leonard K. Eaton, these were usually technically inclined, self-made men; often they were married to forceful women interested in women's suffrage. Avery Coonley, the nominal patron of the Coonley house, was not such a man. He inherited his wealth, but his wife, Queene Ferry, was the daughter of the founder of the highly successful Ferry Seed Company. It was she who commissioned Wright. The relationship of this extraordinary bourgeoisie with her extraordinary architect resulted in the extraordinary Coonley house in Riverside, Ill. It proved to be the largest dwelling that Wright had built to that date.

By the time of the First World War, the Prairie School had largely run its course. Frank Lloyd Wright moved on, but the Coonley house, illustrated with his other major works in *Ausgeführte Bauten und Entwürfe von Frank Lloyd Wright* published by Ernst Wasmuth in Berlin (1910), would have a cosmic impact on modern architecture. An understanding of the Coonley house, therefore, is an insight into the evolution of modern architecture; and to know the house one must know its patroness as well as its architect.

In the interview below, Mr. Waldron Faulkner (fig. 7.1) makes the comment that Mrs. Coonley (1874–1958) moved from one house in Riverside, Ill., that was to become a national landmark into another in Washington, D.C., that was also so fated. This exemplified Queene Ferry Coonley's inherently exquisite taste and explained her lifelong rapport with Frank Lloyd Wright. Mr. and Mrs. Coonley also, quite unknowingly, moved from one community designed by Frederick Law Olmsted to another directly inspired by him.

Fig. 7.1. Elizabeth and Waldron Faulkner in 1975. (Theodore Turak)

Because of Avery Coonley's position with the Committee on Publication of the Christian Science Church, the family moved to the Washington, D.C., area in 1917; they chose the suburb of Cleveland Park for their new home.[1] President Grover Cleveland gave the area its name when he established his summer house, Red Top, there in 1886.[2] The elevated site lying between Massachusetts and Connecticut avenues provided some relief from the District of Columbia's stifling heat. Portions of Cleveland Park have qualities that resemble Riverside. Unlike many contemporary sections of Washington, which were laid out in a grid pattern, the streets of the community's eastern portion were determined by the contours of the land, imparting an informal, parklike quality. This section of Washington was owned and developed by Senator Francis Newlands of Nevada.[3] Although no direct evidence exists that Olmsted actually planned the streets, Newlands was acquainted with and an admirer of the great landscape architect. Letters were exchanged between the two and Olmsted's influence cannot be doubted.

Upon their arrival in 1917, the Coonleys rented Rosedale (fig. 7.2), an estate of several hundred acres. A simple but handsome house, Rosedale was built in 1794 by the Revolutionary War hero, General Uriah Forrest. There he entertained President Washington, just as in later years the Coonleys would host Frank Lloyd Wright. The Coonleys purchased the house and grounds, in a bad state of repair, in 1920. (From the front porch one can now get an excellent view of the National Cathedral.)

Mrs. Coonley's daughter, Elizabeth, married the prominent architect, Waldron Faulkner, whose work may be found throughout the Washington area. His own home, built on a portion of the old Rosedale estate in 1937, is illustrated in the American Institute of Architect's (AIA) *Guide to the Architecture of Washington, D.C.* (Washington, D.C., 1974). However, perhaps his most important building, the Avery Coonley School, stands in Downers Grove, Ill. (figs. 7.3, 7.4). Erected in 1928 for classes ranging from the kindergarten through junior high school, its curriculum embodied the educational philosophy of Mrs. Coonley.[4]

The architecture of the school reflects Mrs. Coonley's taste and must be considered a late manifestation of the Prairie style. Waldron Faulkner placed its principal buildings around a delightful pool and court. There were purposely no historical associations. Its bucolic setting was to be wholesome and its scale

Fig. 7.2. Rosedale Plantation House, Cleveland Park, Washington, D.C., 1794. (Theodore Turak)

Fig. 7.3. Waldron Faulkner, Avery Coonley School, Downers Grove, Ill., 1928. (From Gertrude Hartman, *Finding Wisdom,* New York, 1938)

domestic. The horizontal lines that dominate its composition pick up the rhythms of the Illinois landscape.

Mrs. Coonley's two grandsons, Winthrop and Avery Faulkner, became architects. Winthrop's beautiful house also graces a corner of the Rosedale estate and is mentioned in the AIA's *Guide* for the city.

Fig. 7.4. Avery Coonley School, court. (From Gertrude Hartman, *Finding Wisdom,* New York, 1938)

Fig. 7.5. Queene Ferry Coonley in 1954. (Celia Faulkner Clevenger)

Fig. 7.6. Queene Ferry Coonley in 1901. (Celia Faulkner Clevenger)

This interview expands on the comments Professor Leonard Eaton made in his book, *Two Chicago Architects and Their Clients: Frank Lloyd Wright and Howard Van Doren Shaw.* It adds a few more anecdotes about Wright, but more importantly, it emphasizes the warm and enduring friendship that evolved between Wright and the Coonleys during the construction of the Coonley house. This friendship proved valuable to Wright because Mrs. Coonley later stood behind him during his moments of severe financial crises.

Before proceeding, however, we must consider Mrs. Coonley's background (figs. 7.5, 7.6). She was born in Detroit on 11 April 1874. The success of her father, Dexter Ferry, in the seed business assured her of a comfortable life with the usual social frivolities of her class. She chose instead to attend Vassar, from which she graduated in 1896. Friends of the family warned that a college education would fill her head with dangerous ideas. The prophecy proved true because the very determined young lady decided to enter teaching and take up social work. Her brother drolly observed that "Queene was going to raise the masses." After Vassar her parents permitted her to enter the Detroit Normal School and teach kindergarten (she was an admirer of Friedrich Froebel) as long as she promised to take part in the parties and functions expected of a young woman of her station. Thus, she frequently attended classes in the morning, taught in the afternoon, and danced all night.

Like Jane Addams, Eleanor Roosevelt, and other well-born gentlewomen of her age, she had a strong social sense that rebelled against any injustice deriving from class, race, or sex. She therefore worked for almost a year in a Chicago settlement house, called Chicago Commons, run by the Dutch Reform clergyman Graham Taylor (1851–1938). In a letter to a friend dated 9 October 1898 she described the dismal conditions around her, adding, "But of course all this is just what I came for. I want to understand the other side from what I heard all my life." Nevertheless, she maintained a certain middle-class balance:

> Last night Mayor Jones of Toledo was here. You probably heard of him. A great reformer, a really fine, earnest loving man. After "vesper services" (evening prayer and a little informal talk with Dr. Taylor), Mr. Jones talked about his work in Toledo. Open discussion followed, and once more I had to hear of the vile thief, the capitalist—of how the life blood of the laboring man goes to make the rich man's riches, or how the State must own every-

> thing, the individual nothing, and then it would be according to Christ's word. It's pretty hard for me to keep in sometimes. It surely is not right to censure any one class. No one should say the poor are poor because they are shiftless, no one should say "A rich man can't be a Christian," as one remarked last night.[5]

About this time she met Avery Coonley, the brother of a Vassar friend.[6] He too came from a wealthy reformist family noted for its strong-minded women. His grandmother had been an intimate friend of Booker T. Washington. His mother was closely associated with Jane Addams and Hull House. (Addams spoke at Mrs. Coonley's funeral.)

Avery and Queene became interested in Christian Science before their marriage (1901) and served as board of trustee members, readers, and Sunday school teachers in their church. (figs. 7.7, 7.8). Mrs. Coonley was a Christian Science practitioner between 1903 and 1918, but religion was only one of her many interests. In addition to the activities discussed below, she was at various times in her life: treasurer of the National Women's Party; a trustee of Vassar College; vice president of the Progressive Education Association; a member of the board of visitors of the Zion Research Library of Brookline, Massachusetts; and vice-president of the board of directors of the Madeira School in Washington, D.C.

Fig. 7.7. Group portrait of Avery and Queene Ferry Coonley's wedding in 1901. Man in upper left with cap is Dexter M. Ferry, Mrs. Coonley's father. (Celia Faulkner Clevenger)

Fig. 7.8. Avery Coonley on one of his horses. (Celia Faulkner Clevenger)

Frank Lloyd Wright seemed to have no need for temperamental posturing with Mrs. Coonley. Possibly this was because he saw in her similarities to his mother's family, the Lloyd Joneses, and perhaps even to his mother. Mrs. Coonley was an aristocratic liberal, a reformer. The house of 1907–1908 (figs. 7.9, 7.10) and the "Playhouse" (figs. 7.11, 7.12) of 1911–1912[7] that he designed for her in Riverside were outgrowths of her causes—women's suffrage, Christian Science, and especially progressive education. Her house was thus more than a home; it complemented the Cottage School that she had already founded in the community. As shown in the accompanying photographs, the house served as a backdrop to students' activities. The great court was an ideal setting for theatricals. The drained pool often served as the orchestra to be occupied by an audience. The area before the house thus became the stage and the house itself the *skene* (fig. 7.13).

The Playhouse was not the gift of overindulgent parents, but a structure for the expansion of Mrs. Coonley's educational activities. Even Grant Manson did not grasp its full importance when he described it as a "playhouse and gathering place for the children of the neighborhood."[8] It was a school, and Mrs. Faulkner emphasizes its innovations.

Mrs. Coonley felt that the educational systems of Western civilization had their origins in medieval monasteries and therefore had no relevance to a democratic society. In the *Vassar Quarterly* of August 1921 she described the typical American school as "a building consisting of a group of rooms with rigid little seats screwed relentlessly into the floor; your child who never walks if he be normal and happy, has only a narrow aisle left in which to walk sedately to and from the teacher's desk if he is lucky enough to think of reasons to take him back and forth."[9]

A school must not be authoritarian; it is a children's community (fig. 7.14). Quoting John Dewey she wrote, "School is not a preparation for life, it is life." Discipline was necessary, but it should only come about democratically, "by faculty and children together." There was no place for what today we call sexism. Of her school she wrote, "We had boys and girls. We made no distinction, boys and girls took equal part in all matters of government." They also shared tasks. Girls learned carpentry in the woodworking shop just as boys learned to cook in the kitchen. The school was founded around her four-year-old daughter and moved forward from there: "The needs of the child formed the cornerstone, not the conventions of any system of education. I found games, both in and out of doors. . . . I found animals to care for . . . a garden to work in, the woods, the wild flowers: these proved themselves good."[10]

Her goal was inspired by Tolstoy's idea of a balanced day:

He says a day should have four lines of activities. It must contain,
    First—Physical work; something that takes actual muscular effort.
    Second—Physical work raised to the point of skill, we call it art.
    Third—Some occupation requiring distinct mental concentration.
    Fourth—Some activity along altruistic lines, something for humanity or civilization.[11]

Students were involved in cooking the lunches, making useful objects for the school, and in weaving, printing, and woodwork. When studying literature and history they researched the era, made costumes, and acted out the subject (fig. 7.15, 7.16).

Fig. 7.9. Frank Lloyd Wright, Coonley house, Riverside, Ill., 1907–1908, view from the street. (Celia Faulkner Clevenger)

Fig. 7.10. Coonley house, living room. (Celia Faulkner Clevenger)

Fig. 7.11. Frank Lloyd Wright, the Coonley Playhouse, 1911–1912,
exterior. (Celia Faulkner Clevenger)

Fig. 7.12. Coonley Playhouse, interior. (Celia Faulkner Clevenger)

Fig. 7.13. Coonley house, pool, and court, with Elizabeth Coonley. (Celia Faulkner Clevenger)

Fig. 7.14. Mrs. Coonley's students in corner of the garden. (Celia Faulkner Clevenger)

Fig. 7.15. Coonley house, student performance in the lower living room. (Celia Faulkner Clevenger)

Fig. 7.16. Student performance. (Celia Faulkner Clevenger)

This educational philosophy must have hit a responsive chord with Wright. The Coonley house was, as Grant Manson wrote, "the product of that rare set of factors in architectural history, a liberal client, a great designer and perfect trust between the two."[12] Mrs. Coonley's interest in the Froebel kindergarten method and an organic and natural process of educa-

tion would have linked her in his mind both to Wright's mother and his aunts, Ellen and Jane Lloyd Jones, whose progressive school was among his earliest commissions. Both Wright and his master, Louis Sullivan, hated academic routine and saw nature as the true inspiration for art and life.

It is a little more difficult to see how Mrs. Coonley's Christian Science religion influenced the house, but it too was an important factor. Mrs. Faulkner describes how Wright designed it to fit her needs as a Christian Science practitioner. A deeply religious person, Mrs. Coonley was certainly interested in the "spiritual" quality of her home. Wright's somewhat similar attitudes can be seen in Reverend William C. Gannett's *The House Beautiful,* which he published with his first major patron, William Winslow.[13] Reverend Gannett felt that every element of the house, its setting, design, color scheme, and even its appliances should be expressive of a domestic spirituality.

Wright remembered that in their first meeting Mrs. Coonley commented that his architecture expressed the "countenances of principle."[14] To Christian Scientists, "Principle" like "Love" and "Spirit" is a synonym for God and is capitalized when used in that context.[15] In expressing Principle, therefore, Wright's houses symbolized the divine order of things. The Unitarian Gannett sought in domestic architecture the moral values that Mrs. Coonley, the Christian Scientist, found in Wright's work. In developing infinite variations from absolute principles, Wright created a kind of temple to her ideals.

After reading in Professor Eaton's book that the Coonley's had moved to Washington, I began to search for descendants. At first my efforts were fruitless, but one day I mentioned my quest to a colleague at The American University, Professor Charles McLaughlin. Professor McLaughlin is the editor of the *Olmsted Papers,* which a few years earlier had received some financial support from Waldron and Elizabeth Faulkner. An introduction was arranged and I was fortunate to meet two of the warmest and most charming people I have ever encountered. If Queene Ferry Coonley possessed the qualities of her daughter and son-in-law, I can well understand why Wright formed such an affection for her. The following interview took place at my home in Germantown, Md., on 22 August 1975, when my wife and I entertained the Faulkners for lunch. Both Mr. and Mrs. Faulkner have since died.[16] This constitutes my humble memorial to them.

Turak: First of all, I'd like to ask about Mrs. Coonley herself. She seems to have been an extraordinary person. Reading over an article that she wrote for the *Vassar Quarterly,* I find that she had ideas on women's liberation and feminism that seem up to date in this year of 1975. I wonder, Mrs. Faulkner, if you can tell us everything that you remember about your mother? How was she educated? What produced in her a personality which seemed to click with Frank Lloyd Wright?

Mrs. Faulkner: That's a large question, isn't it? I think that mother's whole family was rather original, not always in the same direction. I've been studying them and find that they did a lot of thinking for themselves and that it was encouraged and enjoyed at home. Mother, I think, had a different form of originality than the others. Women's suffrage was part of it. But I have to say here that she was confronted by my father's grandmother, Susan Avery, who asked mother if she was interested in votes for women. Mother said, "No, she really had not thought much about voting." My grandmother said, "Why, my dear, just because you don't want it for yourself, are you unwilling to have other women have it?" This appealed to mother's sense of fairness so she looked into women's suffrage and went on from there.

Turak: She must have been something of a scholar, did she read a lot?

Mrs. Faulkner: Yes, she did, but I don't think she would have called herself a scholar.

Mr. Faulkner: She was more of a doer, I think.

Turak: An activist, we'd say today. How did her life and her outlook influence the form of the house that Mr. Wright built for her? You might go over how they first made contact and the stipulations that she gave him. Do you recall it all?

Mrs. Faulkner: Only that at the beginning she selected Mr. Wright because she had been to a great many architectural exhibitions and in each case every other architect left something unsatisfied in her. She found Mr. Wright, I think. She had not met him up to that time. She really liked his work. My father was not particularly interested. He went along out of affection for my mother. He wanted something more traditional, but once he embraced the idea, he and Mr. Wright had just as many spirited and amiable conversations as my mother and Mr. Wright. So in the end they were both his patrons.

Turak: What in the personalities of Mr. Wright and your mother led to this extraordinary intellectual convergence? Practically every commentator on the Coonley house brings this up. There really was a meeting of minds between Mr. Wright and Mrs. Coonley.

Mrs. Faulkner: Yes, Mr. Wright said that when she came to him, she found in his work "the countenances of Principle." This was part of her Christian Science in which the concept of God is a much more abstract idea than in conventional religions.

Turak: How did this philosophy or view influence the house?

Mrs. Faulkner: I don't know that I could really say. I think for one thing she had very definite ideas about the practical uses that she wanted to make of the house. She liked the Prairie architectural idea—she was willing to have it extended. There was no basement. It was all aboveground. The only basement rooms or first-floor rooms were my play room and the root cellar—the heating equipment and the storage. They wanted the second floor for family life—they did very informal entertaining.

Turak: Before, you said that it was designed for her function as a Christian Science practitioner.

Mrs. Faulkner: Yes, as you left the living room, you came to a corridor, the first rooms of which were her study. There she received her patients. She asked Mr. Wright if he could arrange it [so that] if she had two patients in succession, the second one [would] not be seen by the first one. In those days, especially, some people were sensitive about going to see a Christian Science practitioner and they didn't want anyone to know. So he had a lovely solution for this. He liked symmetry up to a point. He had two staircases. When you arrived, you were shown up the staircase to the right and seated in the living room. When you left, you went down the other stairway, which was not within view and along a corridor. Neither patient saw the other.

Mother often said that contrary to the popular criticism of Mr. Wright, he was a very good person to work with. That was because they knew what they wanted. They started out with a preconceived appreciation of him and they didn't mind speaking up. [But] my father often had to do the speaking up because my mother didn't want to.

Turak: That's very interesting because generally your mother has been given full credit.

Mrs. Faulkner: My father was very fond of saddle horses, particularly five-gaited Kentucky saddle horses. His mother had been born and brought up in Louisville. He rode before breakfast every morning and took people driving. If you were going to get into a carriage in those days, you really had to have something upon which to climb—so he wanted carriage steps. Mr. Wright was not at all enthusiastic about this. He said, "It's an ugly thing. Look at that line. You'd break it up." Father said, "I take a lot of people driving and I want them to be comfortable." So Mr. Wright said, "I'll tell you what we'll do Coonley, we'll design the house without a carriage step, and if after a year you still want it, I'll design one for you." My father said, "I'll tell you what we'll do Wright, we'll design the house *with* a carriage step and if after a year I don't want it, we'll take it out." This was agreed upon, but Wright said, "I'll design you a carriage step such as you've never seen before." It was eighteen feet long, concrete, about eighteen inches high, and about six or eight feet wide. It had an enormous concrete bowl at one end with earth in it and nasturtiums falling out. At the other end there was a set of demure little steps so that you could quite easily climb from the sidewalk to the platform. It was better than any carriage step I've ever seen.

Turak: Is it still there, do you know? You were there this past week.

Mrs. Faulkner: No, the last two times I've been back to the house the carriage steps have been gone.

Turak: I find this interesting because there are so many stories of Wright's highhandedness with patrons. There was a side to him that many people do not know. He was a very charming man.

Mrs. Faulkner: Oh, he was!

Mr. Faulkner: Not only that. I think that [your mother and father] had a basic understanding with him. They were not formal-minded people. A lot of their friends were horrified. What was it one woman used to say?

Mrs. Faulkner: Yes, one of our neighbors said, "I never can let my husband walk around your end of town at all because he gets apoplexy every time he sees your house." He really

enjoyed working with them and they with him. There was another point upon which they disagreed. I think if Mr. Wright's clients had stepped up and spoken as frankly, but as genially, as father did, there wouldn't have been so many incidents. Father was very disappointed that the house did not have green shutters. He always had been used to a brick house with green shuttered windows. Mr. Wright said that it was unthinkable. It wouldn't go with his style at all. He said, "But I'll tell you why you want those green shutters. You want the variety, design, color, and form that they give to the house. I will give that in the form of an occasional wall ornamented with tile." He brought a design for this and my father looked at it and said, "It's perfectly beautiful, but it looks so expensive. Anyone seeing the house would immediately think of the cost even before they thought of the beauty. This is not the impression that we would like to give." Mr. Wright chuckled and said, "All right, if I make it out of the kind of tile used by the terrace by the pool and bathroom tile, will *that* satisfy you?" But father said that he'd like to see it. So the present design was made from square tile—I don't think that they are exactly like the pool, but they are of the same type, very simple.

Mr. Faulkner: They're almost like a Mondrian mural.

Turak: Spectacular, I saw them in the bright sunlight and they are as fresh and as beautiful today as the day they were put up.

Mrs. Faulkner: I was so pleased to see them again this time at Riverside. I hadn't seen the house for a number of years. We get accustomed to looking at the black and white photographs.

Turak: [Color] is an important factor in Wright's work. I remember the impact that the Winslow house made on me when I first saw it.

Mrs. Faulkner: I remember about mother's study. He wanted a special kind of green painted into the stucco on the wall.

Turak: Fresco?

Mrs. Faulkner: Yes, we had a wonderful painter. Mr. Wright met with him and had him bring all sorts of colors of paint. Mr. Wright himself watched them mixed together. There was green, yellow, rose—it made a charming and varied effect. He loved color.

Turak: What about the house to live in as a little girl? I've seen these pictures with the little girl with a big ribbon. Is that you?

Mrs. Faulkner: Yes, that's I standing by the tree or kneeling by the pool.

Turak: It was a large house, but it seemed intimate and homey.

Fig. 7.17. Elizabeth Coonley at poolside. (Celia Faulkner Clevenger)

Mrs. Faulkner: Yes, it was. It was the only thing that I knew. I really didn't think much about antiques or even the old masters when I first went abroad. They were not part of my early surroundings.

Mr. Faulkner: The very fact that all [of it] could not be seen at any one time or from one point of view helps what you are saying. Although if you add it all together it would be a very large house. But it had all sorts of angles, so that you never saw more than a small part of the house at any one time—which gave it that feeling of intimacy.

Mr. Faulkner: While you're speaking of your father and mother, tell again the story about your mother's research into vegetarianism.

Mrs. Faulkner: Oh yes! Mother lived, of course, so near to Chicago that she would go in for lectures sometimes. She heard a lecture once on the cruelty of methods used for slaughtering animals in the stockyards. She came home absolutely horrified. She said, "Avery, if you had heard the lecture that I heard today, you'd feel just as I do, I just feel that I can never eat meat again. I think we should look into vegetarianism." My father sighed and said, "My dear, we're Christian Scientists and women suffragists, you run a progressive school and we live in a Frank Lloyd Wright house, let's not look into vegetarianism." Father had a lovely sense of humor. One of them could always rescue the other.

Turak: They complemented each other beautifully. What about your mother's ideas on progressive education? And what about the idea of the Playhouse? This was an idea which I must admit I did not fully understand until you explained it to me.

Mrs. Faulkner: This is not understood now. Whenever I go back to Illinois people ask me if I enjoyed playing with my dolls in that playhouse. This was really the only building that mother built for the school that she had in Riverside—except for Thorncroft, which she built for the teachers to live in.

Turak: Drummond was the architect for that.

Mrs. Faulkner: Yes, then she rented other houses, or bought them, and used them for the school. Between them they cooked up the idea of arranging it so that the classes could be there. It was a cruciform scheme. Most of the classes were held in the nave, so to speak. One "transept" was the kitchen, where we studied domestic science, and one was the shop, where we did carpentry and things like that.

Turak: And boys and girls did both, didn't they?

Mrs. Faulkner: Yes.

Mr. Faulkner: It was revolutionary for the time.

Mrs. Faulkner: The "chapel" was the stage. It was lifted up three or four steps above the rest so you could set the thing up as a theater.

Mr. Faulkner: So it was a playhouse for giving plays.

Mrs. Faulkner: Mother objected to the name right away because progressive schools were under fire for being frivolous. She said, "There's a workshop in it after all, why don't you call it a workshop?" So he said, "We'll call it the Workshop *and* Playhouse." But the name was the way it was on the original drawing and it never got changed. I am still fighting the battle about what that was, but it was a lovely building. That was the building we loved so. The windows had balloons in them. Mr. Wright had seen a man selling balloons on the sidewalk outside of his office. He had gone down and asked him if he would sell all of his balloons. Whether the man came up or it was Mr. Wright, I don't know. He let them—they were gas-filled—bob up and down in front of his windows. He got the idea of the stained-glass windows with the balloons in very, very pure colors—red, blue, yellow, green.

Mr. Faulkner: Rather a limited palette.

Mrs. Faulkner: Yes, quite. There were three long windows side by side. There were even strings of balloons showing in the lead below.

Mr. Faulkner: Unfortunately these have all disappeared. I went by just the other day.

Mrs. Faulkner: We were told that they were in the Hirshhorn Museum here. There are some of Mr. Wright's stained windows there but not from the Playhouse. There were clerestory windows at the side, way up high.

Turak: The way the building was used interested me too. The way your mother evolved a system to complement public education.

Fig. 7.18. Elizabeth Coonley next to one wing of the house. (Celia Faulkner Clevenger)

Mrs. Faulkner: The first schools that mother started outside the home were kindergartens for the villages in which there were no kindergartens in the public schools. She was a great believer in kindergarten as the basis – the child's form of liberal arts education. We had in Riverside an excellent kindergarten. We had a very progressive superintendent so [mother] kept me in the public school kindergarten for two years. It was so much better than if I had gone to the first grade as I was old enough to do. But she was such a believer in kindergartens – and this is probably what she would have taught if she had gone on as a teacher, which is what she started to be. She went to the nearest village, Brookfield, and asked the superintendent if he would understand if she built and operated the kindergarten to prepare the children for his school. He was very cordial about it, as were the city fathers. She built a charming little school there. That was also designed by Mr. Drummond.[17] Then another one, a little farther up the line, in a place called Hollywood, Ill., and then eventually another one in Downers Grove, which is still a little farther up the line and which she named after my father – the Avery Coonley School. It expanded and now has eight grades as well as a kindergarten. But this school that she started in Riverside had no kindergarten because the public schools had such good ones.

Turak: Are the other ones still in existence?

Mrs. Faulkner: The Downers school is. We just went to see it last spring. I think she really started it for me. The public school was not as good after the kindergarten, so she started this private school. The first year there were just these four boys and me. Then it expanded. Mr. Ames, the principal of the public school, allowed her to take two kindergarten teachers in the afternoon. They taught in the morning and came and taught her first grade in the afternoon – the four little boys and me.

Turak: Was this before the Playhouse?

Mrs. Faulkner: Yes, it took several years. I think 1909 was the first year of that school. In 1916 I had finished the eighth grade and mother felt either she should give the school to the town of Riverside, as she did the other schools, or close it. She sent me to the Francis Parker School in Chicago. But the town of Riverside was not interested in the undertaking.

It's quite a job to run the school, including the deficit, so it was closed.

Turak: Can you remember "functioning" within the Playhouse?

Mrs. Faulkner: It was like the old churches before the pews.

Turak: Did you study orthodox subjects?

Mrs. Faulkner: Yes, but not in orthodox ways. For instance, we studied literature. When we studied the Greek myths we made the story of Odysseus into a play.

Turak: Are those the photographs you showed me?

Mrs. Faulkner: Yes, when you work on a thing enough to create a new medium for it, you really have to know it.

Turak: Did your mother know John Dewey?

Mrs. Faulkner: I think she may have met him, but I don't think she knew him personally. He was a great prophet of progressive education and she had great respect for him. She was one of the founders of the Progressive Education Association. She was very active in the Association.

Turak: What about the later years, the relationship between your mother and Mr. Wright?

Mrs. Faulkner: After she stopped being his client, she was still devoted to him.

Turak: She seems even to have excused his love life.

Mrs. Faulkner: Yes, mother was very, very straightlaced in all matters of sex. People would say to her, "I don't know how you can go along with Mr. Wright, with these three wives, one of which he hasn't even married!" And mother would say, "Only *one* at a time." I don't believe she would have been tolerant of someone she didn't respect in other ways. But they were devoted, you know. He had some very hard times afterwards and she was one of a group of people who banded together to provide funds for him. That was really how she got possession of those Japanese prints of his.[18]

Mr. Faulkner: He felt very much indebted to her for years.

Mrs. Faulkner: But you know he was a remarkable man. You remember the letter I showed you. He wrote us a letter after we invited him to dinner one evening. By that time I don't believe Taliesin could afford the beautiful stationery he [Wright] designed with an orange oblong in the corner and the letter spacing and design just so. But he still could write an attractive letter. He had black and red ribbon on the typewriter. The whole looks beautiful. I really admired that in him as much as anything else.

Mr. Faulkner: That kind of thing appealed to your mother very much. She had the best taste of anyone I've ever known. One thing that illustrates this is that she moved from one house in Riverside which has become a national landmark to Rosedale in Washington, which has also become a national landmark. These are the two houses that appealed to her—two of highly different character, yet they had the common denominator of excellence.

Mrs. Faulkner: In both cases she rather had to swim upstream. The real-estate agent who showed us around wasn't a bit enthusiastic about her interest in Rosedale. She said, "Of course you wouldn't want that, Mrs. Coonley." Automobile covers came down then, you had to crane your neck to see, but mother would crane her neck and say, "Now that's a nice old place." But the lady would say, "It's run down; it has no central heating; it has no electricity. . . . "

Turak: And now it's a national monument.

Mrs. Faulkner: And it had a barn where father's horses could be stabled.

Turak: Wright's comments about the house were interesting. He showed himself to be a tolerant man.

Mrs. Faulkner: Mr. Wright came to see mother there, and she was a bit nervous about it. She said, "This is not exactly what you designed for me, Mr. Wright." He said, "It's honest for the time it was built; it was modern. It was the best thing they did. It's not copying something from the past."

Mr. Faulkner: I remember the time he came to dinner at Rosedale. Mr. Wright was having an exhibit at the Corcoran Gallery. On Saturday morning we went to see it. Mr. Wright was standing in the wings, listening to the comments. We introduced ourselves. We screwed up our courage and invited him to dinner the following evening. To our great surprise and pleasure he accepted. We had dinner out-of-doors on the lawn. We invited some friends. He was at his best, just delightful. I heard one of the wives say, "Mr. Wright, you wouldn't say that about painting, would you?" And I heard him say, "Well, I never thought of painting as one of the fine arts." [Later,] when we saw the Guggenheim Museum, we realized that he hated pictures.

Mrs. Faulkner: When we were living in New York—we were married in 1926—we lived in Greenwich Village for two years. We met Mr. Wright and the future Mrs. Wright.[19] She still wasn't able to marry him because of the woman who wouldn't give him a divorce. They had a baby carriage. Mr. Wright greeted mother very cordially. He introduced his "wife," made a sweeping gesture toward the carriage and said, "And this is my crime!" Later, when they were married, he sent out the most fascinating wedding announcements with the orange oblong in one corner and in the other corner a photograph of their baby. . . . I must say that what Mr. Wright did, he did with a clear conscience. He was answerable only to Frank Lloyd Wright.

Fig. 7.19. Student performance. (Celia Faulkner Clevenger)

Fig. 7.20. Student performance. (Celia Faulkner Clevenger)

Fig. 7.21. Student performance. (Celia Faulkner Clevenger)

Notes

I would like to thank Mrs. Louise Mann Madden Kenney, a former student, for also helping me make contact with the Faulkner family. I am especially indebted to Mrs. Celia Faulkner Clevenger, who provided me with photographs and family documents. Mrs. Kenney is working on a biography of General Forrest, and Mrs. Clevenger is writing a history of the Coonley and Faulkner families.

1. Professor Eaton wrote that the Coonleys moved in 1912, but Mrs. Faulkner insisted that it was in 1917. Leonard K. Eaton, *Two Architects and Their Clients: Frank Lloyd Wright and Howard Van Doren Shaw* (Cambridge, Mass., 1969), 83.

2. Grace Dunlop Peter and Joyce D. Southwick, *Cleveland Park: An Early Residential Neighborhood of the Nation's Capital* (Washington, D.C.: The Cleveland Park Community Library Committee, 1958), 4.

3. This information was discovered by a former student, David Schele, during a seminar I conducted at The American University. The information was published in *Historic Preservation Study of Cleveland Park, Washington, D.C.* (Washington, D.C.: The American University, 1977), 1–3. This study was edited by three of the students of the seminar, Louise Mann Madden, Sara White Hamilton, and Sheila Dressner Ruffine.

4. Gertrude Hartman, *Finding Wisdom: Chronicles of a School Today* (New York, 1938), xi–xvi.

5. Letter, Queene Ferry Coonley to Gertrude McArthur Slade, 9 October 1898. The letter is in the possession of Mrs. Celia Faulkner Clevenger of Cleveland Park, Washington, D.C. Mrs. Slade was a former classmate of Queene's at Vassar.

6. For more information on Avery Coonley, see Eaton, 82–86. Interestingly, Avery's brother, Prentiss, chose the excellent but more conventional architect, Howard Van Doren Shaw, for his house. Avery, too, would have liked a conventional house had it not been for his wife: Eaton, 217–220.

7. Eaton, 82, and H. Allen Brooks, *The Prairie School: Frank Lloyd Wright and His Midwest Contemporaries* (Toronto and Buffalo: 1972), 87.

8. Grant Carpenter Manson, *Frank Lloyd Wright to 1910: The First Golden Age* (New York, 1958), 197.

9. Queene Ferry Coonley, "The Educational Responsibility of the Mother," *Vassar Quarterly,* August 1921, 239.

10. Ibid.

11. Ibid., 240–241.

12. Manson, 187.

13. Robert C. Twombly, *Frank Lloyd Wright: An Interpretive Biography* (New York, 1973), 38.

14. Frank Lloyd Wright, *An Autobiography* (New York, 1977), 185.

15. Christian Science would have had a certain attraction to turn-of-the-century feminists. The religion was founded by a woman, Mary Baker Eddy. It pleaded women's suffrage and the equality of women before the law and defined God as both Father and Mother. See Mary Baker Eddy, *Science and Health, with Key to the Scriptures* (Boston, 1890 and later), 63, 587, 592. No less a feminist than Susan B. Anthony took instruction from one of Mrs. Eddy's students: Robert Peel, *Mary Baker Eddy: The Years of Trial* (New York, 1971), 223.

16. Mrs. Faulkner died in 1985 at the age of 83. Her husband was 81 at his death in 1979.

17. For a discussion of Thorncroft and Brookfield Kindergarten, see Suzanne Ganschinietz, "William Drummond: I. Talent and Sensitivity," *The Prairie School Review* 6, 2 (1969): 5–19.

18. Twombly, 154. In 1928 Mrs. Coonley, along with Alexander Woollcott, Charles MacArthur, and Darwin C. Martin, saved Taliesin from the bank and paid off Wright's debts. Mrs. Coonley evidently received the Japanese prints in partial compensation for her investment in Frank Lloyd Wright, Incorporated.

19. Ibid. This was Olgivanna Milanoff, whom he married 25 August 1928. The daughter's name is Iovanna.

CHAPTER 8

Douglas Haskell and the Criticism of International Modernism

Robert Benson

Ever since the early 1960s, the discipline of architecture has waged a great debate about the origins and definition of modernism. Much retrospective criticism has accompanied the debate, initiated by such polemicists as Venturi, Jencks, and Stern. Although the controversy has offered valuable insights and judgments and has stimulated a general appreciation for critical assessment, it has also proven the need for a reinvestigation of the modern movement, partly as a defense against the often-exaggerated claims of anti-modernist criticism and partly as an enrichment of twentieth-century historical studies.

One by-product of such studies is the discovery that the debate about the nature and origins of modernism is not new. Even by the late 1920s, the definition of modernism in architecture had not yet been settled in the American architectural press.[1] Although the editors and writers of professional magazines gradually realized that the advent of a modern architectural style in some form was inevitable, the question about its sources in Europe or the United States remained open. On the other hand, rather than take strong positions in a theoretical argument, journalists remained interested, for the most part, in business and commercial productivity, especially during the depressed national economy of the early 1930s. At the same time,

architecture began to receive increased attention outside the professional press. Important debates, in fact, often took place in the popular arena where other political and social programs were being proposed and in journals of the arts.

Much of this was brought about by the commentary of critics such as Lewis Mumford, Henry-Russell Hitchcock, Jr., Catherine Bauer, Henry Wright, Philip Johnson, and others who wrote regularly about modern architecture. One of the most prolific and influential of these writers was Douglas Haskell, architecture critic for the New York *Nation* from 1930 to 1942.[2] Haskell wrote for a variety of publications and treated architecture in political and social as well as artistic terms, that is, as a public art, rather than as the privatized world of capitalist business venture that the professional magazines often fostered. His point of view was therefore well suited to the situation in which architectural writing found itself in the early 1930s and he was a particularly insightful judge of events that were shaping the character of progressive American modernism, as is demonstrated in his numerous reviews and essays.[3]

Returning in February of 1932 from a European sojourn of four or five months, Douglas Haskell found himself back home just in time for the opening of the now famous blockbuster show

165

"Modern Architecture: International Exhibition" at the Museum of Modern Art (MOMA). This was the last exhibit held in the old quarters of the museum in the Heckscher Building, and it ran from 9 February to 23 March 1932, after which it went on national tour[4] (fig. 8.1). The exhibit consisted of ten major models and a large collection of photographs illustrating modern buildings, housing and community planning. A luxurious catalogue with copious illustrations and essays by MOMA director Alfred H. Barr, Jr., Henry-Russell Hitchcock, Jr., Philip Johnson, and Lewis Mumford complemented the exhibited works. A symposium on modern architecture held in conjunction with the exhibit brought attention to its intended scholarly and intellectual character and focused on problems inherent in the modern built environment.[5]

Fig. 8.1. Installation view from the exhibition "Modern Architecture: International Exhibition," 9 Feb.–23 Mar. 1932, the Museum of Modern Art, New York. The model in the foreground represents the Villa Savoye at Poissy/Seine by Le Corbusier; the photographs on the wall picture this and other of Le Corbusier's works from the 1920s and very early 1930s. (Photograph courtesy, The Museum of Modern Art, New York)

Naturally, Douglas Haskell reviewed the show in his column at the *Nation,* and his criticism of it is an important document of his keen judgment.[6] However, in order to assess the depth and insight of his thinking, it is necessary to review the content of the exhibit and examine the reactions to it by other writers for comparison; because over fifty years later, the exhibit is still considered one of the most important and controversial ever to have been organized on architecture in this century. The term *International style* entered into the common vocabulary of the entire discipline; and the accompanying literature, especially Hitchcock and Johnson's book *Architecture Since 1922: The International Style,* which is still in print, remains important reading material for students and scholars who continue to evaluate the subject matter and impact of the exhibit.[7]

An announcement in *Art Digest* said the "exhibition has been in preparation since December, 1930, under the guidance of Philip Johnson, a member of the museum's advisory committee."[8] Reinforcing Johnson's effort, Barr wrote his own foreword to the catalogue and clearly stated the purpose of the exhibit:

> The present exhibition is an assertion that the confusion of the past forty years, or rather of the past century, may shortly come to an end. Ten years ago the Chicago Tribune competition brought forth almost as many different styles as there were projects. Since then the ideas of a number of progressive architects have converged to form a genuinely new style which is rapidly spreading throughout the world. Both in appearance and structure this style is peculiar to the twentieth century and is fundamentally original as the Greek or Byzantine or Gothic. On the following pages Mr. Hitchcock and Mr. Johnson have outlined its history and its extent. Because of its simultaneous development in several different countries and because of its worldwide distribution it has been called the International Style.[9]

Barr reiterated the aesthetic principles of the new style as Hitchcock and Johnson had outlined them and then proceeded to define the broad position that the show would maintain. He made it clear that the style was European despite the fact that Frank Lloyd Wright was one of its primary sources and that Wright was "not intimately related" to it for several reasons, including his romantic individualism and unpredictability. Raymond Hood was also included in the show, but, according to Barr, at a certain risk to the organizers. His career had been inconsistent, Barr said, but seemed now to be moving into the International style camp. Some of the other Americans in the show were George Howe and William Lescaze (although Lescaze was Swiss-born), Richard Neutra (although he was Austrian-born), and the Bowman brothers of Chicago (who had not yet built very much).[10]

In his "Historical Note," Philip Johnson stated that prior to World War I modern architecture was the creation of "great individualists." "Since the War," he announced, "an international style has grown up throughout Europe, not the invention of one genius but the coordinated result of many parallel experiments." After discussing the formation of the new style and the influences on it from cubism and neoplasticism, he concluded that "Since 1922 the new style has not changed in its fundamentals." Mies, Le Corbusier, Oud, and Gropius, he said, were still the leading modern architects.[11]

Hitchcock was somewhat more circumspect in his essay "The Extent of Modern Architecture," and his statements sounded less dogmatic. "Though many architects and critics question the desirability or even the possibility of style fixation," he admitted, "it is true that consciously or unconsciously a considerable number of architects throughout the world accept parallel technical and aesthetic disciplines."[12] Hitchcock's more scholarly and measured judgments lent the show a credibility it might otherwise have lacked.

The most emphatic position statement in the catalogue was that of Lewis Mumford. In his essay "Housing" he wasted little time trying to convince the reader of the legitimacy of European modernism or of his own views but laid out the social, political, and economic basis of a housing program for the United States (fig. 8.2). Even more radical under the circumstances of this show, he relied on various examples—for instance, the community of Radburn, N.J., by Clarence Stein and Henry Wright—which were neither European nor in the International style at all. He thus avoided the stylistic biases that informed the bulk of the show and stressed a much more comprehensive issue of modern architecture. "The new house cannot be conceived except in terms of the new community," he emphasized; "we must take into account all the changes in our habits of working and acting brought about by the motor car, the airplane, the telephone, the giant power line, and above all, by the methods of planned organization that these instruments have helped to create."[13]

Fig. 8.2. Installation view from the exhibition "Modern Architecture: International Exhibition," 9 Feb.–23 Mar. 1932, the Museum of Modern Art, New York. The model in the foreground depicts the Rothenberg Housing Development, by Otto Haesler, architect and planner, in Kassel, Germany, 1930–1932. It is surrounded by photographs of various urban conditions in American cities. (Photograph courtesy, The Museum of Modern Art, New York)

Fig. 8.3. Installation view from the exhibition "Modern Architecture: International Exhibition," circulated by the Museum of Modern Art, New York, and held in Cleveland 27 Oct.–4 Dec. 1932. This view includes a model of the Bauhaus in Dessau, Germany, by Walter Gropius and a series of works by the Dutch architect, J. J. P. Oud. (Photograph courtesy of the Cleveland Museum of Art)

Critical reaction to the show in the popular press was highly favorable. In his review of the opening, *New York Times* art critic Edward Alden Jewell reminded his readers that modern architecture had not always been accepted by the man in the street who "thought it merely a fad, merely a determination to be modish and bizarre." The new International style would now put those suspicions to rest, he assured.[14] In a second review on the following Sunday, Jewell reiterated his earlier comments and stressed that the contribution of the International style was not only its approach to ornament but to materials, construction and function. "It is encouraging, indeed," he wrote, "to see how intelligently such problems have been met. . . . Nor is there involved the slightest loss of esthetic quality."[15] The MOMA exhibit even became Jewell's standard of excellence. Later in the month he reviewed the Architectural League's annual show in the American Fine Arts Society Building and compared it to the larger show at the museum.

> So far as this exhibition is concerned, most of the architects represented might never have heard of advanced ideas such as those embodied in the "international style." Here and there we find evidence of exploration in that direction: John Walter Wood's ferroconcrete house for Sherman Pratt, and occasionally a modern emphasis on the virtue of glass. For the most part the home architecture exhibited pursues conservative or traditional paths.[16]

Thus, taking on the role of institutional architecture critic for the first time, the Museum of Modern Art had produced an assessment of modernism that was convincing to many knowledgeable people. The massive amount of material was presented with legitimating theory and art historical logic. More important, the polemics in the catalogue had introduced a new if not revolutionary vocabulary and rhetoric by means of which others could speak with the same voice of authority as the museum, in effect promoting its position. Few people had the insight, skill, or experience to dissect the powerful combination of words and images orchestrated by Hitchcock and Johnson. The effect was like self-fulfilling prophecy.

Catherine Bauer, writing in *Creative Art,* also praised the exhibition. Although she found the quality of the work somewhat uneven, she had no criticism of the choice, organization, or underlying concept; nor did she find fault with the accompanying catalogue. She thought the show was unified when considered as a whole and that even "the least successful designs achieve a degree of sense merely by being related to the rest of the show." Of course, her personal association with Lewis Mumford and her more than general agreement with him on principles of community planning can only have strengthened her positive assessment of the exhibit as an ideological statement. Nevertheless, she declared with certainty that it was all legitimate material and that it contained "more intrinsic matter for judgment than any league or other hodge-podge has presented to American eyes." She only wondered whether the public was ready to accept the new impersonal, sociological definition of style that it presented.[17] (See fig. 8.3.)

A later review by William Williams in *Pencil Points* was more conservative. With a light touch, Williams criticized what he called the intergeneric quality of the buildings, which, he said, lacked both formal interest and typological identity. He assessed the open plan as inherently nonfunctional and the excessive use of glass as both wasteful and psychologically uncomfortable. He was suspicious of the motives of the designers.

> In modern architecture generally, that is, in the latest phase of it, which is entirely *a la mode horizontale,* romanticism has gone—not sentiment, because anything loved for its own sake is apt to be based on sentiment, and much of the new style is a mannerism loved for its own sake.
>
> Art has become nowadays largely a matter of ideas, and ideas have a way of becoming condensed into catchwords, and catchwords become the basis for new "movements."[18]

Like Bauer, Williams questioned whether the man in the street was ready to accept the intellectualism behind the new style. Yet he was unable to cut through to the heart of the matter: he could not explain what it was that was missing in the intellectual position taken by the curators of the exhibit.

In many ways, the exhibit was truly a turning point, not only because its content had been projected that way by its organizers, but because its scale and carefully designed installation lent it a critical depth and intellectual intensity that neither the general nor the professional public had previously associated with architectural modernism. Yet Haskell's interpretation of the subject matter of the exhibit was very different from that of Jewell, Bauer, or Williams, let alone Johnson, Hitchcock, or Barr.

In his *Nation* review, Haskell's words reverberate with a confidence that seems inspired partly by the very existence of the show itself; for this was the first time that a major institution had launched an effort to convince the public that a new and undeniable attitude existed in contemporary architecture. But Haskell's review also profited enormously from his recent experiences in Europe that had brought him into firsthand contact with much new architecture in Holland, Germany, Austria, and Switzerland. He had, in fact, published a glowing review of the new Van Nelle Factory by Brinckman and Van der Vlugt in Rotterdam with a continental dateline; and he had spent several weeks together with his wife, Helen, living in the new housing complex by city architect Ernst May in the Frankfurt suburb of Roemerstadt, about which he would write several times.[19]

In the opening paragraph, Haskell gave a thumbnail sketch of the rather similar characteristics of many buildings in the show. He questioned whether these visual qualities actually represented a style and agreed that it was at least an important trend that had become fashionable though not yet a sweeping tide of conformity.

> A house that is a sort of box or aggregation of boxes – flat top, flat sides with plenty of glass in them, color generally white, and the whole thing preferably raised on stilts – this, loosely described, is what you were given to see at the Museum of Modern Art. Under the title "The International Style" it will travel thence through the leading museums of the country, on a tour of three years. Whether "style" or not, what the show centers on is certainly the most advanced Continental technique. And considering events, we can be quite sure that houses more or less like these are what the man about town will build.[20]

He complimented the catalogue and the organizers, calling the new forms elegant and recherche, the latter term probably implying that they were intellectually sophisticated rather than natural, naive, or vernacular. He said the new architecture was destined to appeal to "the aristocrat of modern taste," thus suggesting that they were not populist in nature but refined and even perhaps elitist, an idea he also suggested in other articles.[21]

He then reviewed the historical premise of the show: that four streams of proto-modernism, departing from romantic sources in the nineteenth century, had reintegrated into the new style by 1922.[22] He discussed the radical scientific group influenced by engineering and industry and represented by Gropius and Mies, the abstract direction influenced by cubism and

Fig. 8.4. Installation view from the exhibition "Modern Architecture: International Exhibition," circulated by the Museum of Modern Art, New York, and held in Cleveland 27 Oct.–4 Dec. 1932. This section of the exhibit documented the work of Raymond Hood, including his project for a tower in the country, 1932. (Photograph courtesy of the Cleveland Museum of Art)

neoplasticism and represented by Le Corbusier and Oud, the organic impulse initiated by Wright and Sullivan and the stream of the "talented opportunist" represented by the unpredictable Raymond Hood (fig. 8.4). However, he then voiced the most important question raised by the exhibition, its catalogue and its underlying conception:

> Are the paths to constitute a highway?
> Appearances say yes. Never have the various products looked so similar. To those who love uniformity, order, discipline, the result is a triumph. Even the "rebel" Wright, as some of the sponsors exultantly declare, begins more nearly to "fit." Fit what? The new "international style." A classical one, with a "definite aesthetic," and, we may add, a still more definite limited technique. Athens, Rome, Paris. But Wright, the individual, remains a stumbling block. Certain others among the internationalists say he never was and never will be orthodox. A romantic—the last, so it is hoped.[23]

Indeed, it was an exhibit whose premises were theoretical, whose stated intention was to identify the one unified style of the age definitively. Neither of the essays by Hitchcock and Johnson in the catalogue set forth the social, political, or economic rationale of the new style they claimed to have identified. They insisted it was a style because they could enumerate and describe its visual principles, principles that were stable because they had apparently not changed for a decade.

For Haskell, this was much too simple an explanation for a set of relationships that he found far more complex, rich, and diverse and about which he had written many times beginning in the late 1920s. The very fact that it could not adequately account for the place or contribution of Frank Lloyd Wright, whom Haskell had championed during the same period, made it suspect. In the face of the compelling and seductive evidence brought by the exhibit Haskell tenaciously maintained his own point of view:

> I, too, believe, and with still more emphasis, that the paths will diverge. Nothing is established yet, except possibly the common victory over copying the periods and adapting ancient methods. We are at the beginning, not the end, of modern imagination. Technology is far more resourceful than this technique, and the Paris-painting base is not broad enough for more than a school and a couple of decades. Study the models closely—Wright's house for the Mesa, Mies's Tugendhat House, and the Savoye House by Le Corbusier—and you will see implicit differences leading to great new variety and change. You will even see diametric oppositions of attitude and character. All modern.[24]

The Museum of Modern Art had brought together a vast amount of significant work that Haskell admired but that he intended to judge freely on his own terms and according to what it seemed to offer independent of the body of theoretical assumptions published in the catalogue and elsewhere. He did not blindly accept the polemical rhetoric of the catalogue essays, nor did he swallow the proclamation that the style of the age had been discovered once and for all. As far as he was concerned, modern architecture had not yet begun to reveal its real potential.

The comparison of the three houses by Wright, Le Corbusier, and Mies is strongly reminiscent of an unpublished essay Haskell had written in January 1928 with the title "Three Architects," in which he attempted to examine the common bonds of modernism between Wright, Le Corbusier, and Erich Mendelsohn while acknowledging their obvious differences.[25] The choice of Mies to replace Mendelsohn and reconfigure the trilogy indicates that Haskell's perceptions had sharpened but that his instincts were solid. He continued to have faith in a pluralistic and inclusive modernism rather than a modernism of uniformity and exclusion. But this was simultaneously the stumbling block he found for the "man about town" who wants something he can count on. "Well, Paris gives pedigree for the man . . . ," he reflected, "and the new discipline gives the game its necessary rules." Hitchcock and Johnson had provided a way out of the stylistic confusion that had surrounded the definition of modernism in the 1920s, but the way might lead to a dead end at the copyist's draughting board.[26]

In the last paragraph of the review, Haskell said that the housing exhibit had been handled separately and therefore ought to be treated as a separate subject. He called it superb and deemed the method of its display throughout the exhibition magnificent. He also noted that besides Wright, the only Americans whom the exhibit had emphasized were Richard Neutra and the firm of Howe and Lescaze. Their housing project for Christie and Forsythe streets, he said, had "challenging innovations, but certain aspects are highly debatable" (fig. 8.5). He did not elaborate.[27] He further complimented the work of Thompson and Churchill, who "over a period of years [have] done more consistently competent modern work, though on a modest scale, than most of the big noises."[28]

Fig. 8.5. Installation view from the exhibition "Modern Architecture: International Exhibition," circulated by the Museum of Modern Art, New York, and held in Cleveland 27 Oct.–4 Dec. 1932. The foreground model is a four-unit project for a housing development by George Howe and William Lescaze in 1931 at the intersection of Christie and Forsythe streets in New York. The photograph immediately behind it shows the Kiefhoek Housing Development in Rotterdam by J. J. P. Oud in 1930. The other photographs document the Amalgamated Grand Street Apartments, a slum improvement project in New York, and to the far left, a housing development for Cleveland by an unidentified architect. (Photograph courtesy of the Cleveland Museum of Art)

Three other reviews of the "International Exhibition" were published in the April number of *Shelter* along with reprints of the lectures from the symposium. They were written by Frank Lloyd Wright (who disagreed with the exhibit from the outset), Arthur T. North (who took the new style to be either a swindle or a joke), and Knud Lonberg-Holm (who labelled it promotion and advertising).[29] None of the three wrote comprehensive reviews, each using the show as a springboard to present a personal philosophical position about modernism.

Philip Johnson read Haskell's review and was at least impressed with the intelligence and authenticity of Haskell's position, if not with his conclusion. The day after the review appeared in the *Nation* Johnson wrote Haskell to solicit an article for *Shelter* magazine, of which he was an associate editor.

Dear Mr. Haskell:

I enjoyed your review in The Nation very much and am sending you a copy of Shelter so that you can see what this young magazine is trying to do.

I hope that we can have a contribution from you in our next issue. I am sorry we can't pay contributors yet but with the cooperation of people like yourself I'm sure we will have enough success to do so soon.

Any contribution you want to make for the next issue must be here by the 25th of April. And I would very much appreciate hearing from you as to whether or not you can do this to help us make a success of this new venture.

I hope to have the pleasure of talking over the points of this review [in the *Nation*] personally with you.

Very sincerely yours,

[signed] Philip Johnson[30]

Haskell agreed and sent off a piece that appeared as the lead article in the May number under the title "Building with Money."[31] He wrote it as an essay on the value system that links architecture to societal institutions with special emphasis on the encroachment of business attitudes. After reminding the reader of the character of the demands placed on the architect by the Signoria of Florence when they commissioned a new cathedral in the late Middle Ages—"so as to be worthy of a heart expanded to much greatness, corresponding to the city's noble soul"—he quoted Raymond Hood from an interview in the *New York Times*. Hood had stated that the obligation of fiscal responsibility in architectural design leads to a rigorous analysis of materials, to honesty and integrity of design, and to the elimination of whimsy, taste, fashion, and vanity. By practicing fiscal responsibility, the architect is forced to confront the essentials of real architecture and real beauty.[32]

"This has conviction in it, sacrifice, and loyalty," Haskell began. "It is worthy of a good cause. The cause to which it is dedicated is 'good business'." The problem, Haskell charged, is that this attitude makes the architect feel that he is really only a "minor tool in relation to the business man's larger, even more complicated, exact, and beautiful designs of a financial character." Comparing the success of the architect's structure metaphorically with that of business, Haskell pointed out that "the business structure our financial architects have been constructing is suffering not from cracks in the plaster but from the

collapse, story by story, with shrieks of calamity, of whole sections of the frame. Who was it that ever got us into building as a 'business' anyway? We had merely intended to build ourselves homes and places of work. Somehow we were persuaded that the best stimulus for this was speculation."[33]

Haskell's irritation on the subject was not just based on a theoretical position. He pointed out that as projects stood "on their own financial feet" necessary building was not getting done while much, albeit profitable, building was mushrooming. New York, he pointed out, had the world's largest skyscrapers but had not solved its slum problem with the obviously available technology and financial power. Architecture had become a poker game, and buildings were huge, outdoor bookkeeping entries. What he called for was an attitude that could put finance in its rightful second place. " 'Money', like foundations or columns, is merely one element used in the present technique of erecting the necessary shelter. And as such an element it too must eventually be subject to radical redesigning. Not making money but making shelter is the aim."[34] Quoting statistics that showed the extent to which the housing problem had been solved in England, Germany, and Holland, Haskell concluded that the American architect as much as anyone else was responsible for the poor showing in the United States. He saw himself as a poker player, "only a business man," and "not yet a maker."

The essay was in keeping with the strongly liberal content of *Shelter,* which, as a fledgling architectural publication, was probably the most avant-garde in the country at that time. It was also a very clear statement of Haskell's convictions about modern architecture in the light of his recent experiences in Europe, experiences that had also reinforced his analysis of the show at the Museum of Modern Art. In the aftermath of the exhibit, the *Shelter* article was an elaboration on the position he had outlined in his review in the *Nation*. He did not see modern architecture in a formalist cultural vacuum but as the convergence of a nexus of forces, which included economics and finance. The "man about town" could be too easily convinced to accept the forms as a sign of personal sophistication rather than to see them as the result of a new vision for the human community altogether. He had expressed this point of view many times before, but after his recent sojourn, he had become only that much more certain of his ideas. He believed that there was more to the problem of modern architecture than Johnson and Hitchcock had presented in the show, despite the massive amount of evidence they had assembled in support of their ideological stance.

The article in *Shelter* was not the only one in which Haskell took a position on modern architecture in contrast with the attitude expressed by the organizers of the international exhibit. As a matter of fact, on several other occasions he used information and experiences he had collected on his European trip to challenge the conclusions of the great exhibit. In May 1932, for instance, he published an essay in *Creative Art* called "Is It Functional?" As the title implies, the piece is an exposition of issues surrounding the concept of functionalism, one of the central themes of the modern movement and of the International style.[35]

Haskell's intention was first of all to distinguish true functionalism from the cosmetic variety, a subtle but important effort that cut across several buildings and architects treated in the MOMA show and elsewhere. In fact, it is a telling aspect of the piece that almost every one of the examples he discussed was also illustrated in the "International Exhibition" and its catalogue. However, the article was not a retort. Haskell wanted to clarify his own definition of functionalism, particularly as it applied to American architecture. For this he turned to the work of Frank Lloyd Wright, whom the exhibit had slighted, as he had already pointed out, and whose work, he believed, International style theory could not adequately explain. Curiously, he never mentioned Wright by name, except in the caption beneath a photograph of the 1921 Millard house in Pasadena, but the reference is obvious.

He prefaced his discussion with an invented scene in which the reader overhears two American tourists discussing a modern house on the Kurfuerstendamm in Berlin. The first person is totally contemptuous and finds the quantity of glass and the stark planar walls repulsive. In his opinion, the modernist form seems dehumanizing in comparison to traditional architecture. Taking on an air of condescending superiority, the second finds the same building progressive and liberated from the past because of its generous glass and smooth, unornamented walls. Their disagreement over the acceptability of the design leads to the question of its actual or its apparent functionality. Haskell demonstrates that both opinions are based on visual observation and have more to do with the symbolic nature of the form and its presumed functionality than with its true practicality. A wall that looks planar, undecorated, and as though it is constructed of concrete may indeed be functional; but this is not guaranteed by its appearance. In reality, it may consist of stucco over brick masonry and be subject to rapid deterioration by normal moisture. Such conditions are evidence of an "inevitable collision between the functioning of brutal fact and function, the architect's fairy tale," he stated. When modern architecture is at its best, fact and story coincide. But the truth is often not as obvious as the functionalist formal language may imply.[36]

Haskell then offered a working definition of functionalism: "Simply that the house meets exactly the requirements we of this century actually put upon it, instead of fancied requirements or merely inherited ones." Using sunlight as a practical demonstration, he pointed out that recent exhaustive studies of sunlight in residential design would have been meaningless before the availability of cheap glass. Given that material, the studies help determine how to design windows that may not resemble familiar Tudor or Georgian fenestration. But despite the unfamiliar forms produced, the truth of the studies must be respected and trusted. "Whatever is true to its use has character," he postulated; "it has implicit style." As a result, the comfort and flexibility of a truly modern house makes the romantic house seem worn out.[37]

At that point, Haskell moved into the central issue: the relationship between appearance and architectural metaphor. "And yet how was the 'functional' idea to be clothed? It, too, in symbol, precedent and analogy! Try to imagine the purely 'functional' house. The first architects couldn't. But they could say, and they did, 'We will build houses as clean and commodious as the ocean liner, as standard as the automobile, and as light as the airplane.' This gave focus."[38]

In 1922 Le Corbusier wrote about the "machine for living in" and produced something shiplike in the Miestschaninoff house (Boulogne-sur-Seine, 1924), Haskell added. Later houses were more houselike but still not like anything seen before. The ship analogy was a point of departure, not a final destination. In each case, some functions were played up, others were played down. Indeed, it is impossible to express all the functions of any building in the form of that building, he declared. It is never as simple as the epithets make it sound: there is always a choice involved.[39]

Sometimes, he suggested, a look or desired appearance comes about before the appropriate material has been developed. For example, the smooth wall of stucco over brick was more readily available and technically feasible than the metal in the walls of a ship. Yet, the smooth wall of stucco was a point of departure. He illustrated this point with a pair of before and after photographs of Peter Behrens's apartment house at the 1927 Weissenhof-Siedlung in Stuttgart. The original snow-white building had decayed and darkened in the five years after its construction, obviously not a practical wall system even if it had been endowed with the metaphorical language of functionalism.[40]

Sometimes "inconvenient functions are disregarded in behalf of the myth," he continued. He recalled visiting a kindergarten in Vienna with a floor so smooth and polished that normal use — especially by children — would mar it. Its abstract planarity expressed functionalism visually but was anti-functional in reality.[41] This led him to further define the ideal nature of functionalism:

> "Functionalism" properly speaking should indicate nothing but exact technique. That it has become a slogan indicates an infusion by poetry. Each architect a poet according to the depth of his imagination. Those still called "pure functionalists" want to house us in a machine that has "solved" the obvious physical requirements. Then M. Le Corbusier and others, starting with the machine as a poetic idea: "Technical processes are the very seat of lyricism." This has carried the original mechanics far into the realms of human feeling. There are now even systems of esthetics explaining this conversion by the wand of abstract art. They deal with the "international style." We are told that we should "discipline" ourselves to that.[42]

In this passage, Haskell reveals a keen grasp of the romance that had rapidly grown up around the originally objective or *sachlich* concept of functionalism. In his view, a post-functionalist architecture, as Hitchcock and Johnson had defined it, could be explained not as an architecture that had gone beyond functionalism but one that had begun to focus on the romance of functionalism to the disadvantage of function itself.[43]

In his review of the MOMA show in the *Nation* Haskell had already mentioned his doubts about arguing the derivation of twentieth-century architectural style from a school of painting. Here he reiterates his belief that architecture — especially functionalist architecture — does not spring from theories of painting any more than painting springs from architectural theory. Architecture derives its philosophical and programmatic existence from its own internal necessities that are both technical and artistic. Functionalism could only have emerged as an important concept with a much broader cultural basis than that provided by either cubist or purist painting, even though functionalist architecture shared certain formal predilections with contemporaneous abstract art. Indeed, it would doubtless share that foundation with painting and the other arts as well as with the sciences.[44]

Haskell concluded that the poetic imagination of the architect ought to assimilate the more literal aspects of functionalism, but without destroying their practical value. Given this condition, more than one kind of metaphor might be possible as a poetic interpretation of the idea of function, he argued. Would it not be better to go beyond the metaphor of the machine and open up other possibilities rather than eliminate them? Would it not be better to expand the vocabulary and the imagination rather than to limit them?

> But I do not think that the twentieth century is ready to limit its resources. Is not mankind limited enough from the beginning in that its creation always goes largely by metaphor and simile? Can we stretch a single one of these to shelter our whole life? A "machine" in which to carry on a conversation; a machine in which to make love. A subtle machine, the last. Other symbols can be found that carry a share of truth: for instance, there is that of the tree. Too sentimental? Not if you consider how functional it is: capable of converting sunlight into energy, something we can't do without burning the tree itself. It has more than the machine; it has life, and it happens to furnish us not only with ideas of construction and of form, but also with strong suggestions regarding *place*. Enough; I know an architect to whom the symbol has been of use in building superb homes. And I know people who cannot accept these homes as architecture because they don't "seem functional enough."[45]

The unmistakable reference to Frank Lloyd Wright bespeaks Haskell's belief that even those most urgently preaching functionalism and its artistic expression had missed it in their own backyards. Comparing the relative value of machine and tree as architectural metaphors, Haskell would probably have chosen to align with the organic rather than the mechanical for personal reasons. At the same time, he accepted the reality of both and the possibility of their interdependence. Although he did not mention Wright's name, the cutline beneath the Millard house photograph makes it absolutely clear that the alternative—or the complement—to the European mechanical metaphor was the American organic one that had been promoted by both Sullivan and Wright. Wright's Millard house does not have the air of true functionalism at first glance, he admitted, because of its visually deceptive decoration. But in comparison to Behrens's building in Stuttgart, "This is the natural way to build with concrete," he said. "The starting point was not the functioning of the machine, but the organic quality of the surrounding trees."[46]

In this essay as in so many other writings, Haskell again staked a claim for a plurality of approaches to modern architecture. He argued that there is no single or universal metaphorical definition of functionalism. He was willing to concede the validity of the machine as symbol, but did not accept it exclusively above all others. The organic metaphor had just as much validity, but a different approach; and it offered insights and relationships that the mechanical metaphor could not. Both made sense on their own terms; but neither one excluded the other.

More fundamentally, however, the notion of a single modern style—the International style or even the organic, for that matter—could be of no interest to him. Discovering the style of the twentieth century by name and definitive characteristics signified an end, not a beginning. What he hoped to promote was a search to broaden and deepen the process of making shelter that would be as inclusive as possible: "All we can deny is the artist who, with the previous generation, denies the actual function of the house he is building, hides them, fails to let them develop. Develop into what? All we can say is, into a fine house. Beyond that, the answer is still up to the architect's imagination. All we can ask is that his fairytale come true."[47]

Haskell was not the only person who was concerned with clarifying functionalism, of course. In April, *Pencil Points* published an essay by George Howe called "Functional Aesthetics and the Social Ideal."[48] In this piece, Howe stated quite flatly that although the social, economic, and structural principles of architectural functionalism seem to have a wide acceptance in virtually every school of design in the architectural profession, they are also not the central issues. Economics plays an important role because the social ideal is highly economic in character. The economic system may dictate varying means from country to country, but it is almost a universal goal of modern nations to bring better material conditions and living standards

about. In the end, the architectural goals of functionalism are artistic.

> It is therefore important to bring out anew the fact that functionalism is essentially an aesthetic movement. However material the principles it may have laid down regarding the relation of architecture to society these constitute only the subject matter of an emotional expression. To quote Le Corbusier, "The faith of the functionalist is that aesthetic satisfaction in architecture can be found only in the outward expression of the contemporary life process as carried on in and about buildings and that it never was, or could be, found anywhere else."[49]

Haskell stood in agreement with the quote from Le Corbusier but not with the statement by Howe. Howe implies that aesthetics are somehow independent of and possibly even at odds with the practical aspects of functionalism that are accounted for by other cultural agencies. The functionalist fairy tale therefore takes on more significance than the functionalist reality. Haskell maintained that the expression of contemporary life process meant that true functionalism was an integrated expression of technical and aesthetic issues, a kind of aesthetic redemption of the mechanical in the tradition of Louis Sullivan.

Another interpretation of functionalist form was presented by Eugene Schoen in a piece called "Critical Judgment" in the May 1932 *Shelter.*[50] Schoen took issue with the proposal that functionalism could be a manifestation of any social ideal, arguing that it was purely formal manipulation.

> I have no quarrel with the "Internationalists" if they realize that they are only inventing new form through methods of construction; they are not inventing a new Architecture which is always an esthetic manifestation of a social philosophy. Just how much they are contributing to the new social philosophy is very doubtful upon analysis of their work. Just what the cantilever against the direct column support, or the use of horizontal or vertical accents have to do with social concepts I fail to see. Yet that seems to be their main attention.[51]

Schoen's position was farther to the right than Haskell's but shared his skepticism about the purposefulness of the formal and structural vocabulary that identified International style. Moreover, he argues that a new architectural style could hardly have the capability of reordering society, being conversely one expression of more pervasive attitudinal changes in society.

For Alvin Johnson, director of the New School for Social Research and a frequent commentator on architecture, the problem lay in the mediocrity of the product, not in the control of theory by the social ideal. Writing in the same issue of *Shelter,* he suggested that the cause may be that we live "in an age in which professional statecraft amounts to nothing, and each architect is left to jerry together such haphazard conceptions of function as may occur to him."[52]

Haskell had already argued for variety and appropriateness in form, materials, and construction in his critique of the "Rejected Architects," the counter-exhibit of young architects whose work was excluded from the annual show of the New York Architectural League in 1931.[53]

> To one in sympathy with their aims, the show of the refuses was quite disappointing. In practice they are too unanimous. They all use posts and cantilevering—though it is by no means certain yet that this will be the most economical construction. They all use extensive roof gardens—even on a country estate. In form, a great deal of the "rejected" work consisted of mutations of the box, piled up off-center; and although Clauss and Daub made pleasing compositions out of this, they were seldom compelling because they rested on indifferent or extravagant plans. Le Corbusier has captured these designers' imaginations; and until they burst the bonds of foreign restraint they will not do justice either to themselves or to science in American architecture.[54]

Although sympathetic to their work, he nonetheless found them too derivative, too involved with predetermined imagery borrowed directly from their European sources and neither truly functional nor scientific enough. The pluralism that he had always sought and believed to be a natural quality of modernism was lacking, replaced by the acquired language of radical modernist Europe.

The question of the relationship between funtionalism, aesthetics, and contemporary social ideals thus remained open after the exhibit at the MOMA. Since little space had been devoted to that relationship in the catalogue, Hitchcock and Johnson had left their own position in the matter ambiguous. The issue was therefore subject to continued speculation among those who sensed its cruciality to any worthwhile view of modernism. It was principally Haskell, however, who recognized that functionalism, to be more than a slogan identified with modern architecture, could not be one monolithic ideology; and that if it were monolithic, as in the context of the International style theory, it could appear to be a convenient contrivance on the part of Hitchcock and Johnson to rationalize their

own point of view. He was skeptical of those who treated functionalism as a purely aesthetic issue (as in the articles by Howe and Schoen) and disappointed with those who divorced it from art as merely a precondition to a new architecture that had already, in fact, superseded it (as the organizers of the MOMA exhibit had insinuated).

Fig. 8.6. Aerial view of the PSFS Building in Philadelphia by George Howe and William Lescaze. (Photograph courtesy of PSFS/Meritor Corporate Archives)

In June, almost as a response to the piece by George Howe in *Pencil Points,* Haskell tackled the issue again on a more concrete and direct basis. He reviewed the Philadelphia Saving Fund Society (PSFS) Building by Howe and Lescaze in *Creative Art*[55] (fig. 8.6). Labeling the building a dubious success, he nevertheless praised its intention. "In architectural terms," he said,

> this is the first application to skyscrapers of "horizontality." Among the many elements either of structure or of plan that it is possible for a building to "express," this one has chosen to express the floor. It is a filing cabinet of a building. It is a stack of trays, held at the side by the vertical sticks of the rack. That is, the side has columns, showing out beyond the wall; the front has not. Since there is not one daub or hunk of applied decoration, this system is visibly manifest.[56]

Fig. 8.8. Base of the PSFS Building as it appeared in 1949. (Photograph courtesy of PSFS/Meritor Corporate Archives)

Fig. 8.7. PSFS Building, seen from the corner of Market and North Twelfth streets. (Photograph courtesy of PSFS/Meritor Corporate Archives)

Haskell then took the designers to task on several points. He said that the contrast between the verticality of the columns and elevator tower and the horizontality of the floors was "paradoxical to say the least" (fig. 8.7). He found the structure dualistic, with one system of columns embedded in the wall and another system behind it. He thought the facade treatments were disparate and the composition clumsy in the transition between the base and the shaft. The reason for these problems, he said, was intrinsic to the skyscraper as a type. The architects, by trying to be logical, had actually uncovered anachronisms that had been veiled for years by traditional decoration.

But he did not let the architects off the hook that easily. In the catalogue of the international exhibition, Hitchcock had praised the Saving Fund Society building for its "application of an aesthetically logical and consistent horizontal scheme of design to the skyscraper." Although he, too, had questioned the composition of the base and the handling of the elevator tower, he said it was "the one American skyscraper which is worth discussing in the same terms as the work of the leading architects of Europe"[57] (fig. 8.8). Haskell obviously found it less satisfying. He questioned whether the principles of International style could be applied to a building typology, which essentially contradicted them: "The path to simplicity was cluttered a little, I believe, by the architects themselves. They had intellectual baggage from Europe: an 'international style'."[58]

As in many of his reviews, Haskell gave the critique an ironic twist by discussing a tragic flaw in the work: what is commendable in the PSFS is also its Achilles heel. It expresses an approach to modern architectural form consistently, but the design unfortunately conflicts with the building typology to which it is applied, producing something close to an architectural oxymoron. In conjunction with this, the remark about intellectual baggage from Europe illustrates a point Haskell had first made in his criticism of the "Rejected Architects." Too many architects were buying into the formal language of European modernism without the proper grasp of its underlying principles or the willingness to challenge them (figs. 8.9, 8.10). Haskell had gone on record many times in favor of much that was being done in Europe. But he had always called for an authentic approach to European architecture, one in which American designers would employ the principles without the preconceived formal language of the European expression. He

Fig. 8.9. View of the escalator leading to the banking floor of the PSFS Building in 1932. (Photograph courtesy of PSFS/Meritor Corporate Archives)

admired Howe and Lescaze for their willingness to explore important new ideas, but he was convinced that they did not need to rely on the International style or any other preexisting style.[59] These would only get in the way of their own better impulses.

Fig. 8.10. View of the banking floor in the PSFS Building as it appeared in 1932. (Photograph courtesy of PSFS/Meritor Corporate Archives)

Shortly after his review of the PSFS building appeared, Haskell received a letter from Lewis Mumford, who was just completing a four-month research tour in Europe.[60] Apparently the two friends had had little contact regarding the MOMA exhibit between Haskell's return from Europe in February and Mumford's departure in April, although Mumford had obviously read Haskell's review of the exhibit in the *Nation*. The content of the communication must have both amused and surprised Haskell.

Dear Douglas: News from America comes through when one is travelling as sound comes through the wool in a swimmer's ears, when he is too busy fighting the tide to pay attention to what is being shouted from the shore anyway. I saw a copy of Shelter in Zuerich or Vienna with an article of yours in it, but I am eager to learn what you are doing and thinking in private, too. I have had a full and marvelous trip in which architecture and housing had a share, although they did not dominate, and I am more eager than ever to compare impressions with you. The good work I found in unexpected places: in German post-offices, in subways, in one or two Siedlungen, Neubuehl and Roemerstadt, particularly: and much of the architecture which Johnson and Hitchcock have been so loud in praise of seemed a little seedy, or at least, incompletely thought out. Incidentally, however, I felt you weren't quite fair to their museum exhibition in your Nation criticism. God knows their personalities get on one's nerves: but, given a *selective* exhibition, who else could have been chosen as representative except the very men they did choose — except, I grant you, Hood? You were wrong, too, to deprive them of credit for the housing side: it was Johnson's own pet scheme and he carried it through despite every one else's opposition. I say this because I know personally how hard it is to be fair to either of them: they have such terrible intellectual manners, their point of view is so *conventional,* and they are capable of talking so much fish, with an air of authority. Now that you and I have both seen the work, we can at least challenge them on the ground where they have hitherto been pre-eminent, for lack of rivalry . . .

Sophy is coming over now and I expect to get to America by the fifteenth of August. After 1 August Amenia will be the best address.

My greetings to your wife

Yours,

Lewis[61]

The candid, almost gossipy letter reveals that Mumford had definitely been working from a different perspective than Hitchcock and Johnson when he produced his portion of the MOMA show and catalogue — which he refers to as "their museum exhibition." Although he had been a part of it, he considered the exhibit both speculative and tentative as a statement about modernism, thus confirming Haskell's own reservations about its content and theoretical assumptions. Although he gave Johnson credit for his invention and support of the housing section, Mumford openly admits here that his own ideas about modern architecture are not embodied only in the examples the organizers had selected as representative of international modernism. This was especially true once he had seen them for himself and compared what he had been told with what actually existed.

Because of similar experiences, Mumford and Haskell seem to have come to a similar point of view: that continental developments were much richer and offered much greater diversity than Hitchcock and Johnson had allowed; but, as Catherine Bauer had pointed out, the important buildings were not always dazzling. Good modern architecture in Europe could be found in simple, unpretentious places like public housing developments, government buildings, and subways as well as in places like the Van Nelle factory.

Exactly what Mumford meant by seedy is difficult to determine, but it could well describe his reaction to the kind of physi-cal decay that Haskell had discovered in the Weissenhof-Siedlung where the imagery of functionalism — white plaster walls over brick or stone masonry, rust-prone painted metal, flat roofs in the northern climate — proved unable to endure the stress of weather and wear. Nor does he explain what he means by "incompletely thought out," a phrase that could refer to the relationship of details to whole in the program or in the physical structure; or, more likely, to the conceptualization altogether.

As far as his remarks about Haskell's critique of the MOMA show are concerned, it is clear that he had no dispute with the organizers about whether the buildings selected for the exhibit were modern or not. Like Mumford, Haskell was much more concerned about whether the exhibited works truly represented everything that could or should have been subsumed categorically under modern architecture and whether they formed a school that superseded everything else contemporary to them. He was also concerned that others — like Thompson and Churchill — were not equally representative though less highly profiled; and, he wondered if it was conceivable to treat Frank Lloyd Wright as a hopeless romantic who had passed his prime. Whether they had stylistic affinities or not, they were all tied to social and political conditions as well as to scientific and industrial realities, not just to art historical laws in the Wöefflinian tradition. The MOMA exhibit had successfully introduced a large body of modern architecture to the public, but in doing so it had also established a view of modernism that Douglas Haskell found he would have to challenge then and many times in the future.

It was this kind of interchange, due largely to the efforts of Douglas Haskell, that began to urge architectural journalism out of a period of dowdy complacency toward a more dialectical treatment of ideas and concepts. Although the climate for a broad-based architectural criticism in the American press was considerably reduced by the Great Depression, forward-looking publishers like Howard Myers at *Architectural Forum* and culturally based writers like Lewis Mumford, along with Haskell, nevertheless maintained their strong voices and provocative points of view throughout the 1930s and 1940s. Yet, not until Haskell became editor of *Architectural Forum* in 1949, was he able to fulfill his own expectations and hopes for a critical architectural journalism in the professional press, an achievement for which he will long be remembered.

Notes

1. For a more extensive treatment of this issue, see Robert Benson, "Douglas Haskell and the Modern Movement in American Architecture," *Journal of Architectural Education* 36 (Summer 1983): 2–9.

2. Douglas Putnam Haskell, who lived between 1899 and 1979, was a graduate of Oberlin College. He is well known as the editor of *Architectural Forum* from 1949 until his retirement in 1964. He was, however, a Fellow of the American Institute of Architects and a recipient of the institute's critics medal, honors based on a long and distinguished career as an architectural journalist. From 1923 to 1927 he served as editor of a national collegiate publication called *The New Student;* from 1927 to 1929 he was on the editorial staff of *Creative Art;* and briefly from 1929 to 1930 he was an associate editor at *Architectural Record.* He also published in the London *Architectural Review,* Scribner's *Architecture, The Studio, Pencil Points,* the *Journal of the AIA, Parnassus, Shelter, Harper's, The New Republic,* and many other journals. He contributed chapters to several large works and served as editor of *Rehousing Urban America,* Henry Wright's pace-setting study published by Columbia University Press in 1935. He returned to *Architectural Record* as a senior editor in 1942 and remained there until he took over editorial leadership of *Architectural Forum* for Time-Life, Inc., in 1949.

3. For a complete bibliography of Haskell's writings see Robert Benson, "Douglas Haskell: The Early Critical Writings" (Ph.D. diss., University of Michigan, 1987).

4. The itinerary for the exhibition was published in *Pencil Points* 13 (May 1932): 359, 380. It was to be mounted in nine museums and other institutions including the Wadsworth Atheneum in Hartford, Sears Roebuck and Company in Chicago, the Bullock's Wilshire in Los Angeles, the Buffalo Fine Arts Academy, the Cleveland Museum of Art, the Milwaukee Art Institute, the Cincinnati Art Museum, the Rochester Memorial Art Gallery, and the Toledo Museum. In a reduced form, the exhibit traveled to many other cities for another five years.

5. The symposium was held on 19 February 1932 at the Museum of Modern Art. Speakers included Lewis Mumford, Henry Wright, Raymond M. Hood, George Howe, Harvey Wiley Corbett, Henry-Russell Hitchcock, Jr., John Wheelwright and Harold Sterner. Some of their remarks were reprinted as "Symposium: The International Architectural Exhibition" in *Shelter* 2 (April 1932): 3–9.

6. Douglas Haskell, "What the Man About Town Will Build," *Nation* 134 (13 April 1932): 441–443. Other reviews include Talbot F. Hamlin, "The International Style Lacks the Essence of Great Architecture," *American Architect* 143 (January 1933): 12–16; Ralph Flint, "Present Trends in Architecture in Fine Exhibit," *Art News* 30 (13 February 1932): 5–6; William Adams Delano, "Man versus Mass," *Shelter* 2 (April 1932): 16–17; as well as those treated below.

7. See for instance, Richard Guy Wilson, "International Style: the MOMA Exhibition," *Progressive Architecture* 63 (February 1982): 92–105.

8. "Hirams of 1932," *Art Digest* 6 (1 February 1932): 12.

9. *Modern Architecture: International Exhibition* (New York: Museum of Modern Art, 1932): 13.

10. Ibid., 15–16.

11. Ibid., 19–20.

12. Ibid., 20. See also Hitchcock's editorial "Architectural Criticism" in *Shelter* 2 (April 1932): 2. This was a defense of the stylistic premise of the MOMA exhibit directed in particular to the organizers and critics of the Architectural League show. This may not entirely explain the rationale for the show,

but it may indicate how Hitchcock and others at the museum justified the heavily visual nature of the installation and catalogue discussions. Moreover, because the symposium had stressed social responsibility as well as the urban context, Hitchcock and Johnson could argue that the exhibit and its related activities had covered more than just the visual and stylistic aspects of the new architecture.

13. *Modern Architecture: International Exhibition,* 179. The information contained in this essay and the point of view it represented were notably excluded from the simultaneous publication by Hitchcock and Johnson of *Architecture Since 1922: The International Style* (New York: W. W. Norton, 1932), which therefore presented an essentially art historical view of modern architecture out of its social and urban contexts.

14. Edward Alden Jewell, review of "Modern Architecture: International Exhibition" at the Museum of Modern Art, *New York Times,* 9 February 1932, 30.

15. Edward Alden Jewell, review of "Modern Architecture: International Exhibition" at the Museum of Modern Art, an exhibit of Joseph Urban's entry into the Palace of the Soviets Competition at the New York Architectural League and the exhibit "City of the Future" by Hugh Ferriss at the Roerich Museum, *New York Times,* 14 February 1932, sec. 8, 10.

16. Edward Alden Jewell, review of the 47th Annual Exhibition of the New York Architectural League, *New York Times,* 27 February 1932, 20.

17. Catherine K. Bauer, "Exhibition of Modern Architecture: Museum of Modern Art," *Creative Art* 10 (March 1932): 201–206. See Lewis Mumford, *Sketches from Life* (New York: Dial Press, 1982), 459–466, in which Mumford outlines his personal relationship with Catherine Bauer.

18. William Williams, "A la Mode Horizontale," *Pencil Points* 13 (April 1932): 271–272.

19. Douglas Haskell, "A Factory in Holland," *Nation* 133 (18 November 1931): 549. For Haskell's assessment of Roemerstadt and the comparative quality of German and American low-income housing see his "New Mayland," *Nation* 134 (9 March 1932):292–294, and "Modern Architecture, Occupied," (Scribner's) *Architecture* 66 (August 1932): 77–84, which presents a detailed post-occupancy evaluation.

20. "Man About Town," 441–442.

21. Douglas Haskell, "The Closing of the Bauhaus," *Nation* 135 (19 October 1932): 374–375. In this piece, he lamented the loss of the Bauhaus because, among other things, of its threat to Nazi mediocrity: "Yet at the other end of the scale, quite opposed to this elegance or preciousness, to which Mies van der Rohe gives the richest expression and Le Corbusier the most exciting, there stand the socialist workers, with their own rough and ready version of the same 'style' worked out for them by architects interested primarily in sociology and in mass housing."

22. This theory had been established by Henry-Russell Hitchcock and published in several different places, most prominently in his book *Modern Architecture: Romanticism and Reintegration* (New York: Payson and Clarke Ltd., 1929). See also his two articles "Modern Architecture: I. The Traditionalists and the New Tradition," *Architectural Record* 63 (April 1928): 337–349, and "Modern Architecture: II. The New Pioneers," *Architectural Record* 63 (May 1928): 453–460.

23. "Man About Town," 442.

24. Ibid.

25. Haskell wrote an initial draft of this piece in 1927 and titled it "Three Architects of the Machine Age." The revised typescript, dated January 1928, Brooklyn, N.Y., is now located with all of Haskell's papers in the Avery Library

of Columbia University. See also "Douglas Haskell and the Modern Movement in American Architecture," 5–6.

26. "Man About Town," 442.

27. Haskell expressed his specific reservations about the debatable aspects of the Howe and Lescaze project in a footnote to an article he wrote for Scribner's *Architecture* three months later. See "Modern Architecture, Occupied," *Architecture* 66 (August 1932): 77–84, especially the note designated by an asterisk on p. 82. His concern centered on the practicality of rooms facing an outdoor corridor.

28. "Man About Town," 443. Thompson and Churchill, a firm in New York, had produced many small apartment buildings and other small- to medium-sized works.

29. In *Shelter* 2 (April 1932) see: Frank Lloyd Wright, "Of Thee I Sing" (10–12); Arthur T. North, "Old New Stuff" (12–16); and Knud Lonberg-Holm, "Two Shows: A Comment on the Aesthetic Racket" (16–17).

30. Philip Johnson to Douglas Haskell, 14 April 1932.

31. Douglas Haskell to Philip Johnson, 23 April 1932; Douglas Haskell "Building with Money," *Shelter* 2 (May 1932): 2–3.

32. "Building with Money," 2.

33. Ibid.

34. Ibid., 3.

35. Douglas Haskell, "Is It Functional," *Creative Art* 10 (May 1932): 373–378. This is one of the first instances in which a critic attempted to analyze the term *functionalism* both semantically and philosophically in order to make judgments about its value for modern architecture.

36. Ibid., 373.

37. Ibid., 373–376.

38. Ibid., 378.

39. Ibid. There is no direct evidence that Haskell had visited any of the works of Le Corbusier during his European trip. However, according to his wife, Helen Haskell, who accompanied him, they spent time in France and Italy as well as other countries that remain unmentioned in Haskell's writings or personal papers. Therefore, it is possible that he had acquired firsthand knowledge of a few buildings by Le Corbusier. Helen Haskell interview, 14 April 1982.

40. Ibid.; the illustrations are found on p. 374.

41. Ibid.; a photograph (taken by Haskell) of the unnamed Austrian kindergarten is found on p. 375.

42. Ibid., 378. The reference here is probably to the discussion of Frank Lloyd Wright in the catalogue of the MOMA show in which Henry-Russell Hitchcock says, "Architecture to Wright is not a discipline," and then goes on to argue that "those who have aspired to emulate Wright in all the breadth and license of his undaunted genius have never achieved more than a pathetic parody of his work, while those who have purified and solidified their interpretation of his doctrine, seeking more consonance with the second quarter of the twentieth century and less with the romantic absolutes of Man and Nature, have attained throughout the world a real integration of style" (*Modern Architecture: International Exhibition,* 30).

43. The term *post-functionalist* first appears in a review by Edward Alden Jewell of the Exposition of Architecture and Allied Arts of the Architectural League of New York and the "Rejected Architects" show (*New York Times,* 26 April 1931, sec. 8, 10). In the review, Philip Johnson was quoted as an authority on the "rejected architects"–entrants who submitted work to but were rejected by the selection committee for the annual exhibit of the Architectural League. They set up their own counter-exhibit in a storefront on Seventh Avenue across from Carnegie Hall as a kind of "Salon des Refuses." Johnson called them post-functionalists who were working in the International style. This was also the first appearance of the term *International style* in the *Times.* [Johnson used it initially in his review of the New School for Social Research by Joseph Urban. See his "Architecture of the New School," *The Arts* 17 (March 1931): 393–398.] The phrase had already been coined by Henry-Russell Hitchcock in *Modern Architecture: Romanticism and Reintegration* of 1929 (see p. 162). The evidence of this interview and several other articles and documents indicates that Johnson, along with Alfred Barr, was a motivating force behind the counter-exhibit and that he had much at stake in defending the group rejected by the League. On several occasions, he used the event of the "Rejected Architects" exhibit to identify himself as the sole spokesman for an entire architectural movement that was emerging as the result of irrepressible forces of architectural history.

44. The concept that abstract painting, especially cubism, had been a major formative force in architectural modernism was attributable in this context to Hitchcock, who continued to pursue the relationship long after the MOMA show was over. See his *Painting Toward Architecture* (New York: Duell, Sloan and Pearce, 1948). The fact that Le Corbusier was himself a painter and that many of the important architects of the movement were intimately involved with artists of other disciplines in professional, academic, and theoretical interchanges alike, seemed to support the position.

45. Ibid., 378.

46. Ibid., 375.

47. Ibid., 378.

48. George Howe, "Functional Aesthetics and the Social Ideal," *Pencil Points* 13 (April 1932): 215–218.

49. Ibid., 215.

50. Eugene Schoen, "Critical Judgement," *Shelter* 2 (May 1932): 48. Eugene Schoen was a decorative artist whose work was displayed in the Architectural League exhibit in 1931.

51. Ibid.

52. Alvin Johnson, "After Functionalism: Function," *Shelter* 2 (May 1932): 51–52.

53. Douglas Haskell, "The Architectural League and the Rejected Architects," *Parnassus* 3 (May 1931): 12–13. See n. 40.

54. Ibid., 12.

55. Douglas Haskell, "The Filing-Cabinet Building," *Creative Art* 10 (June 1932): 447–449.

56. Ibid., 447.

57. *Modern Architecture: International Exhibition,* 144–145; an illustration of the PSFS building is found on p. 153.

58. Ibid., 448.

59. Earlier in the year, Howe and Lescaze had resigned from the New York Architectural League in protest. All three of their submissions had been barred from the league exhibit at the Fine Arts Society Building, apparently because they were done in modern design, although officials at the League insisted no such prejudices existed. See "Architects' Show Bars Two Moderns," *New York Times,* 28 February 1932, sec. 1:1.

60. See Mumford, *Sketches,* 407.

61. Lewis Mumford to Douglas Haskell (from London?), 4 July 1932.

CHAPTER 9

THEMES OF CONTINUITY

The Prairie School in the 1920s and 1930s

RICHARD GUY WILSON

Continuity, or its absence, has long been a major concern of American architects and historians as they have attempted to create and identify images that express their cultural and physical situation. One example of the lack of continuity is the midwestern Prairie School of Frank Lloyd Wright, Louis Sullivan, and followers, whose considerable success seemed to conclude abruptly about 1916 leaving few apparent successors. Not until the reemergence of Wright in the 1930s is the line of continuity reestablished. Until recently, the intervening years of the 1920s and early 1930s have been viewed by many historians as vacuous in terms of midwestern architecture.[1] This essay investigates the issue of Prairie School continuity not just in terms of visual similarities, but also principles.

The Prairie School did not completely die out with the onset of World War I as some historians have suggested; indeed continuity can be seen in the work of architects of the period; it demonstrates that the apparent decline of the Prairie School has been overemphasized.

Reasons for the decline have been a subject of debate among scholars. Four are commonly given: first, the removal of the more creative members—Frank Lloyd Wright, William Gray Purcell, Walter Burley Griffin, and Marion Mahony—from the scene; second, the increased status of women as decision makers and their preference for design modes other than the masculine Prairie School; third, the removal of journalistic support and the development of a more national, less regional taste; and finally, the failure of the Prairie School architects to develop a committed clientele with the requisite status to continue the reorientation of American architecture away from East Coast and foreign stylistic dictates.[2] These reasons could be expanded, but the implications are clear. For both internal and external causes, personal and cultural, the acceptance of the Prairie School drastically diminished around 1916.

Dramatic changes are apparent between the 1910s and the 1920s in numerous Prairie School architects' work. William Drummond shifts from a flat-roofed volumetric box enlivened by rectilinear trim, as in his own house of 1910, to an English cottage idiom in the 1920s (fig. 9.1).[3] Tallmadge and Watson, a former Prairie School firm, could by 1920 design Colonial Revival residences. Drummond and Tallmadge and Watson apparently felt the earlier Prairie School idiom was no longer apparent (fig. 9.2).

Fig. 9.1. William Drummond, Badenoch house, River Forest, Ill., 1925.
(Richard Guy Wilson)

Fig. 9.2. William Drummond, Drummond house, River Forest, Ill., 1910.
(*Western Architect,* 21 [Feb. 1915], pl. 17)

Fig. 9.3. William L. Steele, Everist house, Sioux City, Iowa, 1916–1917. (Richard Guy Wilson)

Fig. 9.4. William L. Steele, Smith's Villa Branch Public Library, Sioux City, Iowa, 1926–1927. (Richard Guy Wilson)

There are, of course, some architects that continued the Prairie School mode into the 1920s, such as William Steele (1875–1949) out in Sioux City, Iowa. Steele had graduated from Clifford Ricker's architectural program at University of Illinois and was also an alumnus of Sullivan's office prior to his arrival in Sioux City in 1904. But Steele's Prairie School career did not begin until 1915 when he asked George Elmslie to become his associate on the Woodbury County Courthouse. While the courthouse was principally Elmslie's work, Steele felt secure enough in the following years to produce numerous works that fall within the Prairie School idiom, such as the masterful H. H. Everist house of 1916 (fig. 9.3) and numerous other works in the Sioux City area.

The problem of the Prairie School's acceptance as a domestic style is revealed in three branch libraries Steele designed in the late 1920s. The Fairmont Park and Smith's Villa branches are identical, and as Steele claimed, the "architectural style is entirely modern. There has been no attempt to link it with the past by copying. . . . It expresses its function in its design"[4] (fig. 9.4). The Northside Branch of a year later designed in a neo-Tudor idiom, was consciously different (fig. 9.5). The *Sioux City Journal* explained that "because of the location of the new branch library [among houses], it is constructed in the style of an individual residence."[5] Steele was not an ideologue in architecture, and by 1929 his Prairie School career was over. Work diminished in Sioux City, and he moved to Omaha, where in his numerous writings he continued to support the principles of Sullivan, but his architecture reveals little of his Prairie School past.[6]

Fig. 9.5. William L. Steele, Northside Branch Public Library, Sioux City, Iowa, 1927–1928. (Richard Guy Wilson)

Clearly the work of William Steele cannot be considered a very strong extension of the Prairie School, but it does illuminate two of the issues that have to be considered in this discussion. First, the problem of continuity—was it to be merely stylistic, or could the principles of Wright, Sullivan, and followers be carried forward without a specific stylistic guise? The principles can be identified as the usage of simple forms and complex details, an abstract geometrical language, spatial reorganization within the building and a spatial relation to the landscape, common materials used in a direct manner, and an expression of a midwestern cultural and personal situation free of foreign stylisms. Were these principles valid for a different social and intellectual climate? The second issue to be considered concerns influence and creativity. While remaining true to the principles, how could the followers differentiate themselves from the masters? In the terms of Harold Bloom, the question was how to surmount anxiety of influence and develop one's own expression.[7] These issues can be seen most clearly in the work of several individuals from the period: George Grant Elmslie, John Lloyd Wright, Alfred Caldwell, and Alden Dow. Each represents a different source for the continuation of the Prairie School: George Elmslie was a product of the Sullivan wing; John Lloyd Wright was trained in his father's Oak Park studio and later Chicago office; Alfred Caldwell was independent of the normal orbit and came from Jens Jensen's office; and finally, Alden Dow was a student of the Taliesin Fellowship. Visually divergent, these architects attempted to continue the principles of the Prairie School in a new and different social-intellectual climate.

The work of George Grant Elmslie (1871–1952) in the 1920s and 1930s presents one of the clearest connections with the pre–World War I Prairie School, for he had served Louis Sullivan from 1888 to 1909 and then had been in partnership with William Gray Purcell from 1909 to 1918.[8] Formally, Elmslie was committed to the geometrical space-enclosing elements of Sullivan; his architecture was not generated by the open horizontals and verticals of Wright. The First National Bank in Adams, Minn., 1917–1929, designed while the partnership was still in operation, reflects the earlier Prairie School.[9] However, Elmslie's work after 1918 marks a change as he attempts to come to terms with the new period.

The Capitol Building and Loan Association building of To-peka, Kans., 1918–1922, is a curious synthesis of several earlier themes (fig. 9.6). A monumental base derived from the small town banks supports layers of office floors and a gable roof that strongly recalls Adler and Sullivan's Saint Nichols Hotel in St. Louis, Mo., 1892. The tall, gable roof was intended to have sentimental associations, for the clients wanted a building "that reminded people of the American home."[10] The ornamentation has the same split image, contrasting lush Sullivanesque foliage with representational statues and relief panels by Emil Zettler of the Kansas family, the pioneer, and civic virtues. The Old Second National Bank in Aurora, Ill., 1924, substitutes length for height, but continues the high-pitched roof theme, recalling Flemish banking houses (fig. 9.7). On the interior, Elmslie created a lively space with "art glass" and murals by John Norton.

Fig. 9.6. George G. Elmslie, Capitol Building and Loan Association, Topeka, Kans., 1918–1922. (Richard Guy Wilson)

Elmslie clearly sought to temper some of the harsher or more modern aspects of the earlier Prairie School, such as the low-rising roof. The high-pitched roof had played a role in the early work of the Prairie School, and Purcell and Elmslie had used it in their work. In general, however, it had been abandoned as too remindful of the past, and in conflict with the emphasis on horizontality.[11] But the gable was the traditional sign of home in the United States, and in many of Elmslie's projects in the 1920s it dominates. Elmslie handled the gable as an abstract geometrical form, but still it has connotations of Tudor and medieval buildings, a revelation of Elmslie's own stated preferences.[12] The Clayton F. Summy dwelling in Hinsdale, Ill., is compatible in form with its neighbors, though it stands apart on closer inspection in terms of window treatment and details. Residences, though, were not Elmslie's main staple

in the 1920s. More representative are buildings such as the Healy Chapel and Funeral Home in Aurora, Ill., 1927, and Forbes Hall at Yankton College, Yankton, S.Dak., 1929 (fig. 9.8). In both cases, he uses heavy traditional forms and enlivens them through fenestration patterns, treatment of materials, and unique ornament.

A further movement by Elmslie towards acceptance of traditional styles can be seen in the "Church in the Garden," or the Congregational church of Western Springs, Ill., 1926–1930 (fig. 9.9). The vestry certainly had a hand in the choice of the style, but Elmslie willingly accepted the restriction.[13] Following the form of an English Country church but with an abstract handling of the gable, Gothic elements are juxtaposed with motifs that recall the Prairie School.

Fig. 9.7. George G. Elmslie, Old Second National Bank, Aurora, Ill., 1923–1924, interior. (Old Second National Bank)

Fig. 9.8. George G. Elmslie, Forbes Hall, Yankton College, Yankton, S.Dak., 1929. (Yankton College)

Fig. 9.9. George G. Elmslie, Congregational Church, Western Springs, Ill., 1926–1930. (Richard Guy Wilson)

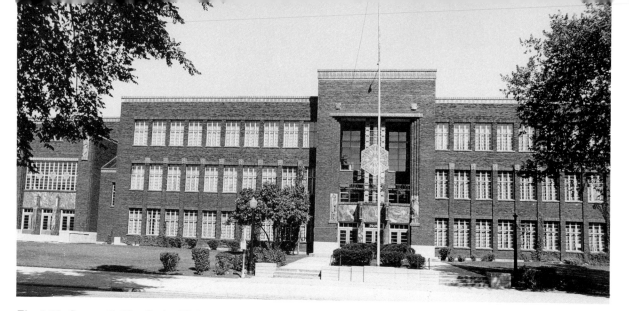

Fig. 9.10. George G. Elmslie for William S. Hutton, Thomas Edison Middle School, Hammond, Ind., 1936. (Richard Guy Wilson)

For Elmslie, as for most architects, work fell off with the Great Depression; and in spite of the publication of some of his work, he was forced back to serving others.[14] His most prominent work is the exterior design on four schools in Hammond, Ind., and Calumet City, Ill., for William S. Hutton, a local architect (fig. 9.10). In these designs, such as the Thomas Edison Middle School, a new energy is present. The entrance is a monumental statement of the Chicago frame with the ornamentation a clearly demarked efflorescence separate from the structure (fig. 9.11). The sculpture by Emil Zettler contains patriotic-mythological motifs common to the 1930s.

By 1937 Elmslie was sixty-five years old; and while there were still a few projects, he largely retired from active practice. Elmslie has generally been viewed as a member of a team; his independent work illuminates his own preference for the medieval and the picturesque. But also his work must be seen in the context of the period; and in that light his exploration of conventional imagery and its transformation gains in richness and comprehension. His job sheet lists sixty-seven commissions (forty-nine for the 1920s and eighteen for the 1930s), with approximately twenty-seven completions indicating the continuation of activity by a major Prairie School figure.[15]

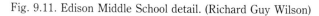

Fig. 9.11. Edison Middle School detail. (Richard Guy Wilson)

A pattern similar to that seen in Elmslie's work of retreat in the 1920s and reinvigoration in the 1930s can also be observed in the career of John Lloyd Wright (1892–1972). Best known as the author of *My Father Who Is on Earth* (1946), John represents a midwestern continuation of the Prairie School principles derived through his father in the 1920s and 1930s. His training, devised by his father, included the Oak Park studio and playroom, Froebel Blocks, Hillside School, readings in Viollet-le-Duc, and then two years at the University of Wisconsin, where he flunked out.[16] In 1911 he joined his elder brother, Lloyd, in southern California and secured a position with a local architect, Harrison Albright, for whom he designed several buildings in the midwestern idiom.[17] John's announcement to his father that he was going to Vienna to study with Otto Wagner resulted in the invitation to return to Chicago to run the office while taking a private course of instruction.

In Chicago with father, John supervised construction and did some designing. He also introduced his father to Alfonso Iannelli, a friend and collaborator from southern California. John's contributions to the Midway Gardens and the Imperial Hotel were probably minimal; however, surviving letters indicate he had a hand in the Bach house in Chicago, 1915.[18] Frank Lloyd Wright's offhand manner with employees' salaries was no more acceptable to his son, and in 1918, while in Tokyo supervising the Imperial Hotel, John was fired in a squabble over back pay. He returned to Chicago, knocked around in different architects' offices, and did some independent work. One of his activities was toy design, and in 1919 he invented the Lincoln Logs, which he manufactured until 1943 when he sold them to Playskool.

Fig. 9.12. John Lloyd Wright, Wright house, Long Beach, Ind., 1923–1924. (Richard Guy Wilson)

For John the complete break and the striving for independence came in 1923 when he moved with his second wife to Long Beach, Ind., a resort and suburban village on the dunes east of Michigan City, about sixty miles from Chicago. For the next twenty-three years John carried on a moderately successful practice in the Michigan City area. His work sheet lists thirty-six commissions received by 1940 and twenty-seven completions.[19] His own studio/house (later a separate studio was added in the rear) is a simple, unpretentious, shingle-covered volume placed on the side of a dune and penetrated by a drive-through arch (fig. 9.12). Traditional in form, the house demonstrates a sensitivity to materials and to setting. An attempt was made to preserve the native trees and shrubs. Evident in the details is his predisposition for complex geometrical forms. The house has a late Arts and Crafts flavor with the straightforward treatment of the trim on the interior. The three-level, living-dining-studio space recalls the Oak Park playroom, a motif that reappears frequently in his architecture (fig. 9.13).

The conservative intellectual-cultural climate of Long Beach in the 1920s precluded John from creating the exotic images his father and his brother Lloyd were able to do in California. Instead he turned to the popular period-house idiom and attempted to merge it with a Prairie School sensitivity to produce an acceptable image.[20] The Zumpfe house is typical: a square volumetric box with a low-rising hipped roof, unassuming except for a few angular protrusions (fig. 9.14). On the interior, the wrought-iron dining room gate, and Alfonso Iannelli's contributions of a fireplace sculpture and leaded glass windows, can best be described as period details (fig. 9.15). More reminiscent of the Prairie School in massing is the C. N. Austin house in Hinsdale, Ill., 1926 (fig. 9.16). However, the plastic treatment of the form recalls the Southern California Spanish Colonial Revival. The siting with the garage to the street and the living spaces to the garden demonstrates his willingness to restudy conventional solutions.

Fig. 9.13. Wright house interior. (Richard Guy Wilson)

Fig. 9.14. John Lloyd Wright, Zumpfe house, Long Beach, Ind., 1925–1926. (*Western Architect* 36 [Nov. 1927], pl. 182)

Fig. 9.15. Zumpfe house interior. (Richard Guy Wilson)

Fig. 9.16. John Lloyd Wright, Austin house, Hinsdale, Ill., 1926.
(Richard Guy Wilson)

Fig. 9.17. John Lloyd Wright, Otte house, Long Beach, Ind., 1928.
(Richard Guy Wilson)

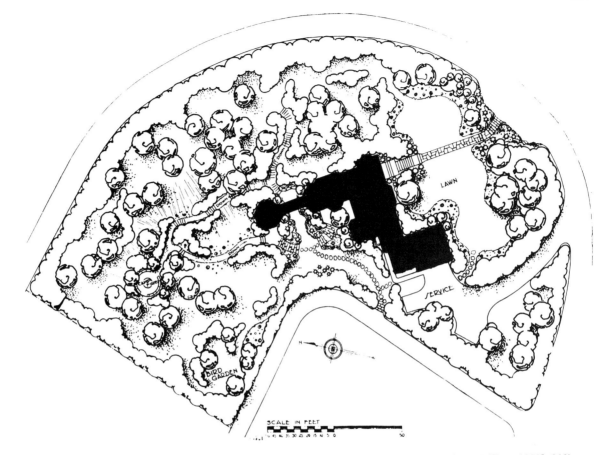

Fig. 9.18. Otte house site plan. (*Western Architect* 38 [Dec. 1929]: 219)

The H. E. Otte commission, "Red Oaks," of 1928 for a large summer house gave John more freedom to experiment (fig. 9.17). Designed to retain several venerable red oak trees on the site, the house is superbly sited and stretches along the top of two dunes. John explained, "Before attempting the design, the exact contour of the natural topography was carefully studied and the building then conceived to grow out of this topography in as natural a manner as seemed desirable and practicable. After establishing the plan and including the various requirements for the owner, I undertook to express the groundwork in the various elevations"[21] (fig. 9.18). Several level changes are contained on the interior and a major axis of over one hundred feet links the entry hall, living room, bridge, and pavilion. The living room, eighteen feet high, has a staircase and balcony at one end. Iannelli provided window glass and light fixtures.

In describing the Otte house, John mentioned the possibility of "an international modern domestic architecture" based on modern needs and universal principles, but still containing "characteristics and mannerisms of the different individual designers." He hoped that "this contribution can be considered an artistic expression in that logical direction."[22] The Otte wall treatment of a continuous unadorned plastic surface punctured by oddly shaped voids is distinctly reminiscent of the work of both his friend Barry Byrne and European expressionism.[23] John's individualistic mannerism is the hexagon that appears in the Otte house not only in windows and doors but also room shapes and, where that is not possible, in the ceiling configurations.

The problem modern architecture faced in Long Beach is illustrated by the O. J. Duke house of 1927 (fig. 9.19). John was offered an open-cost commission if he would produce an acceptable design. After numerous rejections a highly traditional period house design with French Provincial overtones was finally accepted. Siting is sensitively handled and the house has several level changes on the interior, but it certainly has no modernistic images. If anything recalls the Prairie School, it is John's witty insertion of raised brick details in the chimney stacks and the rear wall.

In the 1930s John shrugs off the period house details, and his designs become more geometrically abstract. Two civic commissions reflect the shift: the Long Beach Elementary School of 1927 (fig. 9.20) and the Long Beach Town Hall of 1931 (fig. 9.21). With the school he manipulates traditional imagery, high roofs, a cupola, and thick chimneys, but with the Town Hall he shows no concession to tradition with its severely functional arrangement of volumes and straightforward detailing. Influenced by his father, John's writings are less concerned with modern architecture and begin to promote organic design.[24]

Fig. 9.19. John Lloyd Wright, Duke house, Long Beach, Ind., 1927. (Richard Guy Wilson)

Fig. 9.20. John Lloyd Wright, Long Beach Elementary School, Long Beach, Ind., 1927. (Richard Guy Wilson)

Fig. 9.21. John Lloyd Wright, Long Beach Town Hall, Long Beach, Ind., 1931. (Richard Guy Wilson)

With the depression, housing becomes more of a social concern for John, and he produces solutions such as a $5,000-dwelling that was an attempt "to save the American family of refinement from 'a machine for living'."[25] His answer to the numerous polemical prototypes were three houses actually constructed: the Houses of Steel, Wood, and Tile. The House of Steel for Jack Burnham in Long Beach, Ind., 1933–1934, was erected at the shoreline on stiltlike piles and connected to the higher bluff by a bridge (fig. 9.22). Eight-inch I beams, thirty feet long, form the foundations while the house is constructed of structural steel, with walls of metal lath, covered by sprayed-on insulation, stucco, and plaster. Both the construction and the form of the Burnham house undoubtedly owe something to the California work of Schindler and Neutra. Balancing the volumetric verticality are the copper skirtings that attempt to relate the house to the bluffline and also serve as air-conditioning and heating ducts. Four floors are on the interior, with the major space being a double height living room with a balcony seating area.

The House of Wood for Ken Holden at Birchwood Beach, Mich., also of 1933–1934, is placed on top of a dune and presents a complex geometrical configuration in contrast to its natural surroundings (fig. 9.23). Square in overall plan, the exterior on the first floor is manipulated to create a duodecagon, while the second floor encloses pentagonal, hexagonal, and septagonal bedroom spaces (fig. 9.24). In image the Holden house recalls the Shingle style as well as nautical themes with the prow form on the first floor and the pilot house on the roof. Plywood and shingles cover a stud frame, built-ins are prominent, and in several rooms John created ornamentation that he named "lichenaceous."[26] His father, writing in 1936, claimed the House of Wood displayed "organic architecture instead of modern; . . . the exterior is closely related to the interior and both are directly related to the materials used to make them."[27]

Fig. 9.22. John Lloyd Wright, Burnham house, Long Beach, Ind., 1933–1934. (Richard Guy Wilson)

Fig. 9.23. John Lloyd Wright, Holden house, Birchwood Beach, Mich., 1933–1934. (Richard Guy Wilson)

Fig. 9.24. Holden house plan. (Redrawn by Richard Guy Wilson from *Architectural Forum* 66 [Apr. 1937]:362)

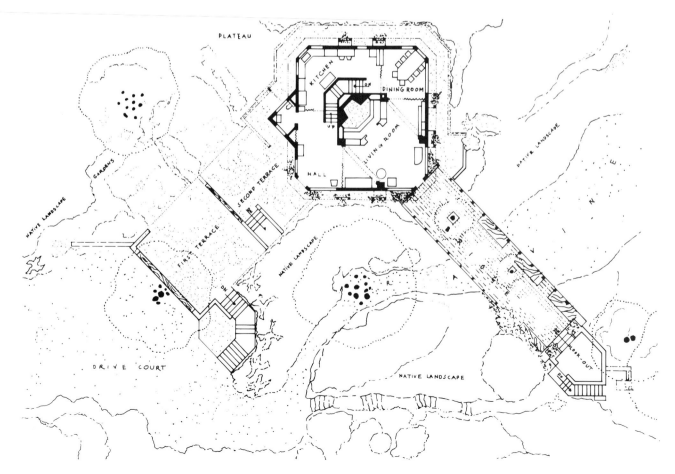

The House of Tile for Lowell Jackson in Long Beach, Ind., 1938, was constructed of structural tile left exposed on the exterior and interior (fig. 9.25). Clapboards were used on portions of the exterior, and floors were of concrete matte and wood. Superbly sited, the interior space is a terrace that spills down the hillside in three levels.

John Lloyd Wright's work in the 1920s and 1930s displays an attempt to remain true to principles of the Prairie School while at the same time asserting an independence from his father. Obviously there is a relation in some work such as the wide balcony of the Jackson house to his father's first Willey house project, but in sum, John remained his own man.

The work of Alfred Caldwell marks the infusion of a new spirit into the Prairie School. He is a member of later generation (born 1903) and consequently did not reach his maturity until the 1920s. Also his training came not through Sullivan nor Wright, but via Jens Jensen. In 1925, after working various jobs connected with landscape architecture, Caldwell approached Jensen for a position. He was taken on as superintendent of construction; and for the next five and one-half years he imbibed deeply of Jensen's philosophy. A total respect for the processes of nature was the basis. The landscape architect was an artist, or more correctly a poet, who would interpret and reveal nature, by using its materials. The result, Caldwell wrote about Jensen's work, must "contain significance, emanation of idea."[28] Jensen also introduced Caldwell to the work of the Prairie School architects, though as Caldwell remembered, "Jensen never talked much about architecture. What was important was his attitude towards things in general."[29] In 1930 Caldwell visited Wright at Taliesin, and though he was invited to stay, the unconventional living arrangements did not appeal and he departed.

Fig. 9.25. John Lloyd Wright, Jackson house, Long Beach, Ind., 1938. (Richard Guy Wilson)

In 1934 at the depths of the depression and after being out of work for several years, Caldwell was hired by the Dubuque, Iowa, Park Board as the superintendent of parks. The park board needed an experienced landscape architect so they could qualify for Civil Works Administration (later Works Progress Administration) funds and put local citizens back to work. The major project was the improvements on Eagle Point Park, a 160-acre undeveloped tract of forest located on high bluffs overlooking the Mississippi River. The park board would have been satisfied with any design, but Caldwell had a greater vision as he explained in a letter: "I have certain ideas, long cherished, too difficult, or impossible of achievement in a large system with its bureaucracies and affinities. In a small park, even with a little money to spend, relatively speaking, much might be done. It is out of the nature of things, that the cheapest and nearest to hand, properly understood, is the best and most beautiful. All ugliness is expensive—certainly expensive to build."[30]

The "City in a Garden," as Caldwell titled his work, is a conceptual realization of his fundamental belief in the unity of man and nature. Great portions of the park remained natural; trails were simply cleared, for, as he explained, "there are no values so potent as the cultural values inherent in the natural terrain."[31] Caldwell described his approach at Dubuque as "nature helping," i.e., using nature's gifts to accentuate the innate beauty present. The stratified limestone outcroppings of the vicinity became the unifying element of the park, for, as he noted, "Here in Dubuque, golden slabs of limestone lie underfoot everywhere . . . [in] long horizontal lines—the lines of repose. . . . The garden [is] laid up in simple abstract forms, a syntax of stone."[32] The stratified layers were an expression "by extension and horizontally, of the breadth of American prairies."[33]

Along the bluff face with a Whitmanesque view to the east was constructed a retaining wall and council rings (fig. 9.26); well back from the face were the park shelters and the ledge and horticultural gardens. In the ledge garden, shallow pools of water spilled down terraces in imitation of a prairie stream, and the plantings were a tapestry of hybrid roses, iris, asters, ferns, lotus, and water lilies. The horticultural garden intended for growing plant materials had as climbers, modern totems—twin, upright, wood posts with orange-faced wooden blocks between

them (fig. 9.27). To Caldwell they suggested the machine in their straightforward appearance and repetitiveness.[34] The three shelters, containing lounges, eating and cooking facilities, locker rooms, and two reservoirs, are impossible to grasp wholly from any single perspective (fig. 9.28). They are extensions of the landscape, long horizontals that appear to grow out of the natural limestone outcroppings. The long roof plane, dynamic in extent, contrasts with the tough solidity of the lower walls (fig. 9.29). One story becomes two, and sheltered terraces open off of each building. An indication of Caldwell's vision is his estimate that, when completed, the City in a Garden would house four thousand people in inclement weather. However, a dispute with the park board forced him to leave in late 1936. Just before the park's completion, President Franklin Roosevelt visited Dubuque, and while Eleanor toured the buildings, he gave an impromptu assessment: "This is my idea of a worthwhile boondoggle."[35]

Fig. 9.26. Alfred Caldwell, Eagle Point Park, council ring with Women's Club, Dubuque, Iowa, 1934–1936. (Dubuque Park Board)

Fig. 9.27. Eagle Point Park construction of horticultural garden, with Caldwell at the right in hat. (Dubuque Park Board)

Fig. 9.28. Eagle Point Park shelters. (Gerald Mansheim)

Fig. 9.29. Eagle Point Park shelter. (Dubuque Park Board)

Fig. 9.30. Alfred Caldwell for the Chicago Park District, Lily Pool, Lincoln Park, Chicago, Ill., 1937–1938. (Chicago Park District)

A logical continuation of the concepts expressing Eagle Point Park can be seen in Caldwell's Lily Pool in Lincoln Park, Chicago, created in 1937–1938 (fig. 9.30). Contiguous with the zoo and yet self-contained, the Lily Pool was constructed with Public Works Administration funds around an old canal (fig. 9.31). Ledges of built-up limestone slabs enclose and define the central space of the pool and suggest a prairie river landscape. The boundary is planted as a riverbank with native trees, shrubs, ferns, and wildflowers, while grasses and lilies grow in the pool. From varying heights, a slab path leads the observer around the expansive and seemingly natural enclave. At the curve of the prairie river the limestone forms a terrace that supports two seating pavilions. Right-angled limestone walls push upward and outward, intersecting pergola roofs of long horizontals and short verticals of open and closed forms (fig. 9.32). Man and nature are contrasted. Against the dismal drabness of the surrounding park and city, the Lily Pool becomes a refuge—a sequestered place of breath and quietude for man in the midst of Chicago.

Similarities between Caldwell and Wright's work, such as the roofs of Midway Garden or the fieldstone at Taliesin, can be observed.[36] However, Caldwell's work needs no defense; his work expands the Wrightian idiom and also is more fully immersed in nature. More significant are the commonalities of interest, both in an organically directed architecture and architecture as social response. Both Broadacre City and City in a Garden are utopian solutions for the social and economic upheaval. The difference is, Caldwell built his. His later career need not concern us here except to note that he went on to become a distinguished professor under Mies van der Rohe at Illinois Institute of Technology after the war and therefore becomes an important link between the indigenous midwestern school and the new architecture from Europe.

Fig. 9.31. Lily Pool, prairie river landscape. (Chicago Park District)

A fourth method by which the Prairie School spirit was continued in the interwar years can be seen in the work of Alden B. Dow (1904–1984).[37]Graduating from the Columbia School of Architecture in 1931, Dow had been a member of the first Taliesin class in the summer of 1933 before returning to his hometown of Midland, Mich. A felicitous opportunity existed in Midland during the 1930s, since his father's company, Dow Chemical, maintained a level of prosperity generally not present elsewhere. Thus he had not only a captive clientele of company personnel and hometown folk, but his personal situation allowed him to run an office less dependent on turning a profit. Joined in 1934 by Robert Goodall (1904–1954), a former Wright associate, Dow became the first of the Taliesin students to build on his own, completing approximately thirty works between 1934 and 1940.

His major work, the studio, 1934–1936, and attached residence, 1940, reposes in a carefully controlled pastoral setting, a corner of his father's garden. Dow's predisposition toward an architecture of repose can be seen in his few completed works before going to Taliesin. Essentially the Taliesin experience gave Dow an underlying geometric order and further intensified the inclination toward creating a continuum with nature. The studio is designed on a four-foot module and constructed of concrete blocks that Dow patented in 1933 (fig. 9.33). Wright's textile block system is an obvious predecessor, but Dow introduces elements such as the diagonal of the pitched roof. In plan the house and studio wander along the pond and through the garden, blending into nature at points, and then withdrawing. The harder order of Frank Lloyd Wright is absent in this pastoral ode. Standing in the studio's pond room eighteen inches below water level, one becomes part of the garden as the stepping stones, elements of the house, spread across the water. On the opposite side in the garden the ruins of the geometric order reemerge giving a sense of archaic timelessness to the entire setting. The element of artifice and delicacy that is present reminds one not of Wright, but of Japan, where Dow first visited when he was eighteen.

Fig. 9.32. Alden B. Dow, Dow studio and house, Midland, Mich., 1934–1936, 1940. (Sidney K. Robinson)

Dow's unique background as a chemist's son imbued him with a respect for science, hence the rationalism of geometry, but he also recognized the individuality of experience and fantasy. His other work in the 1930s can be seen as an attempt to create an architecture of unity that still recognized individual differences. Naturally Dow received large commissions, such as the Dr. C. L. MacCallum (1935) and the A. S. Arbury (1939) residences, but some of his most interesting work was at a smaller scale. These works illustrate the concern of the 1930s for the inexpensive middle-class dwelling. The John Whitman house of 1934 (fig. 9.34), which won the Diplome de Grande Prix for Residential Architecture at the Paris Exposition in 1937, has compressed interlocking volumes encompassing 1,100 square feet that cost $7,700 to construct (fig. 9.35). Integrated vertically and horizontally around a large hall with a dining room attached to one side, the concrete blocks are used for furniture and light fixtures. The MacMartin house is a 38-foot square arranged around a central chimney (fig. 9.36). Attention to details such as the trellis roof, the quiet broad expanses of wall, and the outflung terrace add elements of dignity to the ordinary suburban box. In a sense the MacMartin house continues the theme begun in 1906 with Wright's Fireproof House for $5,000.

Fig. 9.33. Dow studio and house plan. (Sidney K. Robinson)

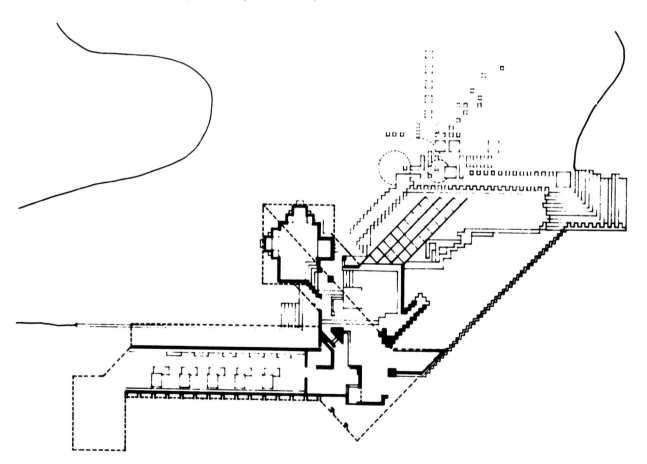

Fig. 9.34. Alden B. Dow, Whitman house, Midland, Mich., 1934. (Sidney K. Robinson)

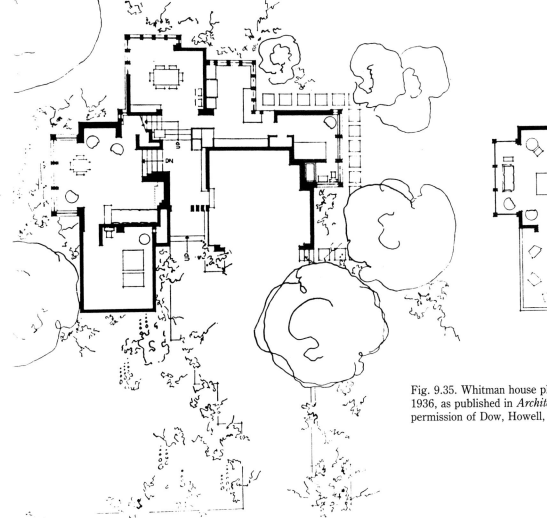

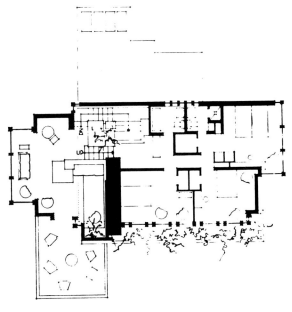

Fig. 9.35. Whitman house plan. (Drawn by Alden Dow Associates, 1936, as published in *Architectural Forum* [Sept. 1936]:199; with permission of Dow, Howell, and Gilmore Associates)

Fig. 9.36. Alden B. Dow, MacMartin house, Midland, Mich., 1938.
(Reprinted from the May 1942 *Pencil Points,* copyright Penton
Publishing. Also with permission of Dow, Howell, and Gilmore
Associates)

Fig. 9.37. William V. Kaeser, Kaeser house, Madison, Wis., 1937.
(Frederick V. Kaeser)

The career of Alden Dow after 1940 is beyond the scope of this essay. His work, while related in the broad sense to that of Wright and the Prairie School, has personal elements of delicacy, quiet, and fantasy that are entirely his own.

To the work just reviewed could be added the work of other individuals that in one method or another continued the Prairie School spirit. The early designs of Bruce Goff and Howard Fisher from the 1920s reveal an acknowledged debt to the Prairie School.[38] There is William F. De Knatel, a former Wright draftsman, whose Walter J. Kohler house in Kohler, Wis., 1938, reveals a creative replay of Prairie School themes.[39] Also in the 1930s individuals emerge, such as William Kaeser in Madison, Wis., and Paul Schweikher in Chicago, whose works are strongly indebted to the Prairie School, yet neither was a student of Wright nor any of the others (fig. 9.37).[40] Outside the Midwest there were independent continuations such as Alexander Trowbridge and Theo White's L. G. Strong house at Gibson Island, Md., 1927, empathetic in its horizontality.[41] On the West Coast, in addition to the work of Wright and his son Lloyd, there is the work of William Gray Purcell, first in Oregon and later in southern California. The early work of Rudolph Schindler also represents a continuation of the Prairie School. And many more could be added.

From the work of these individuals emerge patterns of influence and continuation. Obviously there is a difference between the work of the 1920s and 1930s. The former were in a sense a hiatus for the Prairie School. In many critics' eyes American culture becomes more conformist, consumption-oriented and synthetic.[42] While it is popular to view the Midwest in the 1920s as a vast "Gopher Prairie spotted with Zeniths populated by Babbitts," still there were legacies of progressive thought and ferment in literature that continued. With no strong architectural figures to focus upon, the Prairie School became diffuse. The often thin line that existed between originality and revivalism in the first Prairie School is accentuated in the 1920s. Architects such as Elmslie and John Lloyd Wright consciously investigated the period house and other traditional images and used them to create evocative and idiosyncratic designs. Their work was not so much based on stylistic continuations as on enduring principles.

The 1930s marked a dramatic change, and in spite of the fewer opportunities for commissions, there was a new spark of creativity and perhaps a new Prairie School. One might speculate on the causes, whether the crisis of the depression and the political and social experiments and the turn of American art toward regionalism invigorated the later Prairie School in the same manner as the earlier period of introspection and reform animated the first Prairie School.[43] Broadacre City, a City in the Garden, and the inexpensive housing solutions, whether of John Lloyd Wright or Alden Dow, are responses to economic and social crisis. Frank Lloyd Wright's reemergence in the 1930s is a factor in the new spirit of the Prairie School, but also it can be seen in context and not simply a result of his own indomitable will. Just as his creativity in the Oak Park years did not emerge from a vacuum, so also in the 1930s his rejuvenation can be seen in perspective as part of a movement toward the reassertion of an American-based, organic, modern architecture. Frank Lloyd Wright's status is not diminished, he remains the strong figure against whom other architects swerve and define themselves. But, other sensibilities are in operation as the differing approaches to nature of Alfred Caldwell and Alden Dow illustrate.

The perception of the image of an American-based, organic modern architecture was to be a major issue for the second Prairie School. Already in the 1930s battlelines were being formed between the native American expression and the imported machine image of the International style. In June 1938, *Architectural Forum* published an article entitled "Where Is Modern Now?"; and while carefully avoiding an absolute endorsement of any single style, left the distinct impression that modern meant some form of the European machine image.[44] William Gray Purcell responded with a letter that, while never published, is of importance for the recognition of the gap created.[45] Purcell told the *Forum* editors that in addition to the work of Sullivan and Wright (which they had noted), completely overlooked as a source for modern architecture were his own work, the works of Elmslie, and also that of Drummond, Byrne, Lloyd Wright, John Lloyd Wright, and others. Implicit in Purcell's letter was recognition that the American origins of modern architecture were far different in intent and image than foreign origins. The American sources and continuations were being ignored.

Whether a Prairie School in the same sense as the group of Chicago area architects of the period 1900–1916 can be said to have existed in the 1920s and 1930s is a subject open to debate.

But it is evident that in spite of changes in personalities and stylistic idioms, the work of George Elmslie, John Lloyd Wright, Alfred Caldwell, and Alden Dow can be said to continue the basic principle of the earlier Prairie School: simple forms and complex details, straightforward usage of materials, enlivened interior space, and relating the building to the landscape. Avoiding the shrill clatter of the various foreign imports, the roots of the Prairie School were deep within the native American traditions, and as such the Prairie School continued in the 1920s and 1930s, in a quiet way.

Notes

Portions of this essay were originally presented in Milwaukee in October 1977 and at a conference devoted to the Prairie School. After a hiatus of several years and more research, it has been largely rewritten.

1. Stuart Cohen, *Chicago Architects* (Chicago, 1976); Carl Condit, *Chicago 1910-29: Building, Planning and Urban Technology* (Chicago 1973) and *Chicago, 1930-70: Building, Planning and Urban Technology* (Chicago, 1974).

2. A summary of the explanations can be found in H. Allan Brooks, *The Prairie School* (Toronto, 1972), chs. 8 and 9; Mark L. Peisch, *The Chicago School of Architecture* (New York, 1964), ch. 8 and conclusion; and Leonard K. Eaton, *Two Chicago Architects and Their Clients* (Cambridge, 1969).

3. Brooks, *The Prairie School,* 334–335; and Suzanne Ganschinietz, "William Drummond: I," *The Prairie School Review* 6 (2, 1969): 16–19.

4. Steele quoted in Peisch, *The Chicago School,* 138.

5. *Sioux City Journal,* 1 April 1928.

6. Steele was George Elmslie's associate on Forbes Hall at Yankton College; his Sioux City successor, George Hilgers, was associated on two other buildings, the College Power Plant, 1930, and Look Dormitory for Men, 1931. Steele mentions Sullivan in "Technics and Architecture," *American Architect* 145 (December 1934): 37–38; and "What Does the Architect Have to Offer?" *Architectural Record* 77 (April 1935): 260–262.

7. Harold Bloom, *The Anxiety of Influence* (New York, 1973).

8. Actually the partnership with Purcell did not formally dissolve until 1920, but from 1918 on, Purcell's involvement had been nil because of other interests. See David Gebhard, "William Gray Purcell and George Grant Elmslie and the Early Progressive Movement in American Architecture from 1900 to 1920," (Ph.D. diss., University of Minnesota, 1957).

9. Fred Strauel, a draftsman in the Purcell and Elmslie office, is listed as an associate on the building, *Western Architect,* 36 (November 1927), pl. 187–188.

10. Donald L. Hoffman, "Elmslie's Topeka Legacy," *The Prairie School Review* 1 (4, 1964): 23–24; Brooks, *Prairie School,* 306.

11. Some examples of Purcell and Elmslie buildings with the high gable roof are the Louis Heitman house, Helena, Mont., 1916; the Ward Beebe house, St. Paul, Minn., 1912; and the J. W. S. Gallaher house, Winona, Minn., 1913.

12. Elmslie's "The Chicago School: Its Inheritance and Bequest," *Journal of the American Institute of Architects* 18 (July 1952): 32–34, indicates his sympathies with Pugin and Morris.

13. Information from William Hammond Short, Western Springs, Ill., 22 November 1976.

14. The Western Springs Church was published in *Architectural Record* 70 (December 1931): 416–418; the Healy Chapel in 71 (May 1932): 314–315.

15. "George Elmslie Commissions," Purcell and Elmslie Collection, Northwest Architectural Archives, University of Minnesota, Minneapolis.

16. John Lloyd Wright, *My Father Who Is on Earth* (New York, 1946), 16–17, 60–61, 67–69. See also, Sally Kitt Chappell and Ann Van Zanten, *Barry Byrne, John Lloyd Wright, Architecture and Design* (Chicago, 1982).

17. Illustrations of two of his southern California buildings are in *The Prairie School Review* 2 (4, 1965): 9 and 7 (2, 1970): 16–19.

18. Information from W. R. Hasbrouck.

19. A list drawn up by John Lloyd Wright shortly before his death, courtesy of Frances Lloyd Wright and Leonard C. Rosenberg.

20. Jonathan Lane, "The Period House in the Nineteen-Twenties," *Journal of the Society of Architectural Historians* 20 (December 1961): 169–178.

21. John Lloyd Wright, " 'Red Oaks', Long Beach, Indiana," *The Western Architect* 38 (December 1919): 218.

22. Ibid.

23. Byrne had been a friend from both the Oak Park studio days and also in southern California. Byrne's work, such as the Church of St. Thomas the Apostle, Chicago, 1922, especially the rear elevation, and St. Patrick's Church, Racine, Wis., 1923, are indications of influence. For another example see John Lloyd Wright's apartment house in Michigan City, Ind., 1928, in *Architectural Record* 65 (March 1929): 252–253. See Brooks, *The Prairie School,* 324–325, and Sally Anderson Chappell, "Barry Byrne, Architect: His Formative Years," *The Prairie School Review* 3 (4, 1966): 5–23.

24. "House of Mr. and Mrs. John Burnham," *The Architectural Forum* 62 (June 1935): 535–548.

25. John Lloyd Wright and Hazel Wright, "The Designers Description," *Indianapolis Star* 19 April 1936. His wife's appearance with this design raises the possibility of her contribution to other works, but she is nowhere listed, and they were divorced in 1943.

26. John Lloyd Wright, "Lichenaceous Ornament," *House and Home* 1 (January 1952):136–137.

27. Frank Lloyd Wright quoted in John Lloyd Wright, *My Father,* 115.

28. Alfred Caldwell, "Jens Jensen: The Prairie Spirit," *Landscape Architecture* 51 (January 1961): 105.

29. Letter, Caldwell to Richard Guy Wilson, 9 December 1976; and interviews with Caldwell, 11 November 1976 and 2 February 1977. For more information see Richard Guy Wilson, "Alfred Caldwell Illuminates Nature's Way," *Landscape Architecture* 67 (September 1977): 407–412.

30. Letter, Caldwell to Dubuque Park Board, 24 January 1934. This and all newspaper articles are in the possession of the Dubuque Park Board. I am indebted to Gerald Mansheim for assistance in research.

31. *Telegraph Herald and Times Journal* (Dubuque), undated but circa May 1934.

32. Ibid., 19 August 1934.

33. Ibid., 11 November 1934.

34. Ibid., 4 November 1934.

35. Letter, Caldwell to R. G. Wilson, 9 December 1976.

36. Carl Condit, *The Chicago School of Architecture* (Chicago, 1964), 214.

37. Much of my information is from Sidney K. Robinson, who has extensively investigated the work of Alden B. Dow. See Robinson's, *Life Imitates Architecture: Taliesin and Alden Dow's Studio* (Ann Arbor, 1980) and *The Architecture of Alden B. Dow* (Detroit, 1983). See also, Alden B. Dow, *Reflections* (Midland, Mich., 1970); and Talbot Hamlin, "The Architect and House: Alden B. Dow of Michigan," *Pencil Points* 23 (May 1942): 269–286.

38. Robert Kostka, "Bruce Goff and the New Tradition," *The Prairie School Review* 7 (2, 1970): 6–10; and Cohen, *Chicago Architects,* 20–21.

39. *Architectural Forum* 71 (July 1939): 50–53.

40. Interview with William V. Kaeser, 30–31 October, 1 November 1977. On Schweikher, see "Recent Work of the Office of Paul Schweikher and Theodore Warren Lamb," *Architectural Forum* 71 (November 1939): 351–356; and Cohen, *Chicago Architects,* 25.

41. "A Summer Cottage on Gibson Island, Maryland," *Architectural Record* 70 (December 1931): 425–430.

42. Brooks, *The Prairie School,* 341.

43. Robert C. Twombly, *Frank Lloyd Wright* (New York, 1973), 190–191.

44. "Where is Modern Now?" *Architectural Forum* 66 (June 1938): 465–470.

45. Letter, Purcell to Myers, 25 June 1938, Purcell and Elmslie Collection, Northwest Architectural Archives.

INDEX